YOUR FELLOW AMERICANS

Dispatches from Across the Country We Call Home

PETER SANTENELLO

Simon & Schuster

NEW YORK AMSTERDAM/ANTWERP LONDON
TORONTO SYDNEY/MELBOURNE NEW DELHI

Simon & Schuster
1230 Avenue of the Americas
New York, NY 10020

First Simon & Schuster hardcover edition August 2026

SIMON & SCHUSTER and colophon are registered trademarks of Simon & Schuster, LLC

Interior design by Paul Dippolito

Manufactured in the United States of America

1 3 5 7 9 10 8 6 4 2

Library of Congress Control Number: 2026937122

ISBN 978-1-6682-1434-3
ISBN 978-1-6682-1436-7 (ebook)

For my love, Natalia

This publication is a work of memoir and reportage. It reflects the author's present recollections of his experiences over a period of years. Some dialogue has been re-created from memory, while other dialogue has been edited for clarity and brevity. Some scenes are composites of events. Events have been compressed and in some cases their chronology has been changed. To watch these conversations in full (and hundreds more), check out Peter Santenello's channel on YouTube.

Contents

Introduction

When I was eight, I told my mom I wanted a book about the Soviet Union for Christmas. It was 1985, and in rural Vermont anything on the other side of the Iron Curtain was supposed to be feared. So of course, in my rebellious little kid way, I couldn't think of anything cooler.

I still remember ripping the wrapping paper off the slim rectangular package that cold December morning, flipping the pages, and stopping in awe at a picture of a Russian couple on their wedding day. "They get married there too?" I remember saying out loud. I didn't understand how people from such an evil place could do something as human as fall in love.

Looking back now, I think that's the moment I became obsessed with one day seeing the world through my own eyes.

By twenty-four, I'd saved up enough money from waiting tables at night and cleaning cars during the day to leave North America for the first time. I spent two years traveling overland, from Europe to Southeast Asia, through fifty countries on a budget of $20,000, amazed by how different the world turned out to be from the fear-based narrative I'd grown up with. I learned that politics and people are two different things, and that most people are open and welcoming.

When I came back home, friends would ask which countries I'd liked the most, and I'd say places like Tajikistan or Syria. The reaction was always the same: a confused look, like

Why would you go there? I didn't have a simple answer for them. That's when the dream of one day taking a video camera out into the world began.

Over the next fifteen years, I spent long stretches of time outside the US. My plan was to get in as many experiences as possible before turning forty, doing whatever jobs it took to save up the money, then leaving the US, returning home broke, and going at it again. That drive led me through eighty-five countries, including years living in Spain, Switzerland, Thailand, and Ukraine—where I met and married my wife, Natalia.

Then, suddenly, I found myself on the other side of forty. The pandemic shut down the world, and Natalia and I moved back to the US, to San Francisco, and I found myself asking, "What would be interesting to show people around here?" I thought I knew my own country. Turns out, one of the places I understood least was the one I came from. I'd spent years exploring countries that are widely misrepresented or stereotyped, only to realize my own might be one of the most misunderstood of all. So I decided to take the same approach I'd used overseas and point the camera inward. That journey is what's in these pages—along with everything I found along the way.

* * *

Behind the headlines, statistics, and political hot takes is a huge, chaotic, fascinating country—one that's impossible to comprehend until you've seen it. And even then, after years of digging in, you can look at a map and realize how little of it you've actually covered. America has tropics, deserts, tundra, and endless stretches of rural back roads. New York City's greater metropolitan area alone is home to more people than thirty-five of the forty-four countries in Europe. We've got 575 federally recognized Native American tribes and people from every nation on earth.

I've been making videos about the United States full-time for six years now—driving dusty roads, kicking around downtowns, knocking on doors. I've eaten Sunday dinners in houseboats, mansions, and trailer parks, on reservations and in neighborhoods that don't make the news unless someone gets shot. And what's surprised me the most in all these places isn't the problems, although there are plenty. It's the opposite: It's how often I've walked away from a day of filming more hopeful about America than when I began.

Amish farmers. Cajun fishermen. Chicano artists. Siberian Yupik hunters. Sheriffs. Teachers. Coal miners. Welders. Entrepreneurs. After thousands of miles and thousands of conversations, the thing that keeps hitting me each and every time I find myself somewhere new is how much people here *care*—about their families, their towns, their little corners of the map. About the country we all live in together. This is one of the easiest places on earth to get a smile or have a stranger hold the door open for you. There's a beautiful *you do you* spirit here too. I'm always awed that most of us really do respect others' paths—even admire them—as long as those paths don't interfere with our own. That's what makes this country so dynamic, so interesting. My wife calls the US a "build-your-own-bowl" country. You choose your climate, your culture, your pace, even your politics. If you want to—if you're physically capable and sufficiently motivated—you can design a life that's true to you. Live off the land in New Mexico. Disappear into the Michigan backwoods. Carve a life around the rhythm of the ocean waves. Become someone new in a city with every career opportunity and every culture from the furthest stretches of the globe. That freedom—that possibility—is the real American story. That, and the energy of the people living here. There's a buzz to this place, an enthusiasm unlike anywhere else.

That's why I wrote this book. Just to get under the hood of America—salt-of-the-earth America, the one you only get from people who don't normally get a microphone. To share stories that come through only when you put in the time to listen.

To fit all of America into one book is, of course, impossible. There's simply too much. Too many communities, too many histories, too much square mileage. So I had to pick and choose. What you'll find in these pages are some of the stories that've stuck with me the most on this journey: the places I've loved exploring, the people who welcomed me in, the conversations I kept thinking about long after I'd left town. The experiences that marked me.

I've organized the book into four parts: "Neither Here Nor There" is about groups of people living in the modern world and yet almost *alongside* the modern world, staying rooted in their values and traditions. It's about communities that got me thinking about what I could learn—maybe what we could all learn—from these alternate ways of living in the twenty-first century. "The Underdogs" takes us to Central Appalachia and the Mississippi Delta, regions that have suffered through adversity and been written off by most of the country, and yet are full of grit, sincerity, and loyalty. "The Long Game" is about places that have endured and overcome—like Northern California's Pacific Coast, where the redwoods are older than the Bible, and an island in the Chesapeake Bay where some families have been speaking an Elizabethan dialect of English for nearly four hundred years. The last section, "Pioneering Spirit," explores stories of that classic American thirst for adventure and discovery—stories of people living true to their own tune. People who got me thinking about how to face the future with excitement and an expansive sense of possibility.

While you may recognize many of these places and people from my videos, a lot of what went into these chapters never reached the internet. So much happens when the power button is off: the spontaneous conversations; the funny moments; the times when nobody's filming and the story keeps unfolding; the long, silent drives where I process what I've learned. There are experiences in these pages I never intended to share with anyone—like a cross-country road trip I took with my best friend at eighteen, which ended up setting the course for my life. This book is a mix of all of that: the filmed, the unfilmed, the seen, the unseen. The rawness, the weirdness, the honesty, the humor, the humanity.

As America celebrates its 250th anniversary, I think we could all use some stories that leave us feeling good about our country. I'm not here to tell you this is a perfect place. But I do want to show you that it's a special one. I want to introduce you to Americans you might never otherwise get to know and places that are just as American as wherever you're from. Places that, in some way, are part of your story too.

PART I

NEITHER HERE NOR THERE

CHAPTER 1

Amish Country

Red light. I sat stopped at an intersection, arms draped over the steering wheel. Face close to the windshield, mouth open, eyes wide. Bikes crossed the road that looked nothing like the pastel beach cruisers I'd been seeing everywhere else in Florida: wide seats, low frames, baskets strapped to the front. Some were motorized tricycles; others looked hand-built in a barn. Bonneted women pedaled by in long dresses, men in straw hats and overalls beside them.

Amish snowbirds. Welcome to Pinecraft, Florida.

It was February, seventy-eight degrees and full sun. I rolled the windows down to take the place in: modest homes, a soundtrack of birdsong, and low, friendly chatter in Pennsylvania Dutch (a language that has nothing to do with the Netherlands; it's just German *Deutsch* with an American accent). Across the street, a billboard read SURRENDER TO JESUS in bold block letters. The message fit; the medium didn't. I didn't think the Amish were the billboard type.

It made me curious. If they were preaching from billboards in all-caps Helvetica, maybe they weren't as off the grid as I'd thought.

There wasn't much online about the Amish in their

own words. Some standard documentary-type content with voiceover from a narrator, sure, but most of what was out there were the punchlines: reality shows about twentysomethings leaving the community, viral clips of family chaos. Plenty of talk *about* them, but almost nothing *from* them.

So when my wife found out there was an Amish community a few hours from where we were staying, I knew I had to check it out. I'd been making videos for almost four years at this point, but we'd only been back in the US for six months, so I was in that renewed-awe-for-America stage, excited to see absolutely *everything*. She sent me off with a kiss and a "Have fun!" as I left our hotel, hopped in a rental car, and took off across the state.

I parked behind a small grocery store called Yoder's Fresh Market. This wasn't a tourist trap pretending to be Amish; it was a de facto Amish stronghold. Five men were posted up outside like watchmen at the gates of some backcountry shire, seated on what they told me was the "wisdom bench."

"How can I get over to the wisdom side of things?" I laughed, ambling over. "I gotta age?"

"No," one of them said, lightly teasing. "You're supposed to provide *us* with wisdom." He was a stylish dresser even in the Florida heat—white shirt tucked tightly into pants with black suspenders, squared-off sunglasses. He told me his name was John and that he thought I'd have an easy time finding people open to talking on camera. "We're one big family," he said, nodding toward the billboard across the street. "You can be part of that big family too."

I squinted into the sun. To the left, a photo showed a man with his head in his hands, mid-breakdown. The help came with a number: (83) FOR-TRUTH.

"If I follow Jesus?" I asked.

"Yeah. Exactly like that sign says. Find peace. Surrender to Jesus."

I later learned the Amish credit their entire way of life to the Bible. But that's getting ahead of the story.

"If you want to see a lot of Amish," John added, pointing over his shoulder, "get on the Pinecraft path and go that way."

* * *

I strolled down toward the road. The neighborhood felt pleasant with slow hand waves, soft smiles, and the whir of coaster brakes as occasional tricycles rode by. There was a seasonal stillness to it. It felt like a place where the old-timers wintered while the fields sat dormant up north, waiting on spring.

I passed a small park where dozens of Amish men and women in aprons and vibrant dresses—yellow, pink, sky blue—played bocce with surprising intensity. Another group played shuffleboard. Off to the side, a young man practiced yodeling. It felt oddly normal, despite how surreal it all looked; like a dream, with different centuries overlapping.

A few blocks in, I turned down another narrow street, deeper into the neighborhood. Almost every second house had someone out front. There was a whole lot of sitting: on porches, in folding chairs, on wooden benches hidden in pockets of shade. Then came the laughter, earthy and loud.

I turned the corner, reeled in by the sound.

Four men sat in the shade of a stone-trimmed porch, the lawn manicured like their white beards—mustaches removed and the area around the mouth clean-shaven in the Amish style. The palm trees lining the yard were perfectly spaced; the brick driveway had a single, deliberate parking spot. If this were the wealthy part of Miami, it would have held a Ferrari or a Bentley. But here in Pinecraft, there was a shiny electric trike with chrome spokes and pedal backup.

The men, dressed in suspenders and soft cotton in varying shades of blue, were deep in conversation. The source of the laughter—barefoot, unbothered—noticed me and quieted.

"How's it going?" I asked. A standard, open-ended, Pleasantville-approved phrase.

"Oh, it's pretty peaceful," he answered, real warmth in his tone.

I stepped in closer, and he clocked the camera in my hand.

"Are you putting me on TV?"

I stopped, figuring I was about to get shooed away.

"You don't have to be on any of this . . ." I said, quickly, putting the GoPro down.

"Turn it on, so we can be on!" said the storyteller, cutting me off before I could finish. With the camera rolling, his voice grew loud and wide, like a dramatic soprano's, as he spoke of life back in Ohio: how the hills roll green in every direction come spring, and families gather on Sundays and grandkids help in the garden after church. There's nothing like the smell of fresh-cut hay or the sound of horses at sunrise, he said. But when winter comes, Florida becomes its own kind of sanctuary. No fields to tend. Just sun, neighbors, and rest—a season for playing games, sharing stories, and enjoying the stillness earned after months of planting, weeding, and harvesting. Like the ocean trades places with the land for a while.

Not that life was all idyllic.

"We try and take everything the way it comes," said the oldest man in the group, his beard over a foot long, like an Amish Santa Claus. "If something happens, we try to live with it. We don't believe in fear. You can read that in the Bible."

We talked some more about how they knew people who'd stopped going to Phoenix in the winter, about the drugs and crime in those parts. But they brought the conversation back to fear. It felt as if they had a message that they wanted to tell the outside world.

"Way too much fear now," said the youngest of the group (maybe in his fifties), his voice rising above the others on the word *fear.* "People don't trust each other."

"What about you guys?" I asked. "Do Amish people trust each other?"

"Yes. And we help each other," the storyteller replied.

"We have good, we have bad. We work with what we have, with what we can," said Amish Santa Claus, and everyone grew quiet for a moment.

It was the sort of conversation that's impossible to have if you show up somewhere with a giant DSLR and a full-on camera crew, and why I always self-film.

"I'm sorry if we wore your batteries out," said the storyteller, pointing his finger at the camera. "I've got some in the house if you need them." He broke out in laughter, like he knew how wild the idea of an Amish old-timer having spare camera batteries would sound.

* * *

Until recently, I think Americans mostly saw the Amish as the odd ones. The ones who hadn't kept up. Who'd gotten left behind. Most documentaries "othered" them, approaching Amish folks like zoo animals, safely observed from a distance.

And then COVID happened.

Cities changed quickly—lockdowns, shortages, kids home from school, friends and families separated. People started questioning what really mattered. Migration to the countryside ticked up. Space, nature, a quiet life with deeper meaning . . . it all suddenly became more desirable.

When I posted my video about this Amish enclave in Florida, what struck people most was how removed these folks seemed from the tensions gripping the rest of society. The comments poured in:

"After how the past year has been, I wouldn't mind living like this—cut off from all the insanity."

"I used to drive by the Amish when I was stationed at Ft. Campbell, KY in the early 00's and would feel sorry for them . . . now I envy them."

The vibe had shifted from "outcast" and "weird" to "I want some of that."

So did I.

"If you really want to make a movie about us, go to Holmes County, Ohio," one of the men back in Pinecraft had said. "I'll be back there in the summer. I can give you my telephone number."

* * *

I landed in Columbus, Ohio, in flat midday light that washed everything evenly like a coat of primer. The airport was calm and easy, and within ten minutes I was in a rental car heading south. The farther I drove, the more the landscape seemed to relax into long, flat fields, then shallow dips, then a line of hills: green, rounded, and pleasant to the eye, like something arranged in accordance with the golden ratio.

As I neared Holmes County, I started to feel it. A different pace. Barns with laundry strung tight between posts. Black buggies parked at odd angles near roadside stands. There was a certain rhythm coming through the calm: hard wheels on gravel, wind through cornstalks, the hum of my engine breaking the silence like it didn't belong.

Most people think of the Amish as a Pennsylvania thing, and Lancaster County does have the largest Amish community in the country. But the Holmes County settlement in Ohio isn't far behind, home to nearly forty thousand Amish. Nationwide there are now a little over four hundred thousand Amish spread across some thirty-two US states. They're not limited to a few rural pockets either, and their communities are growing fast. With six or seven kids per family and a surprisingly low attrition rate, the population is doubling about every twenty years. In 1970, there were only about eighty-four thousand Amish in North America. Today that number has grown dramatically.

There is a reason we think of the Amish living in Pennsylvania. When their ancestors first came to America in the early 1700s—many with roots in Switzerland but arriving from German-speaking regions of Europe—they were drawn by Pennsylvania's promise of religious freedom. The colony's founder William Penn, a Quaker and fellow pacifist, had established policies that welcomed religious minorities and offered affordable farmland with exemption from military service. As land opened farther west in the nineteenth century, many Amish families gradually migrated into the Midwest, settling in places like Ohio.

* * *

Before checking into my Airbnb in Millersburg, the Holmes County seat, I swung by a Walmart, which looked to be the best grocery store in town. The parking lot alone was something else. There were cars, sure, but off to the side a whole covered section was dedicated to horse-and-buggy parking. The smell of manure mixed with blacktop heat and the faint sweetness of hay. Horses stood idle, flipping their tails in slow, lazy swats at pickup trucks driving by below the yellow-and-blue Walmart sign. Capitalism doing its thing, adjusting to its customers' wants.

I'd done just enough oddly specific research to start profiling Amish sects by their rides. One buggy looked kind of modern: black and horse-drawn but curved, almost aerodynamic. The frame was covered in taut vinyl, with plastic windows stitched along the sides. The wheels were thick rubber, and there were rearview mirrors. New Order Amish. Another carriage looked almost handmade: matte black and squared off like a shed, with thin steel wheels that gave it a spindly, serious look. Old Order Amish. Too traditional for rubber tires, too traditional for power lines running to the house. Many Old Order Amish don't have phones, although some'll use a shared phone booth down the road. Anything that goes against humility, simplicity, or community is suspect.

I scanned the lot for signs of the group that intrigued me most—the Swartzentruber Amish, the strictest of them all. I'd read their buggies are spartan, like something out of 1781, everything hard and difficult: a flat bench, no windshield. And at home, everything's stripped down to basics: outhouses, water pumped by hand, walls bare except for coat and hat hooks, no screens of any sort. The Swartzentruber are what most outsiders think of when they think of the Amish. Metal zippers are too modern, too convenient, a sign of vanity. Buttons are allowed, but only in certain configurations. Even the stitching on women's aprons has to follow an approved pattern. The Swartzentruber Ordnung—the unwritten set of rules that governs daily life—is so detailed that it regulates everything from the cut of a jacket to how many pleats are allowed in a woman's prayer covering. If Old Order life feels like a considered choice to live simply, Swartzentruber life seemed more like a refusal to change at all.

I didn't spot any Swartzentruber buggies in the Walmart lot—too modern for them, I figured, even though I knew they must be only a few hillsides removed.

I walked through the automatic doors and—*boom*—into a bonkers cultural crossover. Bright neon lights, family-size bags of Doritos, bins of pool noodles, camouflage baseball caps. The hum of American consumerism. The place smelled like freshly mopped tile and air freshener. It felt almost like a movie set, with roughly half the actors wearing bonnets and straw hats. I passed a young man dressed in dark trousers, suspenders, and a fitted green shirt. His beard was neatly trimmed. *Old Order Amish*, I thought. No electricity but room for variation: in shirt colors, beard length, bonnet styles. Lots of Pennsylvania Dutch spoken at home.

Maybe the best way to describe the Amish dos and don'ts is to say that they live in something of a federalist system, like America's. There are overarching rules for each sect, but then bishops in different regions dictate what's allowed in their particular community. It's a lot like how there are dozens of sects of Hasidic Jews, from the Satmar, who are ultra-strict in their devotion to God with few secular distractions, to the Lubavitchers, where the matriarch of a family I visited in upstate New York shopped at Gucci.

Behind a towering cardboard display of family-size cereal boxes and two-liter soda bottles, I spotted a couple in pastels. The woman wore a light blue dress and a white mesh hair covering, pinned neat and flat. The man beside her had on a clean button-down shirt, no suspenders. *Beachy Amish*, I was thinking. More open to the world. If the Swartzentrubers are the most conservative, then the Beachy are the most liberal. A more traditional house might be lit with kerosene lamps at night, but it wouldn't be unusual to hear "Outen the lights" in a Beachy home when it's time to shut off the plug-in lamps before bed. A Beachy Amish family might drive a pickup, have electricity, use the internet (with some restrictions), and get on a plane to fly to Florida for the winter. Which is a long way of saying the Amish, like most things in life, can't be attached to an easy label.

Feeling like a misplaced extra from another movie, I made my way through the aisles to grab eggs, bagels, cheese, and bacon. I only saw one Amish-branded product in the store: a bag of egg noodles with a beautiful horse-and-buggy logo stamped on the front. The fridges had five flavors of kombucha, and for a second I almost turned around to check if I'd wandered into a Whole Foods off the highway in LA. Nope, definitely not.

Near the deli, I spotted a guy in a T-shirt and sandals—one of the few English people in sight. That's what the Amish call anyone outside their world, no matter your skin color or accent. If you're not them, you're English.

He lived in the area, and when I asked him how he liked it, he just said, "Ignorance is bliss. This Amish world here runs all by itself. They're almost completely detached."

* * *

My rental was a beautiful two-story home surrounded by a wide lawn on all sides. Road out front, forest in the back—deep countryside.

I called Marcus, the man I'd met back in winter in Pinecraft. The number he'd given me was for a phone shanty near his home, so it took a couple of tries, but eventually he answered. He told me he'd be heading to a friend's place the next morning to play shuffleboard in a big barn and I could tag along. I asked if I could make a video with him and his friends. He agreed.

It almost felt too easy.

I turned off the lights and lay there, the forest alive with crickets and tree frogs. After years of urban living, sounds like this felt like a brain massage. I fell into a deep sleep.

Until the "meows" came.

These weren't soft, cute meows—they were aggressive, get-out-here-now meows. Still half asleep, I stumbled downstairs in my underwear and opened the back door. Five cats stood around empty food and water bowls. Next to the washing machine, I found a giant bag of cat food, hauled it outside, and shut the door fast as two of them tried to dart in. I filled the bowl, and they swarmed like it was a Reno buffet. The meowing stopped.

Dawn had just begun to tint the horizon. I felt good. There was still time to catch a little more rest.

Bag in one hand, I reached for the doorknob with the other. Turned it left—nothing. Right—nothing. Back and forth, a tiny bit of play between movements—clicking, but no give. The keypad above the handle was electric. A grid of numbers useless without the Airbnb app on my phone, which was inside.

Then I heard it.

I looked around the side of the house. Hooves on pavement. Steel wheels behind. Old Order Amish.

I darted around to the back of the house so fast my underwear started to slide down. I peered my bald head around the corner. The buggy was gone.

The cats had slowed their eating, licking their lips and looking up at me with that silent, judgy cat stare.

What now?

Obvious. Check the windows and the front door.

Another buggy passed. Not yet 6:00 a.m., and the road was coming to life. Amish rush hour.

I peeked around the house again. The coast was clear.

I bolted, all ghost-white chest and legs, toward the nearest window.

No luck. I tried a second, a third. Locked. The front door, locked. At this point, I looked less like a guest and more like a naked burglar.

The cats were lounging now, bellies full. Not a care in the world. The sun crested the trees. My skin caught it, glowing like one of those metallic reflector emergency blankets. The noise of hooves and metal wheels got louder. The Amish were coming, the Amish were coming.

I retreated to the backyard, trying to think. My video shoot—the one I'd flown out for, the one I'd rented a car for, the one I'd gotten almost impossible access for—was about to start. I could ask for help . . . but that meant walking almost naked across the road and down a long driveway to the neighbor's house. The one without electric wires. Deeply conservative, Old Order or Swartzentruber. Yeah, they were going to love that visit.

Or, option two: Smash glass.

I grabbed a rock from the flowerbed, pulled it up over my right shoulder, and threw it at the glass-paneled door, which shattered in a million pieces inside and out. The cats scattered. I tiptoed over the shards, reached through, and unlocked the door.

I spent the next thirty minutes cleaning up: sweeping, picking glass out of corners, trying to undo the mess I'd made. I showered, then called the Airbnb host, told them what happened, and said I'd replace the glass. The voice on the other end sounded entertained, like the story would be told many times to friends and neighbors.

I've filmed all over the world in some hardcore conditions, but somehow it was five cats in the Amish countryside that nearly took me out.

I sped off, late to make my video.

* * *

The drive south to pick up Marcus was a decent haul through rolling hills and green pastures, a soft landscape that makes you immediately question why you don't live there. After about forty minutes, I pulled into a farm, collected Marcus, and headed off in search of his friends. We drove deeper into the hills, talking about the land, the lifestyle, his recent surgery covered entirely by his church. Though Marcus was Old Order Amish, that didn't mean he opposed modern medicine. He'd had the procedure done at a top-tier hospital.

We were about forty-five minutes into the drive, and I figured it was time to start filming. I pulled over and grabbed my camera.

"What are you doing?" Marcus asked curiously. "We're almost there."

"I'm going to start making the video we talked about."

An awkward silence fell between us.

"Yeah . . . I'm really not interested in being in a video right now."

I respected his wish; I didn't think much of it. It was probably better to start with the action of his friends playing shuffleboard, anyway.

We drove the rest of the way, continuing with our small talk, until an oversized red barn emerged from the tree line, big enough to make the big house next to it look small. Inside was a shuffleboard setup and a crew of old Amish buzzards hanging out, cracking jokes, and playing like they were betting on the game. It was perfect. The setting, the energy, the people. *This is going to be amazing*, I thought. Two of the men yelled out when their disc knocked away the other team's, Pennsylvania Dutch and English getting jumbled up together. It felt like another country.

Sensing it was the right moment, I asked one of the men if I could film their shots. The response wasn't a no, but it wasn't a yes either. I read the room and hung back, watched the game, listened to the conversation. I waited for Marcus to give me the green light.

But that moment never came.

He and his friends weren't interested.

After a few hours, Marcus said he was ready to leave. I said goodbye to the guys and drove Marcus an hour back home. He thanked me, and I went on my way.

A few days later, I told this story to a couple of Amish guys.

"Oh yeah," one of them said, laughing. "He used you for a ride. Old Orders aren't allowed to drive, and there's no public transportation out there. They're always trying to bum rides from English."

I smiled to myself. Marcus totally played me.

And just like that, I was back at square one, with no footage, no story, just a bunch of cats and a broken window with mosquitoes flying through it at my Airbnb.

* * *

I did what I do when I'm out of moves: I drove. It was one of those near-perfect days in rural Ohio. Puffy clouds. Soft green fields stretching toward the horizon, cows grazing in the distance. Every few turns, a mailbox came into view: Yoder, Miller, Yoder, Troyer, Miller again, as if the county were a family reunion stretched across four hundred square miles.

One back road led into another, until the signs thinned out and I turned down a gravel lane I assumed was a shortcut. At the end of the lane was a good-size white farmhouse with a tight clothesline behind it, long black dresses and brown work shirts swaying like they were nodding yes or no, depending on how the wind hit.

I felt bad intruding and started to turn around.

A man and woman were in the yard, barefoot, spreading hay with pitchforks. They looked to be in their mid-twenties. He wore a faded black hat and suspenders pulled snug over a plain gray shirt. Her dress was brown, sleeves to her wrists even in the heat, a crisp white bonnet tied low beneath her chin.

They looked at me with curiosity.

I rolled down the car window and waved. "Sorry, wrong turn."

The man nodded once. "It happens." His voice was flat, polite, with a German accent that made it sound like English wasn't his first language. The woman just smiled.

I hesitated, then asked, "Are you . . . Old Order?"

He shook his head. "No. We're Swartzentruber."

After all the buildup, it felt strangely casual.

"Really?" I said. "I've actually been hoping to meet someone from your group."

The woman gave the faintest smile. The man leaned his pitchfork against the fence.

"Well," he said, "you just did."

We got to talking for a bit, mostly about the land—what they grow, how wet the spring had been. They said it's their usual topic of conversation: nature, seasons, chores. They rented the house from extended family for $250 a month—no indoor plumbing, no electronic conveniences.

I asked what they thought about the US now. They just looked at each other and smiled. I asked them if they knew who the president was; they didn't. At one point, I asked if they ever traveled outside the area. The man laughed softly.

"No need," he said.

The woman glanced up at a long white streak trailing across the sky. "Have you ever been on an airplane?" she asked, like this question had been in her for a while but she just hadn't found the right person to ask.

I nodded.

"What's flying through the clouds like? How does it feel to be like a bird?"

I paused, not expecting that. It took me a moment to figure out how to explain something so routine I'd stopped really thinking about it. "Like being in another layer of the world," I said. "Everything below gets small. You can see the curve of the land. Flying through clouds is peaceful, like . . . floating inside a thought."

I told them I'd been flying a lot lately—because of my work, which was the only reason I was standing here now, in the middle of the Ohio countryside, talking to them.

"Ivan might be open to the video thing," the man said. They'd heard of videos but had never seen one. "He's Old Order, but he talks to English people on the phone when he sells his produce and milk."

"Ivan?"

He nodded toward the road. "Down past the sawmill. He's got tall white hydrangeas out front. You'll see it."

I thanked them and got back in the car. In the rearview mirror, the woman was looking up again at the sky with a smile.

* * *

When I first saw Ivan, he was halfway through a hayfield, standing on a narrow cart hitched up behind two chestnut horses. The air was thick with the sweet, earthy smell of summer work. I called out from the edge of his property, but whatever he shouted back got lost in the distance. He waved me in.

Ivan looked to be in his forties: thin, composed, with a light presence about him. He had on a short-sleeved yellow polo shirt and a straw hat that shaded his face, casting a checkerboard of light across sun-darkened skin and a wide, open smile. His kid was with him, maybe eight years old.

I asked if Ivan might be willing to talk on camera, just a short conversation about Amish life. He said he was good with it, as long as he could keep working. As I stepped onto the cart beside him and his son, he made a high-pitched kissing sound with his lips, and the horses moved forward, the soft rustle of cut grass filling the air beneath us.

Our small talk started with what most outsiders fixate on: modern conveniences. I was trying to make sense of it all as Ivan explained that later he'd be using a motor-driven baler and that he had solar panels elsewhere on his farm. In Amish country, I was learning nothing was as straightforward as it seemed.

"Our church allows it," Ivan explained. "Some don't. There are more than one hundred and forty churches around here. Each district has its own rules, set by its bishop." He grinned, then added with a wink, "Sometimes an Old Order Amish person will move to another district just because they're allowed to bale hay a little easier."

"So first it was from Switzerland to America," I said, "and now it's down the road to a different bishop to get around a rule?"

He threw his head back and laughed. "Exactly," he said. "Gotta adapt somehow."

"What does it look like to you," I asked, "living in the Amish world, when you look out and see other parts of the country? What do you think of it? Or are you just in your own world and don't even notice?"

"Yeah, you notice," he said after a pause. "I follow the news some, and it's just . . . I can't imagine the stress.

"Wherever there's people, there's gonna be problems," he continued. But what the Amish had here felt special. He pointed toward a hill in the distance. "My neighbor, William Miller, he was mowing hay, and he had a real bad accident. And just this last cutting, five of us went in and cut all his hay. The next day, there were fourteen of us raking."

"And he's just your neighbor?" I asked.

Ivan nodded. "Us farmers in this area go out through the pastures, over to the farms, and help each other. But it takes a certain type. You gotta like hard work."

I adjusted my footing as he spoke, trying not to wobble as the machine rocked gently beneath us, leaving combed lines in the grass like a freshly brushed carpet. Ivan's son heard a call from his brother and ran off in his tall rubber boots across the field toward the barn.

"I usually wake up a little before four," Ivan said, almost casually. "Wrap up around ten at night. Winter's different—we might turn in around eight, eight-thirty."

I looked out over the field. "It does feel peaceful, though, when you're this connected to the land."

He smiled. "Oh, it's so relaxing. We don't have electricity, so we mostly read. The true books is what we normally do. I like history, World War II. My kids do too."

I raised an eyebrow. Who'd have thought pacifists would love military history?

It's always amazed me how differently so many groups live in the US. Historically speaking, Native Americans have some of the highest military enlistment rates per capita, and then there's the Amish, pacifists to this day. During World War II, they were given the option of alternative service in hospitals or for food programs. As far as I understand, not a single active member of the Amish church fought in Iraq or Afghanistan.

Compared to the other countries I've lived in, America does a great job of letting people live how they want, as long as it's not hurting anyone else. And so the Amish keep on living in the middle of Ohio, somewhat autonomous. Still here . . . but also in their own version of *there*.

"But there's fun too," Ivan was telling me, wiping a bit of sweat from his temple. "Games, sitting around a fire. It keeps you happy. Like tonight, there's singing practice at the church. Every other Thursday, we play volleyball."

We rode in silence past blackberry bushes, the metal rotating rake clattering softly behind us. The barn came into view, low and wide against the afternoon light.

"Ho," Ivan called out. The horses stopped, and he stepped down from the cart.

Everything on his farm was organic, he'd said—the only way to compete with Big Ag.

"They're the big threat?" I asked.

"The biggest threat," he said, guiding the horses toward the barn, their tails flicking lazily. "And they get all these government subsidies . . ."

"The Amish don't?"

"No." He glanced over. "Well, we probably could . . . but we try not to depend on government. We take care of our own."

He said it plainly, like it was just common sense.

"Big farms, a couple thousand cows," he continued. "I can't imagine how they do it. What lifestyle would that be? Even the cows' lifestyle, can you imagine? You'd never get out on pasture." He shook his head, then pointed behind the barn, where a herd of about thirty cows—black-and-whites, reddish-browns, a few creamy Jerseys—spread out across a field, each doing her own thing.

"See those lines on the side there?" said Ivan, nodding toward one of the cows and pointing near the rib cage. "It's always on the left side, kind of looks like ripples. If they have those, they're relaxed. They're happy. And same way with the calves. If they're used to you when they're young and they grow up with you, it's a big difference."

"What about Amish people?" I asked. "Do you guys have happy lines? If you get on that pie program every day . . ." I have to admit the Amish make the best pies I've had to date.

Ivan let out a loud laugh, then turned abruptly, as if an idea had just struck him. "Did you have a ride on those already?" he asked, nodding toward the buggy parked beside the barn.

I shook my head.

"Well, maybe we should hitch up and go for a ride." He smiled. "It's kind of an Amish farm pickup."

He disappeared into the barn and returned a moment later

with a chestnut gelding. The horse stood still, ears twitching to shoo off summer bugs.

"This is Rex," Ivan said, looping the traces over the horse's back. "He was born in the neighborhood, knows all the roads around here. Even stops at every stop sign without me telling him."

The buggy had four steel wheels, a two-row bench, and a triangular orange SLOW-MOVING VEHICLE sign bolted to the back. Ivan led the horse between the shafts, secured the tugs to the singletree, then clipped the bridle reins to the hames. He checked everything twice—buckles, lines, tension—and waved me over.

"Hop on," he said.

I climbed up beside him. The bench creaked slightly under our weight. With a soft cluck, Ivan flicked the reins and Rex stepped forward, hooves clicking steadily on the gravel as we rolled away from the barn.

The buggy rattled, tracing small cracks in the country road. Ivan held the reins in one hand, his body relaxed but alert, like someone used to long stretches of quiet between turns. Though social, he gave off the feel of someone who spent a lot of time in his own head, just the sound of hooves and wheels, and whatever his mind wandered through for company.

The breeze felt warm on my face as we rustled between the cornfields and well-spaced Amish farmhouses that lined both sides of the road. Holmes County felt more prosperous than I'd expected: clean, orderly, rural but not poor. Construction (a booming business for these folks known to be hard workers), furniture crafting, and many kids helping out around the property had gone a long way. Ivan pointed to a 150-acre lot for sale that he thought could fetch $3 million. Farmhouses stood alongside bigger farmhouses, the landscaping simple but beautiful, almost competitively so. Keeping up with the Joneses Amish-style meant neighbors outdoing each other with their flower beds' edging patterns and sheer square footage of green.

When I pointed out a particularly extravagant flower bed with a little buggy sculpture and an elaborate composition of blooms, Ivan smirked. "That's our way to relax," he said, his Swiss heritage poking through.

He nodded toward a tall building—the new one-room schoolhouse they'd recently built to fit the growing number of children nearby. Out front was parking for bicycles and a covered lot for horses. The school, like most Amish schools, was built and maintained entirely by the community, with no government involvement. Classes are mixed ages, usually first through eighth grade, all taught by a single teacher—typically a young unmarried woman, often just eighteen or twenty years old, who's only studied up to eighth grade herself. The curriculum is basic: reading, writing, arithmetic, some history, some High German or Pennsylvania Dutch, though the main language of instruction is English. There are no computers; there is no standardized testing, no high school or college after. At fourteen, most Amish kids start working full-time on the farm, or homemaking, or learning a trade. Legally, they're allowed to do it this way. After a 1972 Supreme Court case—*Wisconsin v. Yoder*—the Amish were granted religious exemption from compulsory schooling beyond eighth grade so they could emphasize practical skills over formal academics. The schools teach what's needed to be a good neighbor, a good worker, a faithful partner, and a reliable part of the community. Amish schools also generally don't include the Pledge of Allegiance. Their allegiance is spiritual first, local second, and national somewhere after that.

The sound of hooves, the wind in my ears, the saturated green and blue of the landscape . . . it felt almost like meditation. Part of me thought: *I could do this. I could stay here for months. Couldn't I?* But like everything in life, there's the honeymoon period, that stretch of time when everything feels new and fresh and full of possibility. Especially in a place as peaceful as Holmes County, with people as kind as Ivan.

Still, I've been through this cycle before. Novelty wears off. And by year three or four, what does it feel like then?

From the outside, this place is easy to romanticize, especially when you're only seeing the good. And for most Amish, it *is* good: Around 80 percent stay in the church, even though many are allowed a period of rumspringa—a chance to experience the outside world before deciding whether to commit to the Amish ways for life. The Amish have built something robust and stable: tight-knit families, shared values, practical support systems. They run their own health care networks, and homeowners contribute to a shared insurance pool, scaled to the value of their property. If a house burns down, there's funding to rebuild and an army of neighbors ready to do the work. Amish auctions draw hundreds (sometimes thousands) from across sects, and English too, bidding on everything from leaf blowers and grills to horses and furniture—sometimes even items prohibited by their own church, just to win and gift them back, letting the auction keep the money. One recent auction raised over $500,000 for the Rainbow of Hope fund, which covers children's medical care.

It seems a lot like the Amish have figured out the answers to problems so many of us are going through today, without even trying. They just stayed looking at their fields while the modern world put its eyeballs up to screens. "Everyone knows each other," a viewer commented under my video; they're "literally hanging out just enjoying one another's company. No phones, no TV, no distractions. It's just so refreshing to see people who aren't messed up by the modern world."

To thrive in a group like this, of course, you have to stay aligned with its values. And I admire that. But it's not for the free spirit. Not for someone drawn to change, to discovery, to unanswered questions that don't start, or stop, with the Bible. Not for someone who wants to try integrating new ideas into everyday life. Not for someone like me.

Maybe that sounds selfish to the Amish. Maybe it is. But the America that lets the Amish be the Amish is the same America that lets us all chart our own paths. So many of our ancestors came to this country looking to get away from monarchs or dictators or repressive landowners. Looking for less top-down control, more life on their own terms. But everything in life is a trade-off. You give something up to get something else. It's all a choice. And the table must be set to allow people to flourish, whatever choice they make. That's the beauty of America.

We passed a buggy in the opposite lane: black canopy, two riders, a wave exchanged without breaking stride. It felt like living in a postcard from another century: simple, timeless. Then a tractor-trailer roared past, dragging its noise and its weight with it, snapping us back to the twenty-first century.

Rex turned down a gravel lane and slowed to a stop. Ivan let the reins slacken and looked off into the trees, head tilted slightly, listening.

"I love bird watching," Ivan said. "If they're migrating, I see a lot of them."

"How many different types of birds are here?"

"Oh, I don't know," he said, squinting slightly. "If you count the migrating birds and everything, two hundred thirty-seven."

"And you know all their sounds?"

He nodded. "More than that." The small wink that followed felt like the first time all day he'd let himself brag.

I looked at him for a moment. There was something utopian about the idea: a man who could sit still long enough to memorize the voices of hundreds of different birds.

Back at Ivan's place, his three sons came rolling up the gravel lane in a small two-wheeled fore cart pulled by a mule. They looked to range from eight to fourteen, all squeezed shoulder-to-shoulder on the bench. The youngest boy jumped off first, cupping something carefully in his hands. He ran straight toward us, a proud grin on his face.

"Ah," Ivan said, already smiling. "Look what he's got—three worms."

The boy held out a pair of broad milkweed leaves. Curled on top were three fat caterpillars, striped and slow-moving.

"What are you gonna do with them?" I asked.

"He's gonna put 'em in a jar," Ivan said with a soft smile. "They eat the milkweed."

The boy turned and trotted back toward his brothers to help with the mule.

"I just . . . I can't imagine not having that," Ivan had said earlier, looking at his sons in the distance, running in the field. "Growing up, I had seven sisters and two brothers. I was in the middle, and there was always something happening. You can imagine."

"Yeah, I'll bet."

"You're never bored. All the cousins . . . we had a lot of fun. Oh, we had a lot of fun." His gaze drifted away as he said it, like he'd stepped briefly back into the memory, and there was a brief pause before I asked, "What advice would you give the outside world? What could they learn from you guys?"

He smiled. "Maybe we should be learning from them."

I laughed. "Ah, I wouldn't say so these days."

He looked around for a moment, thinking. "I think if they go back and base a lot of stuff off the Bible," he said, "morally, I think that would help a lot. But it's definitely not for everybody . . . as you know."

He and I talked a bit about values, about drugs and alcohol. I told him about all the theft at the Walgreens near my apartment in San Francisco, about how stealing up to $950 was just a misdemeanor and so the DA wouldn't prosecute, so the cops gave up on catching criminals who'd be back on the street again that day.

"Steal up to $950 from a store and not get in trouble?"

"I know, it's wild. I've seen people try to return the stuff they just stole."

"That is sad. So sad," he said. Then, more quietly, "But what are they taught when they're young? Do they have a chance? Are they . . . innocently stealing?"

"Innocently stealing?" I repeated.

He nodded. "Were they ever told it was wrong? Or are they taught you're just not supposed to get caught stealing?"

I didn't really know how to answer.

"I mean, us Amish, we're human. There's problems here too," he added. "But . . ."

I looked at him. "What are your biggest problems, would you say?"

I'd learn from comments on this video that there were problems in Amish country with puppy mills—large-scale dog breeding operations, some of which engage in animal cruelty, especially after demand for puppies surged during the pandemic and there was a lot of money to be made. But in all my time in Holmes County, I never saw one. I can't say if it was an uncommon occurrence or a common one. Ivan said he didn't know anyone raising puppies in his area. But these things happen behind closed doors. And I wasn't out there looking for scandal or outrage. I was looking for the good in people. That's mostly what I try to do in my videos.

Ivan thought for a moment. "My biggest problem is being a good father to my children. Just trying to be the best I can, but . . . I'm human. They get frustrated with me, I'm sure. I might work too much one day." Or there'd be other days where "they might have to pitch in and do a little bit more work, because I couldn't be at work all the time." He paused. "And for me, I have to watch I'm not too hard on the kids. So they don't get bitter. I can be too tough sometimes."

"How do you know where the line is?" I asked.

"You tell me."

"I don't know. I don't have kids."

"It's a tough one. As a father, it's hard to grasp that your sixteen-year-old thinks everything you do might be wrong. But . . . they still respect you quite a bit, they still respect you." He said it like he was reminding himself more than me. "It's just . . . it's a tough age."

"It's gotta be tough with all the technology these days," I added.

"It is." Ivan nodded. "It's tough on them."

"They all want that too, don't they? The phones, the screens?"

"Probably at some point," he said. "But if you tell them what the danger is, that makes a big difference."

Then, almost to himself, he said, "I don't know why we humans can't just . . . learn."

We both laughed.

I've moved around too much for my roots to ever go as deep as Ivan's. But I admired the life he lives. It's been five years now since the afternoon we spent together, and I still think sometimes of how much I admire his connection to his land, to his community. I live in Florida these days—just a few hours from Pinecraft, actually—and I've been trying to get better at learning the calls of the birds in my neighborhood. I haven't put in enough time to know the names of many birds yet, but I can now separate many of the different sounds. Before it was just birds chirping; now it's completely separate songs. I've been listening to the noises of palm branches blowing in the wind, to all the soothing sounds that come from my surroundings. Instead of just moving through nature, I'm trying to observe it more. To be present here, in this place where I'm at.

The road back from Ivan's home was empty that evening as I drove away, except for a single buggy in the distance. Its steel wheels rolled steadily along the pavement, hooves tapping out a slow, even rhythm, as the grassy hills glowed orange in the light of the setting sun. It was a rhythm that stayed with me long after the sound.

CHAPTER 2

East LA

Twenty-four hundred miles southwest of Holmes County, Ohio, wheels kept spinning in East LA.

A low throb of bass filled the air, announcing the arrival of a different kind of ride. The lowrider crept in slow: a white '65 Impala with its roof down, a candy-red interior, chrome rims mirroring the flat gray sky. Hydraulics kicked the front end up, then let the car sink smoothly in the back, with all the hissing and mechanical rhythm of a well-thought-out machine. People watched. It was hard not to.

I was killing time outside the King Taco on the corner. A landmark. A neighborhood spot where the guys had told me to meet. Mariachi musicians in full black suits sat under one of the red umbrellas, laughing and eating like they'd been doing so all day. The air smelled of grilled meat, corn oil, and lime: thick, smoky, and unmistakably LA. You could feel a little ocean in it too, carried in on the breeze from miles west of here.

East LA didn't always look like this. A century ago, this neighborhood was mostly farmland. Boyle Heights, just east of the Los Angeles River, was one of the most diverse places in the state. Jewish, Japanese, Russian, Mexican . . . everyone lived on the same block, because it was one of the places they were allowed. Real estate covenants barred non-Whites from buying in some other parts of the city, especially neighborhoods in West LA. So folks built their lives here.

How a century can change a place. These days, the biggest challenge to the local culture is gentrification, pushing out from western parts of LA with all the economic muscle of a robust economy behind it.

The Impala rolled to a stop half over the line, claiming two parking spaces on purpose. Nobody said a thing. Out here, this kind of car parks where it wants to.

The driver—thick mustache, full Los Angeles Rams gear—raised his hand and motioned me over with a short nod. In the passenger seat, I recognized Andy, a guy I'd been texting with for a few weeks. Andy was mid-thirties: shaved head, dark glasses, with a Pendleton board shirt buttoned to the top, tattoos down to his fingertips, and a film camera strapped around his neck. He'd told me he wanted to preserve the essence of Chicano culture through his still lens, and maybe I could help with the motion part.

Ernie stepped out of the driver's seat, a calm but commanding presence. Like those dog owners whose pets end up looking just like them, Ernie's moves mirrored the lift-and-drop of his lowrider, smooth and stoic.

"You wanna get some tacos?" asked Andy, saying *tacos* with that unmistakably Spanish lift.

There's something about breaking bread with strangers that shifts the tone of an encounter, sets people at ease. You're not just passing through anymore—you're part of it all. Breaking bread got me into homes in the high mountains of the Republic of Georgia, the outer worldliness of Eritrea, and across the desert cities of Iran. East LA in its own right was another foreign experience for me.

King Taco was all wall-to-wall tile and laminated menus that appeared not to have changed in over a decade. Tacos cost $1.99, burritos $3.99, prices that made it cheaper to eat here than at home. We ordered fast. A pork tamale. A beef tongue burrito. Chicken tacos. I took a sip of my horchata, which showed up in a blink and tasted like someone's grandma still made it in the back. She probably did.

A friend of Andy's—Ronin, another guy probably in his thirties—was already there, leaning near the napkin dispensers, waiting. He had the kind of presence that didn't ask for attention but got it anyway: black T-shirt, gray sweats, long braids down to his chest. Arms inked in code: old English, Aztec lines, block letters folded into flames. We exchanged the East LA handshake: firm, quick shoulder lean, just enough eye contact to say *We're good.* Then he looked at me straight on, like he was saying *Andy told me to trust you. Don't f**k it up.*

Though I'd been to LA dozens of times, East LA was new territory for me. (It technically isn't even in Los Angeles proper. It's just outside, an unincorporated part of Los Angeles County.) For a video maker, LA is a treasure trove: so many unique lifestyles running in parallel, the frame always interesting, sounds and colors overlapping, an ordered chaos I first learned to appreciate watching director Robert Altman, whose roaming camera technique probably influenced my filmmaking style the most. Altman's best known these days for *M*A*S*H*, but *Short Cuts* has always been my favorite of his. His busy visuals and overlapping dialogue make his work feel interactive, real.

That afternoon, I was at King Taco because there was a story about Chicanos I wanted to make . . . but that wasn't the whole reason. Amish country had stayed with me. The way people there moved through life—unforced, purposeful, like they know something much of the modern world forgot. When I got home, I got to wondering if that same sort of grounded culture could exist outside a rural setting. Maybe it did—right here in my old California backyard—in the way these guys poured their souls into chrome, hydraulics, pressed Dickies pants instead of buggies, farms, and suspenders.

There was something about the places that seemed to mirror each other in ways I couldn't quite explain but also couldn't ignore. Two cultures built around craft and belonging, around people trying to hold on to what matters most before it gets swallowed up by the rest of the world. Maybe there was some wisdom out on these streets.

The guys and I scored the one empty table outside the restaurant; families filled the rest. Toddlers hanging off chairs, tías wiping mouths with paper towels, plastic bags already packed with extras for tomorrow sitting beside half-finished plates.

We laid our spread out across the plastic table. Andy passed around the little salsa cups. "You gotta ask the people which do they prefer, the green or the red sauce? You're gonna get people to battle it out."

I smiled. "I'm red sauce for life."

A paper-lined tray dropped in front of me. More crispy, golden tacos, still sizzling. I hadn't ordered them.

"That's for you," Ernie said, a smile hitting his eyes. "I told him to hook you up. It's birria. Crunchy on the outside, juicy inside. Dip it in that cup right there, it's called consommé. Don't be shy with it, you gotta get it messy."

He waited for me to pick one up, still dripping with oil, the tortilla clasped around shredded beef and melted cheese. It cracked at the bite, meat spilling out, red broth running down my fingers. The crisp shell gave out halfway through, onion, cilantro, grease, everything landing on the wax paper in a little collapse of glory, just how it's happened thousands of times before from the exact seat I was sitting on.

"You know, it's funny," I said. "I just made some videos about the Amish, and to be honest, I can see a lot of similarities out here."

Ronin raised his eyebrows, clearly surprised. Which was fair. In Holmes County, the colors had been muted apart from the blooming flowers: worn denim, raw wood, sun-faded buildings. Here, color shouted: candy-colored paint, gold rims flashing, murals telling stories of saints, struggles, and pride. Back there, silence did the talking; here, every block had a beat. And yet.

"I mean, check this out," I continued. "Just like the Amish, people out here can be a little hesitant to approach you . . ."

"For different reasons," Ernie said.

"Exactly. And both of you kind of share a stronghold of roots that can't be shaken. Even the Spanish accent in your English, yeah?"

"Oh yeah," Ronin said, nodding as he set his taco down—overloaded and coming apart like mine.

"Actually, my Spanish isn't so good. I didn't grow up speaking it. English is my first language." Ernie said this with a heavy Spanish accent.

"We all kinda got a hint of accent here," Ronin added. "My first language is English, both of my parents were born here in California. People still call you Mexican, though. No matter what you tell them."

"You can say whatever you want, but at the end of the day, you're gonna be considered Mexican here," Andy said.

"What do you want people to call you?" I asked.

"I'm fine with Chicano," said Ronin. "That's how I see myself. In America, they say you're Mexican. You go to Mexico, and they say, 'You're American.'"

He'd later lift the cuff of his gray sweats to show his family's story on his shin. On the left, the Mexican flag draped above rows of men bent over in the fields. "That's my grandfather," he'd say, tugging higher. On the right, an American flag and a soldier with a helmet. "My pops, he was in Vietnam." Half Mexico, half America—one body, both histories.

I'd read more about Chicano culture after returning home. The word itself once came from outsiders as an insult, then got taken back and worn with pride. The culture emerged from the kids of immigrants who grew up in neighborhoods like this one, who spoke both languages but belonged fully to neither, so they made their own. Although it's worth remembering that not every Mexican American family crossed a border to get here. For a few, the border crossed them. The map moved, not the people—whole communities (some eighty thousand people) ending up on the American side of a line suddenly redrawn in 1848 after the Mexican–American War. All of California and Nevada and Utah, much of Arizona and New Mexico, parts of Colorado and southwestern Wyoming . . . all that was once Mexico.

Chicano is what happens when heritage collides with survival. In Mexico, culture is rooted—regional, specific, centuries deep. In Southern California, it had to adapt. The same ingredients but cooked up a little different. It's Catholic votive candles next to Dodger caps, abuelas who bless their grandkids before they leave for work in warehouses or movie studios or schools, still praying in Spanish but dreaming in English.

East LA wears all of it like a badge of honor. Just over a hundred thousand people live in this part of the city, and a good amount of them carry that mix: Mexican ancestry, American reality, Chicano identity. In California as a whole? Many more. The census won't tell you who's Chicano, because it's not a box you check. It's a personal decision. And most Mexican Americans nationwide wouldn't consider themselves Chicanos; East LA is the culture's ground zero.

"Neither here nor there," I said through a full mouth.

"Exactly," Ronin replied, nodding like we'd just defined something that didn't need more words.

* * *

"You ready to cruise?" Ernie asked, opening the Impala's door and adjusting the front seat so I could climb into the back. Not that I couldn't have done it myself, but it felt like you had to earn a little more trust before touching his car uninvited.

"Only thing I ask: Please be careful with the seat belts. Try not to sit on them." He sounded chill as ever, but I had no doubt he'd go mental if someone sat on the metal buckle and indented his fresh leather seats.

The Spyres' "Looking for a Place" cracked out of the speakers as I sank into soft leather. Pure, sweet soul carried by low, intimate vocals. There was a weariness to them, a longing. Played here in East LA, it makes you picture the eclectic streets, night cruising, the city moving at half speed. Played in Holmes County—not that the Amish would—the melody would have drifted over open fields, jarring the quiet porches like a fire alarm.

The hydraulics let out a hiss. The Impala bounced once, and the engine rumbled through the frame. Ernie hit the gas and we glided out, Ronin beside me and Andy in the front passenger seat.

It felt like floating.

Tall palm trees lined the street, soft sun rays poking through the hazy air—the golden hour, which was almost any time of day in the low California February sun. No wonder Hollywood loves this place. Set anything against this backdrop and it'll feel like something worth watching.

I pointed at a black panel with two rows of toggles lined up, like cockpit controls.

"What's that?"

"A switch box," Ernie said. "Flips the hydraulics on and off, gives you bounce. Back in the day they used to pull us over for driving too low. That was illegal, so we figured out a way to drop it when we wanted and raise it when we had to."

Savvy, I thought.

He told me about how guys used to bring home parts from the aerospace jobs and machine shops that are abundant in Southern California: hydraulic pumps, metal tubing, aircraft-grade switches. All of it then adapted for style and cultural flair. The switch box was the brain and every flick on it controlled bounce, lift, or lean.

"Cruising got banned too," he added. "They said it was a gang thing, but most of it was just culture."

Lowriders gained popularity after World War II, after Mexican American veterans came home to the barrios of East LA with some money, new skills, and a taste for style. They'd seen the world, fought for their country, and returned ready to create something of their own. Chevys, Buicks, Cadillacs, and Oldsmobiles became that canvas.

At first, it was about cruising slow instead of racing fast—*low and slow*, as the saying goes. While other young men in SoCal were becoming hot-rodders, jacking their vehicles up, or chasing speed, Chicano drivers were dropping theirs to the pavement, gliding through the streets like kings. It was a way of saying: *We're here, and we'll make you stop and look without us having to say a word.*

Police didn't see it that way. In the late '50s and early '60s, California passed laws banning cars from being too low, like Ernie said. So Chicanos got creative. They installed hydraulics—repurposed postwar aircraft landing gear—that let a car lift itself at the push of a button. By the '70s, lowriders with narrative paint jobs were embedded in Chicano culture. Saints. Family. Aztec imagery. Chrome halos around the Virgin of Guadalupe. Every car a moving altar.

We passed a three-story mercado: red-tiled arches, the smell of tortillas and spices drifting into the street. We then hit Soto Street southbound, five quick blocks to jump onto Whittier Boulevard. First thing you noticed was the massive El Arco arch overhead, a monument of identity, like a Chicano Statue of Liberty. Neon taco trucks jostled outside liquor stores, laundromats, and pupuserías. A few carts sold bombas: water cans on ice, tamales wrapped in banana leaves, bacon-wrapped "ditch dogs" still steaming. Flags in the windows—Mexican, Salvadoran, Honduran, American—waved above metal gates and marquees fending off the weak winter afternoon sun.

I spotted a purple late-'60s Impala, two lifted mid-'70s Chevys, and a green '71 Buick Riviera with blinding gold rims. But there was something familiar missing.

"I haven't seen one homeless person," I said, nodding toward the sidewalk devoid of sleeping paraphernalia, which was unusual for early 2022. "If we were in Santa Monica, there'd be someone horizontal right here."

Ronin looked around, then back at me. "You don't really see Mexicans or Chicanos begging," he said. "They'd rather clean windows, sweep driveways, or sell hot dogs instead of waiting for the handout. It's probably pride, but it's also the code—you work for your money."

My door panel vibrated with bass, a Roger Troutman tune, drawing looks as we pulled up outside a small storefront. From the street, it looked like any other East LA corner shop. Weathered signage: CIGARETTES, USB, LPS. Freddy Fender playing in a pleasantly screechy voice from a sun-bleached speaker mounted above the door. It was only inside that you realized the place was a neighborhood archive. Racks of flannels, posters of Pedro Infante, candles, rosaries. Eastside lowrider art mixed with black-and-white flyers and old-school turntables behind glass.

Ronin led me to one of the walls, where faded newspaper clippings declared: DRAMATIC PHOTOS TAKEN AT SCENE OF SALAZAR'S DEATH. "This was during the Chicano Moratorium in 1970," he explained. "Over twenty thousand marched through East LA, protesting the Vietnam War." He tapped one photo—deputies in riot gear. By afternoon, LAPD and sheriff's deputies had moved in, claiming a nearby liquor store robbery required them to disperse everyone. Instability followed. "It was supposed to be peaceful, but the sheriffs unleashed tear gas and billy clubs on the crowd. People fought back, and it turned into chaos."

But by 1970, the Chicano Movement—El Movimiento—was in full swing. It was part of the larger civil rights movement of the 1960s, focused on social, political, and economic issues affecting Mexican Americans. There were farmworker strikes and boycotts led by labor leaders like César Chávez and Dolores Huerta, student walkouts, and efforts to reclaim ancestral lands across the Southwest. But alongside all this was also a flourish of Chicano art and literature. By the mid-1970s, the word *Chicano* had evolved into both a political statement and a cultural identity.

Ronin leaned in toward another clipping, deputies in riot gear aiming their launchers toward a café. "Ruben Salazar was in here, just where we stand. He was a journalist trying to speak up about what was happening. Stepped inside to take a break, and a deputy fired a tear gas round through the door. Hit him in the head, killed him on the spot."

Outside, the speakers rolled out the Monitors' "Greetings (This Is Uncle Sam)."

The car was waiting. The boulevard rolled on.

* * *

The pine stood tall against a pale blue sky, just off N Indiana and Folsom. A landmark with no plaque.

"Is that the tree from *Blood In, Blood Out*?" I asked.

"Yeah," Ronin said. "That's the one."

Blood In, Blood Out is the story of three cousins from East LA whose lives take very different paths. Set between prison and the streets, it's about family and loyalty and how our choices ultimately define our lives. A three-hour movie that came out in 1993, though most people missed it when it dropped, it was a box office failure, turned into a Chicano cult classic.

"Why that movie?" I asked. "Why does it stick? Why is gang life always the headline?"

Ronin shrugged. "I guess it's loud, dramatic stakes, good scenes. Nobody wants to watch a guy hold down a job for thirty years. That doesn't make interesting cinema." He nodded toward the houses across the street. "But it's not just about gangs. That movie had art, family, betrayal, pride. Gangs were part of it, but they weren't the whole thing. That's what people get wrong."

He began telling me how most of what people call "gang culture" didn't start out that way. He said that back in the day, these were just neighborhood crews: guys who grew up on the same block, went to the same school, the same park. They'd hang out after church, start sports teams, name their crew after the barrio or a nearby street. White Fence, Maravilla, Dogtown—all those started as tight-knit cliques, not criminal empires.

"There were always fights," he said, "but it wasn't organized like people think. Not at first."

A lot of the older guys—veteranos—came back from Vietnam with medals in their pockets and no work waiting. Some became mentors to the newer generation, steering them off the street, but the pressure kept building. Cops would roll up and ask your name just for standing outside, and if five guys from the same neighborhood kicked it too often, they called it a gang. And it's true, the Chicanos had their fair share of hardcore gangs.

"Once the police started treating everyone like criminals," Ronin said, "people just rolled with it. Like, if we're gonna get labeled anyway, might as well own it." He told me how pachuco culture played into it—slicked-back hair; zoot suits with high-waisted, wide-legged pants tapered at the ankle; street slang—and how even the early look became a problem. "Too proud, too loud, too brown. There were always guys doing dirt," he added. "But most were just trying to look out for each other."

We passed a building where layers of blue spray paint tried to wipe out the black underneath. Gang-related Chicano hieroglyphics, Ronin had said. You had to know how to read them.

"Back then, gangs came out of pressure and defense," he told me. "Now it's about power, drugs, and money."

Power, drugs, money. So many of America's so-called south sides or east sides in you-name-the-city are struggling with crime tied to these three things. I've been to many of these areas, places where residents are often warm and inviting and eager for more policing to bring a sense of security to their children's lives. But they're also places where the most hardened criminals hold the most power, dragging everyone else down, creating a chaotic order built on fear. These are the neighborhoods where a fifty-two-year-old is now scared of the fourteen-year-old with a gun and a still-developing brain spinning off who dissed them on TikTok. The hierarchy isn't built off years of reputation and respect anymore; it's built off who's willing to do the craziest or scariest stuff.

"Don't believe everything you read, though," Ernie added. "Not everyone in the barrio is in a gang. But it's easier to get in the mix than you think."

"Exactly," Ronin echoed. "It's all about influence. If I come around and I'm older and I have nice cars and I have women and I have jewelry and I dress nice—and you're poor, you have none of that stuff—you're going to listen to me. You're going to be like, 'Oh man, that guy's so cool. I want to be like *him*.'"

"What age do kids start getting into gangs?" I asked.

"I would say toward the end of elementary school into junior high, so probably as young as ten to twelve. All boys are looking for someone to identify with, and if you don't have a male figure in the household, joining a gang is very inviting."

I'd seen this before in other places, the criminal element showing young men leadership, attention, and the "love" they might not get enough of at home.

"The truth is, for a lot of people, it's generational," Ronin said. "My father said, 'I didn't have to join a gang to see what it was like to stab someone with a bayonet,'" speaking about his time in Vietnam. "But for a lot of people, it just comes from the generations: If your grandfather was in a gang, and then your father was in a gang, then maybe you feel inclined to join the gang, because it feels almost like a tradition."

"Is that why you stayed out of it too? Because of your father's example?"

Ronin paused. "I got caught up in the drug business when I was younger. And I realized that it's true what they say, 'You got death or prison.' Most of my friends that I grew up with, they're no longer living, and a few of them are never getting out of jail."

"What made you change?"

"I was about twenty-four. Facing twenty years. I got really lucky, I had a great lawyer. But in that moment, I had to make a choice: 'Is this what I wanna do, or do I wanna change?'"

He chose change.

"I got the option to start in the motion picture business. I started working for a writer-director, Mark Brown. I worked for him as an intern, then background. The first movie I did was *Hancock* with Will Smith." He smiled a little at that one. "After that, I did assistant camera. I was PA for two years for *Judge Judy* and *Judge Joe Brown* at KTLA. And I did *Divergent*, *Insurgent*, *Allegiant*, *Black Panther* . . . even *Alvin and the Chipmunks*."

He didn't sound like a guy chasing stardom, more like

someone who'd steered himself out of turbulence and now had the self-confidence to chart his own course.

"What do you like most?"

"Acting," he said. "That's what I really love. I booked a pilot just recently and made more money than I've ever made in my life. I'm gonna reinvest that and do more acting. It's easy to go back and do the same thing. It's hard to do something that you've never done before. It's scary, but you just gotta have faith and trust." He looked distant for a minute. "I respect guys in the game. But I don't need to be in the mix anymore."

"At the end of the day, Chicano culture is all about respect, right?" I asked.

Ronin nodded. "That's everything. In most neighborhoods—especially where people don't have money or material things—respect is all they've got. Their name, their reputation, that's the real currency. And that's how this bubble within LA operates."

I'd been thinking a lot about bubbles since getting back from Ohio, about the good and the bad. You can't really preserve a culture without some degree of isolation from the cultures that surround it. Think of Chinatowns in big cities, where some people barely leave the few blocks near where they live, and speaking English isn't necessary. That kind of insulation keeps a language alive, a cuisine, a tradition, a way of life that feels familiar. Same goes for gangs. Once you're in, you're surrounded by people who move the same, talk the same, expect the same. There's an order: territory, loyalty, reputation. It all becomes normal. Outsiders don't come in, and insiders rarely step out. I've been in parts of East New York where a teenager could change the trajectory of his life if he just took the subway a few stops farther. If he focused hard on self-improvement and working his way up. One of the biggest economies in the world is right there at his fingertips. But you can get stuck in what you know.

I think it's fair to say that most people talking about American culture can't point to where the Hopi people live or talk with experience about Chicano culture or the calm of Molokai, Hawaii. They may hear of these far-off things from time to time, but in many ways they're as sheltered as a kid who's never strayed far from Appalachia or Wilshire Boulevard or Newport, Rhode Island. If you're speaking to the country from behind a lens, live on air every weekday evening, you're going to spend your days commuting from your home to some news studio in an urban center. You're not spending a week or two each month connecting with your fellow Americans somewhere far in the interior. But I think if someone's going to speak to the country, a prerequisite should be being curious about this country, and the various people, perspectives, and cultures in it.

Growing up in the United States doesn't make anyone an expert on this place. To understand all corners of it takes a lot of curiosity, and a lot of listening. I'm on the road now over a third of the year, and traveling the US is helping me understand that I'll never understand *everything*. The more I see, the more I realize I haven't seen. America goes granular; it breaks into millions of shards of individual stories. It took me until my forties to fully grasp this, but when I now look at a map, I realize how much of the country I haven't experienced, how many stories are out there, how much there still is to explore. How the place is way too complex for any one mind to fully comprehend.

My aim has always been to get out of *my* bubble. And I've been amazed over the years at how many people have welcomed me into *theirs*. And I think it's true that you can learn more about yourself in a week of looking at your community as a spectator than in a decade of living in it as a participant. Experiences outside the norm sharpen things. You start to observe what's real and what's just habit dressed up as cultural identity. That's what I respected about Ronin. He'd gone out—to Hollywood—and actually looked back at his old neighborhood from a distance, clear-eyed about both what leaving meant and what staying demanded.

He kept the pride, the discipline, the loyalty he grew up with, but he left the rest—the drugs, the hollow noise, the gangs. There's something to admire in that: a man who loves his culture, truly, but who can recognize the aspects of it that no longer serve him. Who goes searching for more and finds it . . . but doesn't lose the parts of home that helped to get him there.

* * *

We cruised slow, cool air drifting in as the last light faded, pink haze just starting to rim the sky. Palm trees slid by on both sides, tall and motionless, their silhouettes reflecting off the polished car hood like they were painted on. Everything felt slower in the best way, slow enough that I could notice being *present* in a way I hadn't felt in a while.

Almost every building we drove past had a patch covered in perfectly executed murals—DJs spinning records, Saint Mary holding hands in prayer next to Santa Muerte wrapped in roses, dragons spitting fire. More cars were showing up. First just one, then two, then three lined up along the curb, bouncing, gleaming, cruising at 5 mph.

"Car show on this block tonight," Ernie said over his shoulder.

By the next intersection, the whole block was lit. We were

gliding behind a bright orange Monte Carlo, front end lifted high, rear bumper almost tickling the pavement. Through the back window, I caught flashes of the interior: orange tuck-and-roll upholstery, a chain-link steering wheel, little Saint Jude swinging from the rearview mirror. A green Buick on deep twenty-inch gold rims sat parked at an angle, its paint job glittering with metallic flake that caught every bit of fading sunlight. A boxy, dark-blue Caprice with TAXI written across the side rolled by.

People were everywhere—families in foldable chairs, drinks in hand, some waving, others just watching. Vendors were set up under LA Dodgers tents selling framed art of La Virgen, Aztec warriors, and calaveras wearing LA hats. A few tourists hung back, fluorescent storefront signs reflected in their wide eyes.

Street music came from every direction: voices singing in Spanish, funk classics, West Coast oldies. Someone's trunk cracked open with bass thumping. Hydraulics hissed, kids ran between bumpers, a honk blared every time someone spotted a familiar face.

Andy waved into the air. "When you hear the Spanish music, like for example this right here—that's called a *corrido*. Corridos are basically . . ." He seemed to be searching. "It's a drug ballad."

"A drug ballad?"

He nodded. "Yeah. They're probably singing about a drug dealer or drug dealer situation, or someone big in that business."

I learned later that drug ballads may be corridos, but not all corridos are about drugs.

"Do the dealers pay for the song?"

"For the most part, yeah." Andy shrugged. "There's some where the groups will just make it for them, like a way of commemorating them."

It was hard to square the culture's warmth and hospitality with these hints of bad-boy admiration for drug dealers and gangbangers.

"And then some of them are just about love," Andy said as a new rhythm kicked up nearby. "We're not only drug dealers—we're also lovers."

"A lot of emotion?" I laughed.

"Yeah! We're passionate about everything we do."

A police SUV rolled by in the opposite direction, met with claps and whistles.

"Nice rims!" I shouted, trolling the officers.

"Make it bounce! Make it bounce!" Andy called, pumping his hand up and down in the air.

The cops smiled behind the glass, like they wouldn't mind bouncing too if they weren't on the clock.

"I've never experienced anything like this in my life," I said, unable to stop smiling.

Andy laughed. "Doesn't look like a bunch of scary gang-bangers, huh?"

"These neighborhoods are getting slowly gentrified," Ronin added, "so people do this weekly"—trying to show this place is still theirs as well. "All these lowriders you see? It's not just fun and bonding for the community; they're a form of art too."

"That takes up all your money." Ernie smirked from behind the wheel.

I grinned as a Bel Air convertible with a spotless white-and-mint-green two-tone paint job rolled by, straight out of 1953. "I can only imagine."

Andy waved to two ladies in sunglasses and rhinestone-decorated tops.

"That's Sandy and Vanessa—president and vice president

of an all-women car club. And the lady in the Charlie Brown top? She's an OG. Works in the legal department at Boeing. She always says her lowrider's her stress reliever. I bet most of her workmates in her corporate job have no idea she lives this life too."

The culture was having a resurgence, they'd told me earlier. Chicanos once caught up in turf wars had grown up, raising families of their own. Former enemies could now relax, spend time together with their kids. The recession in 2008 had led a lot of people to sell their cherished rides, but the comeback in the winter of 2022 was real. *Peak Chicano*, Andy told me.

I looked around at the packed sidewalks, lowriders lined up in both lanes.

"The turnout is insane."

"And you'll catch everybody here, you know?" Andy said. "Samoans, Cambodian brothers will be up in here. We don't discriminate when it comes to this culture right here. And nobody picks things up like the Japanese. We've got a Japanese brother named Hide, speaks a little Spanish, swears he's Mexican at heart. He used to trip when our homies would hug him and kiss him on the head. He wasn't used to that. And it's wild how many people follow my photography account from around the world. They love the aesthetics, the vibe, the details. There's just so much flavor in it, you know? We're passionate people. We're passionate about everything we do."

Passion. If the Amish have mastered tranquility—life at the pace of sunrise and sunset—then I was realizing, cruising down Santa Clara Street as twilight fell, that Chicanos have mastered something just as rare: a joy in motion. In color. In flavor. In sound. Maybe today the lowrider's the center point, but I'd begun to suspect the car was sort of like the tortilla, just the thing holding in all the other ingredients. When really, it's about neither. The car, the taco . . . they're just the vehicles to bring everyone together.

"I get so many tourists wanting to ride in my Impala," Ernie said as we rode on down Santa Clara. "And I love it. I want to make it my full-time job—cruising people for their special occasions, proms, city tours . . ."

"It is kinda special, huh?" I heard Ronin say beside me. "Sometimes we're so deep in it, we forget what makes it that way."

CHAPTER 3

An Island in the Bering Sea

In most of Alaska, you don't drive to places—you fly in.

So, here I was on a small Bering Air plane, one of those older commuter types with stairs that fold straight out of the fuselage. There were only about a dozen seats, and they looked like they'd been pulled from a Greyhound bus circa 1979. At boarding, I'd watched a few passengers shove Walmart bags and taped-up boxes with Costco goodies under the seats like they were settling in for a ride across town. There was no safety briefing and no exit-row speech; no one told us to fasten our seat belts. It felt like a city bus with wings.

The trip from Florida to where I was headed takes something like 21.5 hours, with three layovers. As a bird flies, traveling from Miami to Casablanca, Morocco is closer than Miami to Savoonga, Alaska, USA: 4,300 miles to 4,700.

I'd been realizing that many Americans—and this included me, until a few years ago—think they've seen the United States because they've been to cities, some rural spots, national parks, maybe done a few cross-country road trips. But America gives the gift of a lifetime of discovery to those who seek it. You could spend years just exploring Alaska's islands. The state has approximately 2,670 named islands. (Maine has thousands more.)

I hadn't even heard of Saint Lawrence Island, not until I stumbled across it on Google Earth late one night. Zoomed out, it was this giant land mass in the Bering Sea; zoomed in, the details barely filled in. There were just a few road lines, no street view, and no house numbers. Two faintly marked villages, Savoonga and Gambell, were separated by empty tundra and mountains. There were some churches, a post office, a tribal office, a grocery store. No cafés. No hotels. No Airbnbs. This stretch of frozen earth was once the bridge between worlds, the place where humans crossed from Siberia into North America along the Bering Land Bridge some twenty thousand years ago. The earliest human footprints on the continent would have been left here. How wild is that?

My mind started spiraling. What did this place look like back then? What did the wind sound like? The sea? Had anything changed? And had the Siberian Yupik—who live here now—been walking this same ground ever since? In the months since visiting Amish country and East LA, I'd thought a lot about the idea of being deeply rooted in a place. I wondered what it would be like to belong somewhere for thousands of years. What do roots mean when measured in geologic time? What can a place teach us when that connection is older than memory itself? In a country so big it still has parts almost nobody knows, I loved that the only way to find answers to these questions was to go there myself.

It wasn't my first time traveling somewhere blindfolded. Back in my twenties, I'd spent a few months in former Soviet countries in Central Asia with nothing but a backpack, a Russian/English dictionary, and an adventurous spirit that stranded me in high places like the towns in the Pamir Mountains of Tajikistan. It had taken me weeks to get the visa I needed to enter the country that, after the US invaded Afghanistan to overthrow the Taliban, had become the number one heroin route out of the region. There was big money to be made, and everyone wanted in—from local militias to the Russian military. Still emerging from a civil war, Tajikistan's federal government wasn't fully in control of its own borders. The semi-self-governed region I was going to required a handwritten note of approval to let me enter, followed by a stamp over the note in my passport. In my quest to get as far out into the world as possible, this was it.

But each morning, at the Tajik embassy in Uzbekistan, I'd be told the only man in Tajikistan who could approve my visa—Gafrov—wasn't ready to do it. And every day, there was a new excuse.

"We can't reach Gafrov. He's gone fishing."

"Gafrov won't be in for the rest of the week."

Or simply: "Gafrov needs time to think."

Even the Uzbeks thought it was a wild idea to cross the border; more than a few locals told me you couldn't pay them to go. And so, like any adventure-seeking guy in his mid-twenties, the more impossible it became, the more I wanted it. I ended up staying with this local who claimed his mom worked with the guys at the Tajik embassy and could get me a visa . . . only to instead get poisoned, robbed, and then brought back to life. But that's a story for another time.*

* Gafrov did eventually grant me a visa and write a note in my passport allowing me to travel through Tajikistan's autonomous region of Gorno-Badakhshan. But DHS later held on to this "terrorist document" when I applied to renew my passport. So if anyone from the agency happens to be reading this, please return this one-of-a-kind historical passport back to me.

What I'm trying to say is that for the last five years, I've tried to explore America the way I used to explore the rest of the world, venturing out as far as possible, the more difficult the destination the better, the more unknown the culture the more interesting. And I was beginning to realize that getting to Saint Lawrence Island might be a lot like getting into Tajikistan. "Technically it's America, and Americans can fly there. But once you step off the tarmac, you're on private land. Everything: The villages, the gravel roads, the trails, even the coastline is private," read this blog post I stumbled on. "It's like stepping onto a ranch in Montana with a NO TRESPASSING sign."

On Google Earth, I could see that right in the center of the village of Savoonga stood a large building with a gray roof—the only part visible from the aerial shot. This was the final boss between me and the edge of America: the Tribal Council of Savoonga. My communication with the Tribal Council president had been spotty at best. Over the last few months, I'd sent messages, left voicemails, talked with him on the phone, and eventually gotten something resembling an approval to step foot on the island. (Native speaking can be less than direct, floating toward the abstract or to stories.) There'd been no discussion of where I'd be allowed to go when I got to Savoonga, or even where I'd sleep. But it was enough to give me the confidence to buy my airline tickets and go for it.

My checked bag was mostly warm clothes, a sleeping bag, and a blow-up mattress, since I thought there'd be a high probability I'd be sleeping on someone's floor. That was it, mostly—but not all.

"Well, that's going to cost you extra," said the check-in agent after I put my bag on the scale. "What do you have in there, anyway?"

Traveling the world has taught me the wisdom of bringing gifts, and with Saint Lawrence Island so far north, I thought it would be a good idea to bring something that might be scarce up there. Packed between the layers of fleece and wool was the produce section of a grocery store.

* * *

As we neared Anchorage, I'd started to get a feel for what "north" actually meant: scale. The rivers looked wider, the mountains longer and taller, the gaps between signs of life grander. It didn't take much common sense to look below and realize humans were insignificant here. Wolves, bears, moose were in full control in the wilderness. Nature rules in all places, but in Alaska, its dominance was obviously supreme. My humanness felt . . . less important. The vastness of the place made me all too aware that I was like one ant in a very big anthill.

From Anchorage, I'd caught a flight to Nome, then piled onto the small plane bound for Savoonga. Miles up in the air, the sky beyond my window was a deep, piercing blue.

"I've been on and off the island maybe fifteen times this year," a woman was saying, like it was routine for public transportation to cost $360 a ride. "For any real medical procedure, college stuff, larger shopping runs."

The thought was surreal to me.

Mid-flight, I pulled down the tray table, which creaked like a folding chair. The back of the pleather seat in front of me was loose, held on by Velcro tabs uneven from being peeled and restuck so many times. I tugged a tab, curious. Underneath was a worn canvas panel, covered in handwriting—names, initials, flight dates.

Jazlyn Ungarook, from Barrow, AK. 06/30/19, 3:33 a.m. (An

odd time for a flight, until you learn that the two most common phrases when it comes to air travel here are *weather delay* and *cancellation*.)

I scanned the cabin. A younger guy in the back was watching me. He unzipped his backpack and started digging through it.

"Here," he said, tapping the shoulder of the older woman in front of him. She took the pen from his hand and passed it to me without looking up. "You can write your name and the date there too."

Others looked around from across the small fuselage to see if I was going to. I glanced back at the guy who gave me the pen. He gave me a little nod, like I had his approval to join the locals and tag the plane. Grandma in her wool mittens looked up and gave me a little nod too.

I added my name and the date alongside the others, then pressed the flap shut and clicked the tray back into place. It was official. I was here.

* * *

The sea gave way to a thick, green landscape. Waves crashed hard against the island's rocky edge, mountains trailing off into the distance like the spine of something ancient. From the air, the island looked enormous—wild, rugged, alive.

When we landed, I pulled on a wool hat and jacket while other passengers disembarked in flip-flops. It was mid-July. The sky was so clear it felt almost otherworldly, streaks of white clouds stretching flat across the horizon. Behind the plane, the tundra rolled out in soft green swells like the flow of the ocean on land, the wind whistling with no break in tone. Something felt off, but I couldn't place it. There was a strangeness I didn't yet have language for.

Then I realized: no trees. Without that reference point, the scale was impossible to understand. I couldn't tell if I was looking fifty miles out at far mountains or five.

"Peter?" someone called from behind.

I turned and saw a young Siberian Yupik man with a patchy beard and mustache, squinting in the sun. His red hood was up against the wind.

The Yupik people are indigenous to western Alaska and far eastern Siberia—Arctic coastal people hardened by the cold, the wind, and the sea. Their features carry that heritage: broad faces, high cheekbones, dark almond-shaped eyes, and straight black hair. Their skin tells the story of generations living between the ice and the sunlight reflected off the sea—a people who belong completely to a place that would mentally break most outsiders in a couple of weeks.

"My name is Sunny," he said, grabbing my bag. "Come with me."

I followed Sunny over to his four-wheeler, which was parked next to a rusted metal shipping container. He looked to be in his late twenties, with a wide smile and an easygoing demeanor.

I settled in the back. The gravel crunched under our tires as we pulled away.

Town unfolded into a few spacious dirt streets lined with elevated, one-story wooden houses, all neat rectangles painted in bleak colors: gray, off-white, beige. The ocean shimmered on the horizon, an exalted sapphire blue against the flat landscape—a patchy sponge of permafrost terrain. Snowmobiles and four-wheelers—some functional, some clearly not—were scattered across the open yards. Some homes had trampolines out front; others had animal skins hanging from porch railings.

We reached the Tribal Council building, the metal door

swinging open lighter than I expected. “This way,” Sunny said. We passed tables stacked with boxes of clothes and food, empty buffet chafers idle between meals. Pictures of locals covered the walls—fishing shots, elders with their grandkids. A few men sat in folding chairs, talking through the day’s happenings: a neighbor leaving the island for a hip replacement, a new proposal for a job training program.

“Nice day, isn’t it?” said one of the men—the tribal president, I’d learn, the dark frames of his rectangular glasses slightly obscuring his eyes. He motioned me to a seat across from him. But instead of the questions I’d been expecting, he reached for an unplugged electric guitar on the wall. Held it in his lap, plucked a couple of strings, played a few notes of Tom Petty.

No one spoke. Everyone’s movements were slow. In my travels, I’d noticed this across many Native American communities—a kind of calm, unhurried presence that’s just pleasant to be around. Time slows down; sometimes it dissolves completely. I tried to slow myself too—my breathing, my hand movements, my head turns. Natives more than any group I’ve been with expect younger people to listen without interruption and not ask too many questions.

The tribal president was softly strumming the guitar now, murmuring a few lyrics under his breath, just loud enough to be heard. He was actually pretty good.

“Sunny, take Mr. Peter over to his stay,” he finally said, then looked at me. “Your room will be forty dollars a night. You can stay here for your three days. And if you want to come back later for hot dogs, we’re eating around six.”

* * *

Sunny and I pulled up to a gray building on stilts, a rusted metal ramp leading to the door. The house to the left was boarded up and leaning slightly—like it had surrendered to the wind years ago.

"Just leave your bags inside the front door and I'll show you around town for a bit," Sunny said, handing me the key.

I walked up the ramp, the metal flexing slightly under my steps. A paper sign taped up on the door read MEDICAL CENTER CLOSED.

I glanced back at Sunny. He grinned.

"I wouldn't recommend sleeping in the room on the left," he shouted. "That's the old emergency room, bunch of people died there."

Inside, I flipped on the long fluorescent lights overhead, which flickered on with the harsh brightness of a surgical room. It looked like the clinic had only recently shut down. The reception window still held paperwork, a bottle of disinfectant wipes, a coffee cup. But no people. A worn WELCOME sign hung above the entrance to the room Sunny had pointed out, the letters outlined in black and dripping downward—just enough to make you unsure if it was supposed to be ice letters melting or the blood-dripping font of a heavy metal T-shirt.

I dropped my bags and walked back out.

"It'll be an interesting experience for you here," Sunny said with a mischievous smile, popping in one wired EarPod. "Hop on."

The population of Savoonga is roughly eight hundred. There are no sidewalks, no traffic lights, no road signs. Almost every house looks the same. Same shape, same color palette beaten pale by wind and salt. Exposed plumbing and water lines run above ground, stretching awkwardly between buildings spaced far apart. Buried pipes don't work out here—too much permafrost. A pipe's heat can thaw the frozen ground, causing buildings and roads to sink.

The four-wheeler's tires splashed through puddles collecting in potholes. In the gaps between homes, the tundra kept pushing back into view—green and endless.

The vast openness reminded me of a patch of dusty no-man's-land I'd passed on that Tajikistan trip, a Mars-like landscape: just dirt, stretching as far as the eye could see, crashing into mountains that looked like shards of broken glass shooting into the heavens. Here, the climate was different, but there was a strange kind of shared exposure to it all—not threatening, just absolute, as if the place had no outer layer. No fences, no hedges, no real divide between private and public, just wide-open turf with everything left out: woodpiles, busted appliances, fuel drums, bones, sleds, buckets. You could read a life from the objects alone. It felt like stepping into a town without secrets. Riding exposed on the back of a four-wheeler only sharpened the feeling. It was like being inside someone's dream. I let go of any sense of agency and gave myself over to the island, fully in the moment, not knowing what the next one would bring.

"This used to be our old fire hall," Sunny said, shifting into tour-guide mode, pointing to a faded red building on the right. "And next to it was our washateria." It stood nonoperational, the windows boarded up, a bent metal pipe curving out from the side. "It's where we'd wash our clothes, take showers and stuff. We didn't have indoor plumbing yet."

"So that's where everyone in town would go to shower?"

"Basically, yeah."

"When did people get indoor plumbing, hot water?"

"I wanna say . . ." He squinted, thinking. "Maybe 2008?"

We passed an American flag flapping off the side of a utility shed. Depending on where you are in Native country, flags might be a popular thing. As of 2026, the US has 575 federally recognized Native American tribes, 229 in Alaska alone—and if there's one thing I've learned, it's that they can be drastically different from one another.* It'd be a culturally eye-opening experience for a Cherokee kid in North Carolina and a Hopi kid in Arizona to travel to each other's lands.

"Here are some of the oldest houses in town," Sunny said. "You can tell how they're dipping in the soil from the permafrost melting. These ones are about sixty, maybe seventy years old."

He pointed at the side of one. "See that old jug near the wall? That was for stove oil. Most of us have what we call a laser heater."

We made a sharp turn, and I grabbed on to the metal bars at the back of the four-wheeler. They were cold, and the wind cut across my exposed fingers.

We cruised around a little more.

"This is the school, K-12." Sunny pointed to the largest newish-looking building in town, powered by wind turbines

* A person might prefer to be called Native American or Native or Indian or Indigenous or First Nations, but there's no consensus, and anyone telling you there is one hasn't talked to enough Native people in enough places. I've asked the question of preference hundreds of times on different reservations and have consistently gotten inconsistent answers. I was even told by a Lakota medicine man that I'm the Native American and not him, since the country was founded after his lineage. That said, most Native people prefer to be referred to as a member of their particular tribe: Crow, Lakota, Zuni Pueblo, Navajo, Hupa. Think of Europeans: You'd probably say that someone is German or Italian, not simply that they're European.

with a playground set behind. "Sometimes the snow gets all the way up to its top. Basically one big igloo in the winter."

Hoping to show me some action, he drove around to an empty basketball court. Usually there'd be kids playing there, he said. We reached the edge of town and continued on a dirt road, the sea below us on the right and nothing but tundra ahead. He started telling me about the blizzards that come in winter, winds 110 miles an hour sometimes.

"So you just have to hunker down?"

"Oh yeah," he said. "Some of us brave the storm for a pack of smokes."

We both laughed.

"One year it was like a hundred," he said. "I was like, 'Man, I'm going.' I was walking at like forty-five degrees—leaning into it. I've seen people sliding back, you know. Just for a smoke."

I laughed again, then noticed a long white bone lying off in the distance, curved like a canoe paddle and tapering to a blunt, rounded tip.

"That's a jawbone of a whale," Sunny said. He cut the engine. "We can walk on the utility lines—just be careful, they might be slick."

We hopped off and started walking along the raised metal pipes—flat-topped and wide enough to walk on comfortably.

"I read you guys do a whale hunt every year?" I said.

"Yes. Every spring we hunt the bowhead."

I'd seen a whale skeleton once at the Natural History Museum in London, suspended from the ceiling under a spotlight. It felt bizarre to see one here, just lying out in the open like a leftover piece of plywood. It felt more real, and more impressive.

"Looks like it was about sixty, maybe sixty-five foot long."

Sunny said. "Nothing out of it is wasted. It feeds the whole village."

"One whale feeds the village for the whole year?" I asked, impressed.

"A couple of whales, actually." The International Whaling Commission sets catch limits for aboriginal subsistence whaling, with only a certain number allowed to be "struck" per year, even if the hunting party doesn't land the animal successfully. *No pressure.*

"But we still rely on seal, walrus, reindeer, birds," Sunny was saying. "We try to get the bigger whales—the older ones. Give the younger ones a chance to grow, mate, reproduce. The kill's not pretty, but we're very respectful of them too; we give thanks. When we get 'em, all of us gather and share a bite. Right out on the water, we take muktuk—the whale blubber—and eat it."

"The whole town participates, or just a few hunters?"

"The whole town goes and helps. We do it by manpower. The women get the share first."

"So there's chivalry here in the culture?"

"Oh yeah, women are just as important as men, yes. They keep our clothes in check, dry, ready for the next hunt. They take care of the kids, obviously. Each role is important, especially out here. No-man's-land, you know? Could you imagine living out here without any help from the outside world?"

Saint Lawrence Island isn't a reservation. Nearly the whole island—about 90 percent of it—is owned collectively by the people who live here. The land in the villages of Savoonga and Gambell isn't bought or sold; it stays in the community. You won't have a deed to the cliff your grandfather hunted walrus from, because one doesn't exist. The land belongs to everyone and no one at the same time. The remaining roughly 10 percent of the island is federal—a lot of it situated around a former Cold War radar site. But the rest—over a million acres—is privately owned by corporations representing the two villages. And what's unusual is that the people here still use it the way they always have—not for development or tourism, but to simply live. To hunt, to fish. If they lose those traditions, they lose the whole point of being there.

I'd learn later that there *was* quite a bit of help from the "outside world": funding for education, for health care (including flights off the island for doctor visits), food stamps for those who qualified. A regional nonprofit that supports tribes in the Bering Strait helps with wildlife management, education, and social services—things you might expect from a tribal government. But in subsistence hunting and hunkering through the extreme winter, the people here were on their own.

We climbed back onto the four-wheeler. Sunny pressed the throttle, and we sped on. The sea was coming closer quickly, expanding out like an endless desert. The bright Arctic sun cast long shadows, pulling back a little on the raw exposure of the place.

"That line over there is Russia," Sunny said when we stopped again, pointing out toward the horizon.

I followed his finger and saw it—a faint dark strip in the distance. Something in my brain flipped. On a map, I'd always known how close Russia is to Alaska. But it needed to be seen to be understood. Out here, I was one thousand miles closer to Moscow than I was to Washington, DC.

"You know, that's where our people come from," Sunny said, still pointing across the water. While the earliest people moved through this part of the world some twenty thousand years ago, the Yupik arrived much later—about two thousand years back. "Some are still over there," he continued. "We used to have a festival each year; '95, I believe, was the date it stopped. They would come over on walrus-hide boats. They'd dance here, we'd spend time together." Have bonfires. Crash in one another's homes. He wasn't sure why the tradition ended, although he did hear one of the boats didn't make it back to Russia one year. The Bering Sea was pretty mean, he told me.

"Do you think it'll ever come back?" I asked. "Or are the relations between the countries just too bad now?"

"Some of the youngers, they're trying to bring that back. Bring dancing and share our culture, how it changed through the years." One of his neighbors had gone to visit Chukotka some years back, in Russia's Far East.

"In many ways, we don't see Russia or America—we just see where our people live. Don't get me wrong, I'm proud to be American. I'm happy I'm American. But it's almost like . . . blood first. I don't see them as Russian, if that makes sense."

Identity can be a surprisingly flexible thing; the lines between nation-states don't always separate people in lived reality. Pashtuns in Pakistan may have more in common with Pashtuns in Afghanistan than with the non-Pashtun people of their own capital city. Still, I wondered if long-standing cultural ties always outweighed the national cultures layered on top of them. Siberian Yupik in Russia grow up watching Russian movies and reading Russian news. If Sunny's generation was able to start the walrus carnival back up again, some of its visitors would probably only speak Russian.

"I was told we have it much better than them," Sunny said. "We've got indoor plumbing, four-wheelers, snowmobiles, a steady connection of resources. I heard they have much less.

Plus, the US lets our culture be. Over there, I was told, there's more pressure from the state, on their language and traditions."

There was a moment of smiles and stillness. The sound of the small waves crashing up on the rocks, the fresh cold breeze keeping my eyes watering.

"You know what I just realized?" I said. "I've been on this high of being here, but . . . you grew up never knowing what a tree was like. You've never touched one?"

"Not one."

"Not even back in the mountains?" I asked, just making sure.

"Nope," Sunny said with a smile. "Only the dead ones you see washed up from somewhere else. A lotta stuff floats up ashore from Asia." He pulled his phone from his pocket. "Shoot, I gotta head home to see the family. Are you ready to go?"

The place felt too special to leave just yet.

"I'll just stay out here and walk back into town in a bit," I said, shaking his hand. "Thanks for cruising me around."

Gravel kicked up behind his tires as he stepped on the pegs of the four-wheeler and hit the throttle, the hum of the engine fading slowly into the wide open. I stood there for a moment, trying to process everything—a blend of *How did I not know about this place?* and *This country is so amazing.* The air was sharp, the saltwater smell so pure that I felt this sense of somehow becoming untethered from everything. The sound of gentle waves crashing into the rocks pulled me into a kind of hypnosis. Time dissolved. I wasn't sure if I sat there for a few minutes or an hour. There was a melody to this place: the slow way the people spoke, the ocean's rhythm, the stark beauty.

Eventually, I started making my way gradually along the shoreline, falling into the pace of the island, following the black sand and scattered rocks. Scraps of driftwood and sea-tossed planks lined the edges of the bluff. A few wooden structures leaned out toward the sea; I guessed they were old hunting blinds for seal, left there to gray and warp in the salty air.

I came to a place where wooden boats were pulled up above the tide line, resting on the sand like a scattered fleet. The boats were red, but unevenly weathered—some still shiny, others worn and chewed by the sea. In the distance, a young couple with two small kids walked the shore. I waved; they waved back.

I noticed a few of the vessels were tied off with rope to a massive white skull roughly the size of the boats, like something a child might press out of a piece of Plasticine.

"Do you know what that is?" I called out as the couple got closer.

The man, a kid on his shoulders, looked down at the bone, then back at me.

"Stegosaurus," he said, deadpan.

"Stegosaurus?"

"Yeah, the dinosaur," he said.

"Oh. Did it thaw out of the ice here or—"

"No. We hunt them."

Unable to hold it in, the woman broke into laughter. I laughed too—half at the joke, half at how confidently he delivered it. For a moment, he'd had me wondering if this was like how Indigenous people in Siberia came across woolly mammoths preserved in the permafrost.

He told me his name was Nick and that he was a police officer on the island. His wife, Ashley, held up something that looked like a small potato with a root sticking out the top. "We just picked these from the sea."

"What are they?"

"Depuks," she said. "They're sea peaches, but we call them crunchies. Do you want to try?" She handed one over.

"They're a little sandy," she added. "I tried to wash them in the ocean."

The crunchie was something between a carrot and a radish—mild in flavor, but with a salty finish. Earthy and oceanic at the same time.

I thanked them and wandered back down the long dirt road toward town, trying to catalog all the gridded streets in my head. I didn't want to miss anything in Savoonga during my time here.

* * *

The sharp ping of BBs hitting metal rang out, followed by whoops and shouts from a group of boys locked in competition. A kid who looked maybe eight tore past me on a mini motorcycle, his two friends and a barking husky chasing behind through the gravel. They looped around the building like it was a racetrack—dust flying, all noise and laughter.

An older boy, maybe eighteen, stood nearby folding up a fishing net methodically. He wore a blue Huskies jersey that caught my eye.

"Washington State?" I asked.

"Yep," he said. "I got a scholarship there for wrestling. I play basketball and Eskimo Stick Pull too, but wrestling's my top sport."

"You gonna go?"

"Ah . . . I'm still thinking about it."

The boy on the mini motorcycle reappeared, windblown hair sticking out from his hoodie. (No helmet on this kid, just a few scuffs on his clothes.) He skidded to a stop next to us, using his feet to brake. His buddies caught up seconds later.

They all circled around the athlete. It was clear he was a bit of a hero to them.

"Derek Jr.," said one of the boys, still catching his breath, cheeks purple-red. "Tell him about your first one."

Derek Jr. looked over the group, then back at me.

"I was sixteen. We got a couple whales that year. I killed two of them."

The boys went quiet, wide-eyed, ready for the story again.

"What's it like—killing a whale?" I asked.

"Kinda feels spiritual," he said. I'd heard that in Siberian Yupik tradition, it was only the people selected by the spirit that were granted the honor of killing a whale. "And there's a whole bunch of adrenaline rushing throughout your body. When I was striking, I was kinda shaking because of the excitement of it. When I killed it, it felt fun . . . and at the same time, kinda sad. But I'm grateful. I do feel sorry for the whale sometimes, but I'm also thankful—to feed my community and keep our way of life going for generations. It's a beautiful thing."

He said it so simply and eloquently, like most of the people I met out here. Everyone's manner of speaking was so pleasant, the calm pace of their words bringing the listener in closer, eagerly waiting for where they were going next in their story. In Hoboken, New Jersey, where my Italian American relatives are from, it's all about fast-talking, exuberant hand motions, even a slap on the shoulder to bring you back if you turn your attention away. A sensory assault—and often wildly entertaining. The Siberian Yupik approach is the opposite, but I find it more effective.

"It's very risky, though, right?" I asked Derek Jr.

"Yep. We hunt in eighteen-foot boats. They'll swing their flippers, and it doesn't take much to tip one over."

The real threat, though, to him, was that people concerned

about animal cruelty might try to take away the tribe's right to hunt. I could still hear his words in my mind as I walked away: "Some people think it's outrageous, even horrible, but other people have different ways of life. This is ours. And we'd love to keep it."

* * *

That evening, I pushed open the creaky clinic door, exhausted. I checked my phone for the first time all day—no signal. It was around 9:00 p.m.; I'd missed hot dogs. Bags in hand, I stepped inside my room, opened my massive duffel full of fruit, and started eating—apples, oranges, almonds, grain bars. Then I just sat on the edge of the bed, reflecting on everything that had happened. It reminded me of traveling the world, absorbing months of information between one sleep cycle. Some of my most tired days haven't come from physical strain but from mental stimulation. New smells, new tastes, new traffic patterns . . . a full barrage on the senses. Just when I'd thought I had a good understanding of my country, I was realizing, again, that I didn't. The same flag flew above my hometown as here—but everything felt so different.

I used to not think of the flag as such an important visual, but I've changed my mind about that. I feel we need shared visuals as part of the connective tissue that reminds us our own bubbles aren't everything—that anywhere the flag flies is just as American as wherever we're from.

I got into my night pants and a sweatshirt and slid under the covers, my brain burning a little trying to wrap around that truth.

* * *

I woke to a sharp, hollow rhythm echoing through the building. *Bang, bang, bang.* Through the cracks in the blinds, I could see it was still light outside.

For a moment, I couldn't tell if I'd slept an hour or half a day. Then I remembered—it was summer, and we were far enough north that the sun barely dipped below the horizon. I glanced at the digital clock on the nightstand: 2:03 a.m.

The noise came again, but different. A faint whistling. I could tell it was coming from the end of the hallway.

I got up and opened the door. The hallway was dim, but not totally dark. Enough late-night daylight leaked in through the windows to guide me. To my right was the old emergency room. To my left, the sound. I followed it slowly down the hall. It made a softer knock now.

The floor creaked as I got closer. It felt like that scene in *The Shining* with the kid pedaling down the hallway on a trike. I got to the last door on the right and turned the metal knob—it felt colder than the air temperature. I pushed the door open.

The noise stopped.

Inside were two empty beds, stacked chairs, and a stale smell I couldn't place. A chill moved up my spine, like I'd interrupted something or arrived too late. I stood there for a moment, waiting for more noise.

Nothing happened.

Exhausted and in a daze, I walked slowly down the hallway and went back to bed.

* * *

Bang, bang, bang!

I snapped awake, eyes wide. Light was pouring through the gaps in the blinds. The clock read 9:07 a.m.

Another knock, this time toward the front door—sharp, impatient. I walked to the door and opened it.

A rush of cold air swept in, stinging the skin on my arms and ankles. Outside stood an older man, face deeply lined, wiry gray hair and beard poking out from under a beanie. He gave a crooked smile when he saw I was still in pajama pants.

"Oh, sorry," he said in a voice both gravelly and gentle. "Didn't mean to wake you. The Tribal Council needs to see you."

I rubbed my eyes. "Yeah, sorry . . . I didn't sleep too well."

"No wonder," he said, casually. "This place is haunted."

I threw on pants and a thick sweater, splashed water on my face, brushed my teeth. When I came back out, he was standing with his hands in his pockets, staring down the hallway. He told me his name was Dean.

"You get noises from the east side of the building," he said, nodding toward where I'd heard them. "You hear knocking?"

"Yeah," I said.

He smirked. "It echoes, and the sound goes all the way down the hallway." Dean walked to the far end, stopping just short of the door I'd opened last night.

"They'll whistle too," he added. "People in the village hear them. We all feel it's haunted, that's why it's empty. Nobody wants to stay here. The best thing to do about it," he whispered, "is get some small flowers from the tundra to put at the base of your door at night to act as a defense against the negative spirits. It won't make them go away, but it will help."

I just stood there, red-eyed and still a little foggy, trying to process these matter-of-fact instructions about how to win over a ghost. "That's it?" I said, at last.

"Yes. Don't be scared, and don't even try to confront it.

Don't look straight at it—even though you can't see it, it doesn't do well with direct confrontation. It will come at you and get into your head."

He nodded like he was shaking something off. As I ran back to grab the bag of fruit from my room, he gave one last glance up at the WELCOME sign hanging above the emergency room.

"I almost died in there," he said.

He closed the door with force, and we started walking toward the Tribal Council building as he told the story: how a whale had landed at Kukulak, how the ice had packed in, how the cold and his high blood pressure brought on a stroke, his face pulling sideways, falling over and over into the snow.

"Well . . . there you go," he said, abruptly, as we reached the building. "You can go alone from here." And he hustled off, quicker than he'd left the haunted hallway.

Same as yesterday, there was no one just inside the door. I waited a beat, then followed the sound of women's voices to a small office, all whirring printers and stacks of paper leaning against cardboard file boxes. Things looked and felt bureaucratic.

"Ah, here you are," said a woman seated behind a large desk. Short haircut, a streak of gray, eyebrows sharp and angled like punctuation. Adora.

I handed over the bag still full of tropical fruit unusual in these parts: papayas, mangos, passion fruit, not a bruise on any of it after five thousand miles. I was a bit proud of the offering.

Adora looked down at the open bag in front of her. Her expression didn't change. There was just a brief, awkward pause, with a look that said *Gifts aren't going to get you anything here, Lower 48er.*

"What are you planning to do here on the island?" she asked.

Her forehead was pinched, her voice more interrogation than interest. In a way, it felt like the high school principal's office, like I was back in tenth grade and trying to get out of something . . . only I was pretty sure I didn't do anything wrong yet.

"I'd like to make some videos of the island," I said. Had the tribal president not told her?

"Were you up at the market yesterday videoing the pop delivery?" Adora asked, her voice freezing the Bering Sea ice out the back door.

As a dry island (outside of some local moonshine), sugar is the next most popular drug here. When shipments of soda come in from the mainland, there's a mad rush. It sells fast, as there's no guarantee of when the next shipment will fly in.

"No," I said. It'd probably been one of the pilots from the mainland, but with a White guy hanging around town saying he wanted to shoot some footage, I got why she suspected me.

She nodded her head like she wasn't convinced.

"So why do you want to video here?" she asked.

I started trying to make my case without it sounding like a sales pitch, talking about the beauty of the place, about how I went around the country trying to show America from locals' perspectives. I had two more days of filming, but nothing really planned. I could tell she was looking for the lie: scanning my fingers to see if they were clenched, my eyes to see if they were all over the place. Then things went still, and she looked right through me to see if I'd flinch or fidget in the tension.

Eventually, she sat back in her chair, considering something. "You know, we could go on a four-wheeler tour looking for reindeer," she said. "But you'd need the right permit to do so."

I looked around the room at the papers stacked high and knew this was the one place to get a permit in Savoonga.

After a fair amount of back and forth—and $400 split between the Tribal Council and a few of Adora's relatives—a four-wheeler expedition into the mountainous interior was arranged for the next morning.

As a rule, I never pay people for content. I've always felt that once money enters the exchange, the dynamic shifts. It stops being an authentic interaction and becomes a transaction. Someone's there to perform a service; there's almost an employer–employee dynamic. There have only been a few exceptions, like the time I paid a woman on skid row to show the fentanyl in her hand. I wanted to see the drug responsible for killing so many Americans. But this felt different. Different because a few hundred went toward an actual permit and gas. And different because, frankly, I didn't have any other option.

* * *

Back on the streets, I figured I'd knock out a few essentials—breakfast, flowers for the spirits, rubber boots for the expedition tomorrow. I cut around the back of one of the buildings, where I'd spotted a patch of wild purple flowers the day before. They stood low and defiant against the tundra wind, their smell sweet and bright. I picked a few and carried them gently in one hand like something precious.

Inside the general store, prices were about three times as much as on the mainland. I avoided the pop aisle, grabbed eggs, and headed out. I still had some of my produce back at my place.

That's when I saw Derek Jr.—the teenage athlete I'd met the day before—walking up the road, windbreaker flapping behind him.

"Hey," I said. "Good to see you again." I told him I was

working on a documentary and asked if he could think of anyone who might want to talk on camera. He was polite, but his mind was already halfway to the sea.

"I'm heading out for halibut," he said. "But you can stop by the house and talk to my family. I'll let my dad know. His name's Derek too." He gave me directions that would mean nothing anywhere else: second street on the right, brown house with a sled out front and a pile of spare tires next to some whale bones. "Don't knock," he added. "It's just something we don't do in our culture. Just open the door and come in."

On my way back to the clinic, I stopped by Dean's place. He'd told me he was a carver, that I should come by and see his stuff. He unwrapped a figure from tissue paper like it was a relic: a smooth, polished whale, carved out of ivory from the previous year's hunt, he said, and mounted on a fossilized walrus cheekbone. "I cure ivory for about a year before I work on it," he told me, rotating the beautiful piece proudly in his hands. The whale looked like it was in motion, arched slightly like it had just breached from the sea. It was detailed but not overdone, the way it often is with skills passed down through many generations and given a modern twist. I picked the figurine up, no bigger than my hand, and knew I wanted it. So I bought it. Dean smiled as he wrapped it back up. It sits on my desk next to me as I write this book.

* * *

After a warm breakfast cooked in the clinic's kitchen, I placed a small bouquet of flowers outside my room—figuring I'd be proactive and show the spirits I was taking them seriously—then headed out to meet Derek's folks.

The temperature had dropped from the previous day to

around fifty degrees and the sky had gone flat gray, the air damp with sea mist. In front of Derek Jr.'s place, the dirt road just stopped at the top of a cliff, an expanse of sea opening up below. It was quite possibly the best ocean view from a trailer.

The home was rough, utilitarian, built to endure the Bering Sea wind. A sheet of weathered plywood served as the doorframe, leading into a small mudroom crowded with practical gear—snowboards, gas cans, boots, a chainsaw, plastic totes. I put my hand on the door handle and just walked right in.

Inside, a man and a woman in their late thirties sat with a boy who looked around ten. They glanced up as I entered—not surprised, like I already belonged.

"I did it right, yeah?" I asked.

"Yeah." Derek Sr. smiled. "That's how we do it."

The house felt warm, tight, and lived-in. Kids' certificates and school awards were taped to the walls, alongside whale baleen and hand-drawn basketball posters. Natives are known for their love of hoops. I'm not sure how that came about, but it's become one of the common threads tying tribes together, despite their differences. A PlayStation controller lay on the floor. A few pieces of clothing hung from a line near the ceiling, drying in the heat.

Derek introduced me to his wife, Audrey, and then pulled out his laptop to show me some hunting footage. Thick snow. Uneven terrain. "Hunters will walk out—sometimes all the way to the sea—to hunt walrus and seal. But they'll drive up to the smooth ice first, then start walking around these chunks," he said, motioning to the jagged slabs on-screen, "to get to the edge."

I asked how often he and his neighbors ate traditional food.

"Some families like to eat it every day," Derek said. "Especially when the store runs low—like when the weather's bad and no supplies come in."

"A lot of people in our villages get food stamps," Audrey added. "We live in a high-cost living area. That runs out, so there's people that, no matter what, they live on a daily basis eating the native food." Folks mostly ate whale raw, but you could also fry it with rice or bake it with Shake 'n Bake.

"How's your housing situation here?" I asked.

"Bad," Audrey replied. "We've been on a housing waitlist for eighteen years."

"Eighteen years?"

"Well, I stopped putting in my application several years ago. I was promised to get one, but they gave me a false hope."

"Why is there a problem with building more housing?"

"I would like to know that myself," she said. "Not a priority, not important. Our government not hearing us out. I don't know whether it's because we're Natives and we're pushed aside . . . but then there's also some people in the past"—people in town—"that mishandled the money. There're different and good people in charge now, so hopefully things will change. But I think it has a lot to do with the bigger government in Washington, DC."

I nodded. It hit me then how alone this place really was. And yet the biggest problems people in Savoonga were facing were unmistakably American: housing shortages, grocery prices that made your eyes widen. You could fly for nearly a day to the farthest edge of the continent and still hear about the exact same struggles.

I hesitated for a second, not wanting to sound naive, but the question felt natural.

"And it's only Siberian Yupik people living here?" I asked.

"Me and Derek are native to Saint Lawrence Island, but we're one of the few kids from the eighties that are mixed. I'm mixed with Black—my biological father is from all that, and his mom's White."

"My biological mother is," Derek clarified. He didn't know her.

"Are mixed marriages common now?"

"Not when we were kids," Audrey said. "But it's starting to get common. The only different people is the outside visitors, usually teachers or health care providers, the pilots that fly on and off the island. Otherwise, our whole town is just us."

"Do you like it that way?" I asked.

Audrey paused for a second. "I don't know . . . I want to move on, and be in the suburbs. I've told Derek that many times. Housing's a problem, power outages at certain times of the year, the long dark. . . ."

Many people from the island have moved to places like Anchorage for more job opportunities, more reliable utilities. There weren't a whole lot of places to work on the island other than for the Tribal Council or the school—and even there, a lot of teachers were imported from the Lower 48.

"Here's the shot of the village in late May," Derek said, turning the laptop toward me so I could see. The drone shot showed the entire village of Savoonga wrapped in white—low buildings laid out in tidy lines in the endless snow. There was no sign of plowing, just four-wheelers parked and snowmobiles on the go. Meltwater had spread across the roads into wide, murky pools that reflected power poles and rooftops. The densely packed snowbanks still stood about six feet tall.

"In winter, this village gets almost buried in snow," he said, "sometimes all the way to the rooftops."

"Global warming is real, though," Audrey said. "We've had some odd winters."

"You really feel that here?" I asked.

"Yeah, with our food. The ice goes away before the hunters can get female or baby walrus, and that's what we prefer." She was reminiscing now. "I used to go trick-or-treating on a snowmobile. It'd be so winter, like five feet of snow. And then in my twenties, I started to take notice that winter started happening in December more. And then for a couple of years, we didn't get ice on our ocean. It's usually completely frozen."

"How about last winter?"

"Pretty close to normal," Derek said.

"Yeah," Audrey echoed. "It was finally a normal year."

A thin whistle of wind slipped through the edges of the window frame, carrying with it the distant sound of music.

"There's a wedding going on," Audrey said. "I can show you if you want."

She zipped up her jacket and we stepped out into the chilly afternoon air, walking side by side down the wide dirt road. The music got clearer with each step—upbeat and cheerful, floating lightly over the stillness of the village.

"You can't get too close—only Yupik people can take part in the ceremony. But we can stand here," Audrey said as we stopped beside a row of parked four-wheelers. Just beyond a nearby house, I could see the wedding procession starting to form. Behind Audrey, another American flag flapped in the wind over the USPS building.

"Traditionally, the groom's family goes over to the lady's family, bringing goods over," she explained. "Then he's gonna work for her family for one year, helping her family out with anything that requires a man to assist. Stove oil runs, errands."

"And if he does a bad job, what happens?"

Audrey laughed. "We don't think of bad jobs. So what they're doing right now"—she peeked around the house—"is what's called tukfightugh. If you translate it, it means *buy*. They bring presents, a dowry. Before that, the groom's family goes to the bride's family to ask if it's okay to do the tukfightugh. Her family will also gather presents for when she goes to his family. Just like the groom, she's going to work too—but not hard labor, 'cause she's a lady. That's the last step. That's when his family gains the daughter. Not everyone does traditional weddings, but . . ."

I felt like I was watching a cultural event I'd expect to see in Myanmar or Kyrgyzstan.

"How about your family?" I asked.

"Yeah, they did me. I was feeling uncomfortable. . . ." She found it all a little embarrassing at the time, but Audrey started thinking differently about tradition as she's aged.

"We plan to do that for our kids," Audrey said, then paused. "When I was a kid, it was more traditional on the island. Our culture was more alive. We used to speak our language—our kids knew it. I was a kid that spoke nothing but my language, and English was really hard for me. I went to elementary school, and I was like, 'What is this new thing?'"

That's probably not going to happen much anymore, with the internet and video games—the modern world doing its thing. And yet.

"It feels very connected here," I said, "on a deeper level that's hard to describe."

"Everyone knows everyone," Audrey said, "so we try to keep things kind. If tension shows up, we change the subject, bring it back to something good. When the weather's gonna turn bad and it's gonna be bad for long, there's gonna be power outages, water and sewer freezing up in the pipes, no phone access, no internet access. Then we look out for each other. We go see the old lady over here, make sure she's okay."

There were some core values it seemed no amount of modernity would change.

* * *

That night, the village streets stayed alive well past midnight. Kids laughed, and four-wheelers revved and spun burnouts outside my haunted house, headlights sweeping past the patched-up window blinds. I couldn't tell if it was the wedding still going or just the younger crowd making the most of the midnight daylight. Either way, they'd catch up on sleep when the winter came.

The spirits came back not long after I started drifting off, creepy whispers I could hear from down the hall. But they spared me the banging this time.

The next morning, Jason—a relative of Adora's—picked me up for the reindeer expedition. He was a heavier man in his forties, with a rifle slung over one shoulder.

"You think you'll get one today?" I asked.

He smirked. "We'll be lucky if we even spot one."

We started driving and, just like a flock of geese, two other four-wheelers fell into formation around us—one driven by Adora's son Tanon, who was maybe in his twenties, with his mom riding on the back, the other carrying a woman named Brenna and a young kid. I wasn't sure who these two were exactly, perhaps cousins or neighbors. Our wheels kicked up dust in front of weathered wooden buildings and scattered shipping containers, as neighborhood kids darted across the road behind us.

Once we crossed the edge of Savoonga, human habitat just

stopped. There were no power lines, no cabins dotting the countryside, only open tundra and faint four-wheeler tracks. Just a clean break from settlement to wilderness. The land stretched flat for miles, broken only by shallow pools, boulders strewn in random places, and distant mountains streaked with pockets of midsummer snow. It reminded me of the desert: You're exposed, humbled, made small. Only in the desert, I'd often felt dried out, stripped bare by the sun. Out here, I felt rinsed clean, emptied in a different way. Tundra beauty doesn't come on strong. It slowly seeps in, reminding you how insignificant you are and how much peace you can find in that.

We must've been driving for an hour now; the hum of the engine had started to feel like part of the landscape itself. Eventually, we met up with a small group out on the open plain who were heading back to town. Adora began speaking with an elderly woman in Siberian Yupik—their voices rising and falling in a rhythm that sounded like poetry.

"Hey, try this," one of the women said, plucking a purple flower from the field of green. "You can suck on it."

I put the stem in my mouth.

"Poisonous flowers right there," Tanon said from behind me.

Everyone turned to watch how I'd react.

"Right, is this where the story ends?" I asked. "I get poisoned on Savoonga, you guys take off? The reindeer eat me?"

Adora cracked up, and the others followed. I think I was earning some cred.

Our four-wheeler posse left the open tundra and began to climb beneath a sky that seemed to change by the minute. As the elevation rose, the grass thinned, and the island's volcanic past began to show. Sharp black rock poked through the earth at our sides; massive cones loomed dormant in the distance.

So much of this island was formed by volcanic activity—the Kookooligit Mountains made from lava flow beneath the Bering Land Bridge. Ancient fire in a landscape now dominated by glaciers and wind. Sentinels. Some of the oldest islanders.

The expedition turned into a childlike joyride, revving across snowbanks, zigzagging through slush, skidding on ice. Laughter echoed off the empty rocky mountainsides.

"This is so amazing," I said to Jason. "The private island. It's all for you guys."

I heard a shout and turned to see Tanon off his four-wheeler, pointing toward something white in the distance, a single pale shape against the dark lava rock.

We pulled up. The snow was gone here, and on the rocky surface lay a white skull with broad, curled antlers.

"Probably got attacked by wolves," Jason said, trying to ramp up the suspense. (I'd later learn there aren't actually wolves on Saint Lawrence Island.) He hopped off and crouched next to it. The reindeer skull's hollow nasal cavity gaped like a silent scream, and the antlers arched outward like gnarled branches. Around the base, tufts of pale fur still clung to black volcanic stones, like the ghost of the animal hadn't fully left.

"So, you guys are always living with life and death here, huh?" I said.

"Yep," Jason replied without pause.

He grabbed the antlers with both hands and lifted the skull high, the way someone might hold up a trophy or a sacred relic. The greenish tinge of moss ran along the base of the bone, a faint outline of the island's past winters. He placed the skull on top of his head and grinned, baring his teeth like a deer. It looked a bit ridiculous, and we all started laughing. Nothing here stayed serious for long.

Tanon took the skull and looked somber. "Looks like it's got some kind of worm." He turned it upside down and brought the teeth closer to me.

"Oh, that . . ." I leaned in as he pointed to a small worm curled near the gumline.

"Guhh!" he shouted, suddenly thrusting the skull toward me.

"Ahhh!" I jumped back as everyone doubled over, choking with laughter.

"You finally got me," I said, wiping my eyes. "Took you, what, ten tries?"

Tanon was beaming, all glimmer and pride now that one of his pranks had finally landed.

* * *

We climbed through rocky ridgelines. Far below, the land we'd come from stretched out like a green Eden, reaching toward the Bering Strait. At the top of the hill, the island opened up into a sweeping vista. The world looked immense from this height—untouched, unconquered. I could see now why this was the sixth-largest island in the country, nearly three times the size of Maui in Hawaii.

We rode over a pass and down a little ridge. A golden band of light slid low across the horizon, casting a soft, honey-colored reflection across the still surface of a lake below. Behind us, the hillside was layered with thick, cream-colored snow, each stripe separated by bare bands of dark volcanic soil.

Tanon and I parked and wandered down to where the slope dipped into the lake's edge. There, a narrow corridor had formed where melting water had carved a gap into the snowbank—about eight feet tall, with sheer walls of packed snow glowing faintly blue at the seams.

He climbed in first, disappearing between the frozen walls. I followed, sloshing through the shallow icy water. Inside, the splash of our steps was amplified by the stillness: no birds, no voices, no wind. I ducked low and laughed out loud, partly from the cold, partly from the sheer absurd beauty of it. The North was taking hold of me.

The path widened just ahead and I caught a glimpse of the sky glowing beyond us. For a moment, it felt like stepping through a portal—out of time, out of place.

Jason and Adora started speaking Siberian Yupik to me, asking me to repeat long words that were impossible to get right, having fun as I fumbled my way through.

"How many letters are in your name, Jason?" I asked. He stayed quiet for a long moment, staring at me, holding the silence until the laughter started to build around us.

"Ten hundred."

It was easy entertainment. Jason locked eyes with me and gave me a fist pump. Maybe it doesn't sound all that funny on paper, but delivered in true Siberian Yupik fashion, it landed hard.

At some point I wandered off behind the hill to heed nature's call. When I came back, Tanon looked up and said, "We thought something took you."

"Something?"

"We have yetis here."

"Yetis?" I smiled. He didn't.

"My uncles thought they seen a fox here once, and shot at it," he continued. "But when it stood up, the eyes were too close together, and it was twelve feet tall." He said it without a hint of humor. "Next day, they seen big footprints in the same spot."

I heard the flick of a lighter as Adora lit her cigarette.

"I've heard stories from the elders," she said, blowing a cloud of smoke, "about those little men." She raised her hand to about three feet, showing their height.

"What are they?" I asked.

She shrugged her shoulders. The sun still had a little ways to go before setting, casting a warm golden light that softened her face. "We don't know what they are. They always see 'em. Not just here in Savoonga, in other villages too. The one they've seen here, and the one in Gambell, both had seal skin. And a tall hat, made out of seal skin too."

I'd heard stories of the little men across different Native cultures: the Yunwi Tsunsdi of the Cherokee, tiny protectors who help kids lost in the forest; small figures who throw rocks from Shiprock at those who disrespect Navajo land; in Hopi tradition, the Ant People who once sheltered humanity in underground caves during the destruction of previous worlds. But Adora was one of the best storytellers I'd ever encountered. Though our relationship started off rough, things had thawed. The cadence, the pauses, the vivid details in her voice and eyes as she told a story—it was captivating.

"What's their purpose?" I asked. "What are they doing?"

Adora pursed her lips and held my gaze, not answering.

"Have you seen 'em?"

She held another pause, then spoke.

"My niece seen them when she used to work at the school. Broad daylight—eight or nine in the morning. She was going up the stairs, she's seen this small, little man just standing there. All black in torn-up clothing. But she didn't see the face, it was all just . . . black."

She had more stories.

"Every year, we used to go camping on the island. One time, my youngest brothers were playing hide-and-seek. When it was getting dark, they went back to the cabin. One of my brothers wasn't there. They kept yelling out his name. No response. They told my dad, my older brothers, and they all went out, calling his name again. When they finally found him, they asked, 'Where have you been?' And he said . . . 'Them little people were there.' When he tried to go back, they wouldn't let him."

"They wouldn't let him go back?"

"Yeah. Tried to take him somewhere. But I guess when they heard the adult voice, they went away."

Water dripped steadily from the ice shelf into the lake, the subtle rhythm adding to the story's mystery. Off in the distance, some of the others were skipping stones.

"What's your advice for dealing with ghosts and spirits?" I asked Adora.

She exhaled a long stream of smoke from her cigarette. "Once you're scared, they'll bother you more. But you can tell them, 'In Jesus's name, go away.'"

"So just tell 'em to go away?" I asked.

"In Jesus's name."

There was an art to living in peace with the natural (and supernatural) world, to being as open to the unseen as the seen. To living in harmony with things that could easily be the death of you. The long, dark, frigid winters. The whales you depend on for sustenance that could flip your boat with a single flick of the tail. The malevolent spirits that sometimes seemed as real as day and yet at the same time invisible, leaving you questioning your own mind. To live out here in the middle of the sea, some forty miles from land, on the edge of America, on the edge of Russia, required getting comfortable with your own smallness and fragility in a way we don't often have to if we live in a big city or off in a charming countryside, with all the built-in safety mechanisms of modern life.

But I couldn't get lost in my thoughts for long, because Adora had another story to tell.

"My father-in-law was the mailman," she said, during the era when mail was still delivered by dogsled. "He used to bring mail from here all the way to Gambell back in the seventies, which was roughly sixty miles. One time he heard something behind him heavily breathing. Getting louder and louder. Even his dogs were barking. So he just got up, hitched the dogs, and left without looking back. One of his dogs got attacked."

She dropped her cigarette, and it hissed into the snow.

"Was it an animal or a spirit?"

"He didn't bother to look. And one time he noticed he was up in the air, going around with his dogs."

"Up in the air?"

"Yeah," Adora said, motioning in a wide circle with her arm.

"Like hallucinating?" I asked, trying to track what she was saying.

"Nuh-uh. It was real," Tanon said.

"That area over there . . ." Adora pointed over the mountain. "I think it could tease you or something. You're like, in a fog. You would try to go one way, but back-and-forth feels the same. It swirls you around until you accept you're in it . . . and make a choice to stop noticing."

* * *

There was a long pause giving the story time to settle. Jason raised his binoculars and looked in the other direction—fixated on the endless sweep of land beneath the heavy sky.

"You see quyngiq?" Adora asked.

"There's lots—look," Jason said, handing her the binoculars.

Her face lit up in a soft smile of awe.

"Take a look," she said, passing me the binoculars.

At first, all I could see was the brown foreverness of the land. Then, far off in the distance—nearly lost to the scale of it—I saw them: a wavering black line drifting across the valley floor. A massive herd of reindeer.

"How many?" I asked.

"Hundreds, maybe a thousand," Adora replied.

They stretched like a shadow over the tundra, moving in slow motion, like a school of fish slipping through water in a tight, instinctive formation.

I handed the binoculars over to Brenna, who was scrolling through her phone, finding music. Beyoncé pierced the silence. Then the Eagles. The cultural juxtaposition was incredible: one foot in the traditional, the other connecting us with the mainland.

Everyone took a turn with the binoculars, and even though they'd seen reindeer their whole lives, there was still a childlike wonder in spotting them again—like the novelty never wore off.

The reindeer weren't native to Saint Lawrence Island, they'd tell me. The deer had been brought over a hundred years ago by a missionary named Sheldon Jackson as part of an effort to establish a stable food source after a devastating famine. Sure, maybe this wasn't an "authentic" Siberian Yupik reindeer hunt—it wasn't something Adora's and Derek Jr.'s and Sunny's ancestors had been doing for fifty or eighty generations. But traditions, I was realizing, don't have to be ancient or even inherited to have power. Everything's got to start somewhere.

Many of the old Siberian Yupik traditions—the language, the walrus carnival—hadn't held up against the tide of the modern world. And yet core habits endured: hunting whales, telling stories, that fantastic sense of humor. And who knows? Maybe I was already witnessing other new traditions being created to replace those that'd been lost. Maybe people of Sunny's generation *would* get back in touch with their Russian kin across the sea.

It reminded me of the Amish and the Chicanos, each community trying to protect its own rhythm inside a country that's constantly shifting around them, all of them showing the same instinct I'd been noticing in pockets across the country: Finnish culture holding on in Michigan's Upper Peninsula, ranchers working hard to keep the Wild West alive. . . . People proud to be American, but also proud to have been born and raised with other overlapping identities.

Which, I suppose, is how we all live. As citizens, but also as ourselves.

I took one last glance at the herd through the magnified view, still drifting like a dark ribbon across the open land.

"What now?" I asked.

"Well, no way we're getting anywhere near them today," Jason said. "So now we just enjoy the wild."

PART II

THE UNDERDOGS

CHAPTER 4

Deep Appalachia

I woke up in a small town in Virginia called Bluefield, right over the state line from a different town in West Virginia with the same name. Nestled in a remote valley, these Bluefields felt like a nation of their own in this far-flung corner of Appalachia. It was about as rural as you can get. Ancient, forested hills rose behind my little Airbnb rental—tulip poplars, sugar maples, a few proud, surviving American chestnuts that had probably been here long before the first house was built and would likely outlive the last.

There's something magical about Appalachia in the summer: the scent of cut grass drifting in the morning air, the lonesome call of a mourning dove mixing with the bright chatter of cardinals. As I sipped a cup of hot tea on the porch, neighbors were tending to unhurried tasks around their yards—sweeping the front steps, uncoiling a garden hose, rolling a wheelbarrow half-filled from yesterday. Across the road, kids swarmed around a trampoline, ready for the day's first bounce. The place reminded me of my childhood in Vermont in the 1980s, a free-range kind of life I'd assumed kids didn't get much of anymore, though maybe they still do in a place like this.

I drove about fifteen minutes to the downtown of West Virginia's Bluefield, its glorious old redbrick architecture a reminder of its boom years as a regional economic hub. One building caught my eye, its black iron fire escape something you'd expect to see in Brooklyn or the Bronx. A black-and-white mural on a side wall depicted Bluefield in its prime: early model cars rolling down a wide street, a steam locomotive billowing smoke into the dark clouds above. Trains still rumble through Bluefield these days, but they're almost like apparitions of the past.

Bluefield's rise came from what lay buried in the surrounding mountains: coal. In the early 1900s—when miners worked the nearby Pocahontas Coalfield—up to 40 percent of the fuel for the entire United States passed through town. Once drawn by horse and buggy, after the Norfolk and Western Railway came, coal moved faster, and more people started to stick around. Businesses that financed, supplied, entertained, or housed the wave of bodies flowing into the region prospered. Coal country royalty—bank presidents, civil engineers, enterprising merchants, mine owners—built grand houses now listed on historic registers. Ornate archways and engraved door handles marked them out, details that no longer exist at scale today, simply too expensive and labor-intensive to produce. People started calling Bluefield "Little New York," as it was one of the first cities in the region with a recognizable skyline.

I think it's easy to forget sometimes that it was the crazies who built this country. Risk-taking Scots, Italians, and Poles (just to name a few) who upended their lives to come to a new world, often without understanding the language or how they'd earn their keep, only to find themselves tunneling into the earth, searching for the energy to power an industrializing nation. People who threw it all out there for the chance of becoming something more, boarding ships across the Atlantic or hopping trains north from the cotton fields of the Deep South, with nothing but the courage to start over, and zero guarantee that things would work out. And in Bluefield, at least for a while, they did.

Neither of the Bluefields are thriving anymore, but they get by. There are places to eat, and there is somewhere to catch a movie. Interstate 77 brings goods in and out. The Walmart on the outskirts of town sells avocados. But downtown Bluefield in West Virginia—or *Best Virginia,* as locals like to say—was empty that Saturday morning, so I wandered off and walked up a hillside to a cemetery overlooking the valley below. The hills in the distance broke into narrow, shaded valleys—what people here call hollers. I'd heard about them: winding off the main road, some short, some stretching for miles, most eventually dead-ending. In some hollers, families had been rooted in place for as many as four, five, six generations.

I walked past a home where a surefooted man in his thirties balanced on a ladder, setting up lights on a newly built patio. We said hi to one another, shot the breeze. He told me he was having a party that evening; he'd like me to stop by if I could. He seemed like the type of guy who, if I told him I had a problem with my front door not working, would come over with his toolbox and fix it.

I could suddenly see myself posting up here for a week, crashing the party that night, making some local friends, heading out to swimming holes for dips in cool mountain streams to cut the summer heat, like I had in my childhood. Forgetting about the outside world altogether.

In my mission to better understand this country, I'd been seeking out places that got me excited. Places that promised adventure, escape, or the unexpected. I'd found struggles in all of them, for sure, but there was always something aspirational about the lives people were living there too. Lately, though, I'd been thinking especially about the regions that get dismissed—sometimes even mocked—by the rest of the country as places where nothing much good ever happens. As full-on underdogs. "You're from the hills of coal country West Virginia? How cool!" isn't the go-to response for many people from elsewhere. I wanted to get beyond the stereotypes, to get to know locals living out here firsthand.

The road trip I was about to set off on would take me through what's arguably the poorest region of the country these days, one that had such a huge role in building America and yet in recent decades has seen the worst decline.

I told the man my plans.

"Have you been to Welch before?" he asked.

I hadn't.

"Some interesting folks out that way," he said, lifting his chin slightly. "Good people, but they've been through a lot."

The following morning, I set a course northwest toward Welch.

* * *

It was a pleasant drive, though the weather was on the verge of turning nasty. Churches speckled the sides of the road—not big ones, but big enough to have a lot of cars out front. It didn't look like religious attendance was thinning out around here.

Deeper into the valley, the train tracks started running parallel to the road. A rusting coal bridge crossed high above, precarious but intact, its old steel beams fused into nature. Rows of houses lined the route, some grander, others modest. Many sat empty, their wood siding moldy from the humid air, windows as dark as the sky above. Tropical-looking kudzu vines—what people call "the vine that ate the South," with almost no exaggeration—had taken over. Broad, waxy leaves smothered houses and porch railings, wrapped themselves around old trees, and swallowed power lines in a thick, green embrace. It was as if nature was getting revenge, taking back what had always been hers.

A steady rain started to fall.

I stopped at a gas station and got to talking with the attendant inside, a woman in her mid-thirties. She was open about the lack of jobs in the region, how people were barely getting by.

It made me wonder: Why stay? In a country built on the idea of leaving everything behind to start again, why cling to a place that had fallen so far? Why not do what her ancestors had done, pick up and move on?

"Roots," she said, with a shrug.

Maybe it wasn't just the houses the kudzu wouldn't let go of. She made me even more curious about what made this place so special, to keep people so attached.

I asked if I could record some of our conversation for a video I was making about Central Appalachia. Her demeanor changed, her shoulders and forehead tensing up.

"Don't film me," she said. "I know how people show us."

I understood what she meant, and I knew there was no way to prove myself any different in that moment. This is a part of the country that demands reputations be built on actions, not just words.

I thanked her for the chat and went on my way.

* * *

I'd been warned by people outside of Appalachia that the locals here would be closed off to me due to stereotype fatigue. It was a shame, because even after a little time here, it was clear that the reality didn't quite square with that image. People were open and talkative off-camera. But when I'd mention filming, the mood often changed.

The road to Welch continued on through a narrow valley, verdant lawns running up to steep hillsides. If this lush land were in California, it would have been worth a fortune, but out here the dirt was dirt cheap.

Coal trucks rumbled by, tall and heavy, their battered open-bed trailers coated in black soot, blowing grit across the roads, onto the siding of homes, and probably into the lungs of the people living inside of them. I passed an abandoned Walmart on the left side of the road, an outline of the name still visible on the facade. One thing you don't see often in America is a Walmart that's gone out of business. Usually, it's the Walmart that stays alive when everything else dies off.

It made me think about company stores, the original one-stop shops of the Gilded Age. Back in those days, coal miners were paid in scrip—a kind of private currency only good at company-owned entities. The tools to do your job, paid for in scrip. Rent for your company-owned house, paid for in scrip. Most months ended not with a paycheck but with deeper debt, and if something happened to you, your house could be taken back lightning quick. It wasn't uncommon for a miner's widow to be pressured to send her sons into the mines or risk losing the roof over her head. *I sold my soul to the company store* isn't just a line from a song—it was the business model.

But the rules of scrip quickly dissolved when it came to

company profits. That money left town in dollars, funding lifestyles in cities like New York and Pittsburgh.

And this system wasn't some Appalachian outlier. The same setup ran through the redwood mills of California, the paper towns of Florida, and the lumber camps of Washington State.

A few miles farther, I finally entered Welch, a town of roughly 3,600 people nestled in the hills at the confluence of the Tug Fork River and some small creeks. I parked at an empty lot next to an outdoor basketball court with a high fence, barbed wire wrapped around the top. An old stone building sat behind it, which I guessed was the McDowell County jail.

I was told back in Bluefield that some of the homes go for $25,000 out in these parts, and that was for a home you could move right into. Some properties went for as low as seven dollars a square foot, and the run-down ones—the ones that needed serious work—were practically being given away. In a country of sky-high housing prices, here was the other extreme. The poorest county in West Virginia, with a median family income of $31,984, had more empty houses than people to fill them.

I ambled around the almost empty streets, imagining what they might have looked like back in the day. There was a grand, Renaissance-style bank; a boarded-up, three-story, flatiron-style drugstore; an empty Odd Fellows temple with clouded windows, the stonework darkened by age. I passed empty storefronts, some with CLOSED UNTIL FURTHER NOTICE signs slapped in the windows, five or six at a time, like just one wouldn't do. Others had windows blown out, as if a natural disaster had ripped through.

I could walk straight down the middle of the street without

needing to dodge a single car, the quiet broken only by old signs creaking in the breeze and the soft flap of an American flag hanging from a lamppost above a banner: THE CITY OF WELCH SALUTES PHALANDERS F. "PHIL" LAW. VIETNAM VETERAN. PROUDLY HONORED BY A GRATEFUL COMMUNITY it read, but it didn't seem like there were a whole lot of people left around to be grateful.

Still, there was something . . . charming about the place. Maybe it was the calm that came from the lack of urgency for anything as if the whole town were on standby.

I wandered past a gas station where two guys in their early forties stood beside a pickup, sipping tall cans of Monster Energy. One of them—shirt cut off at the shoulders, lean arms marked with ink—nodded first, jaw tight behind a patchy goatee. He wore a backward cap and stood like someone used to scanning a horizon, like he'd been in sketchy situations before.

"Iraq from '05 to '06," he said, catching me looking at his military tattoo. "Baghdad."

His name was Adam. The other guy, Jason, nodded along.

"Around here, it's military or mines," he said.

Though coal mining isn't what it was in boom times—partially because of competition from cheaper forms of energy like natural gas and renewables, and partially because advances in technology allow companies to do more with fewer workers—it's still the main economic driver of the region. I'd heard entry-level mining pays $85,000 right out of high school. Still, companies are having a hard time finding young people willing to do the work. Maybe it's the uncertainty: the fear that your skills, your worth, could vanish with a single letter from the company saying the mine's done. Or maybe it's the mix of hard manual labor and real danger underground, difficult work in a society that's grown more comfortable and less willing to grind.

"You ain't got time to spend no money," Jason said. "Just ain't nothing enjoyable about it to me."

"How many hours a week?" I asked.

"Sometimes sixty-plus," he replied. "Underground."

"What does that do to your sleep cycle?"

"It's terrible. You're always tired. Like a zombie."

Adam grinned. "I did a whole three weeks in the coal mine."

"What work did you like better, military or coal mine?" I asked Adam.

"Military," he answered, no question. "You can't find that brotherhood anywhere else."

Still, Jason said people looked out for each other in the mines. "It's a tight community," he said, nodding toward the road back into downtown Welch.

"If you get outta town, up in the hollers, it's even tighter," Adam added. "You be a kid down there and get in trouble down here, time you get home, about five people done called your mama. Everybody knows everybody. That's not a good thing, sometimes." He laughed.

I pointed out the bars on the gas station windows. "Is there a lot of crime here?"

"Not really," Jason said. "It's just this area right here. Probably in the early 2000s it was pretty rough. But now, everything's kind of calmed down, settled down. The population's been gradually going down since the fifties. Before, you walk out here, every one of these streets will be full, it'd be bumper-to-bumper traffic."

I asked if young people stuck around.

"Our generation, most of 'em left here," Adam said.

Jason nodded. "And for the ones that stayed, they don't really get out much. Most of 'em can't even change a flat. It's a different breed than how we was raised."

"But they'll tell you how to play any PlayStation game," Adam added.

I'd thought, probably naively, that the farther out I went into nowhere, the more I'd see kids on BMX bikes or playing around in the woods. But video games and the internet had charged through the front door, just like they had in most every other community across America.

I asked if they planned to stick around.

"If I didn't have three babies here, I'd done been gone," said Adam.

"I've been gone a few times," said Jason. "Always end up back."

* * *

I passed some cheerful Mormon missionaries (who I've always respected for getting out of their comfort zone) on my way up to a high school on a hill overlooking town—a massive, ivy-draped brick structure built to last forever. The windows were a mix of busted-out and brand-new, as if someone had started to care but then run out of money or interest.

It's the cycle of life, everywhere always at a different point. Was Welch at the bottom, I wondered, or did it have further down to go? Maybe someday people would see this place as a kind of escape: a rural haven like Amish country. Somewhere to go to live a quiet, affordable life in the countryside. Some small industry would have to move in first, though—something to keep the lights on.

One of the doorways of the school sat chained shut, the handles looped together with a piece of metal wire like a rancher had closed a gate. Weeds pushed up through the cracks in the concrete, brushing against the rusted barrels crowding the entrance. Inside, through the cracked glass, I could see the hallway and a staircase. Lockers that had been opened and slammed shut a million times. I could almost hear the laughter bouncing off the stairwells. The bell going off: three o'clock, end of the day. Gonna get out in town, have a milkshake, maybe an adventure.

I'd think back to that old schoolhouse a couple of days later, when a local told me one of the rivers around here had once flowed full of coal runoff. "Back in the day, this river ran black," he'd said. "Didn't matter if it rained or not."

The river water ran clear now, but there were few people still around to see it.

* * *

On my way out of Welch, I turned onto a narrow side road—the kind you don't end up on unless you've taken a wrong turn or you just want to exhaust all things a place has to offer. It was wide enough for one vehicle, with a moss-stained stone wall on one side and thick trees on the other.

Up ahead, a man was hunched under the hood of his pickup truck, working on something. I rolled down the passenger window.

"How's it going?"

We fell into small talk.

"What, a car every twenty minutes?" I asked.

The man laughed softly. "That's about it in these parts."

He worked six days a week in a coal mine, he'd told me, squinting in the sun and wiping his hands with a rag nonstop, like there was always another layer of oil beneath the last.

"Five in the morning to five in the evening. And all the overtime I want." There was no complaint in his voice. No boasting either.

"If it wasn't for coal mines, a lot of these people around here would be starving to death. They wouldn't have electricity, they wouldn't have heat. And here you got the government and everybody wanting to shut the coal miners down, do away with this, do everything electric. Well, you gotta have coal to run many of our electric plants. You've got to have coal to power electric cars, and you've got to have it to make steel too."

It's true. The technology is changing, and hydrogen might be the future when it comes to making steel. But transitioning at scale will take years, investment, and a whole lot of infrastructure. Right now, many blast furnaces need coke, which comes from coal and is the only thing that burns at the intense 2,800°F needed to melt iron ore to make the steel molds. Start looking for steel, and you'll see it everywhere—car doors, elevator shafts, surgeon's scalpels, washing machines. Without coal from places like McDowell County, a lot of the basics we take for granted just don't exist. Even so, US coal consumption has declined roughly 60 percent over the last twenty years.

"And a lot of your coal goes to China?" I asked.

The man's gaze sharpened a little. "Yeah." China consumes 50 percent of the world's coal—more than the rest of the world combined—while the US burns roughly 8.5 percent. Although those exports were down too. A lot of the American coal industry's struggles lately have been due to global oversupply and competition from fracking, not just clean energy.

He paused a beat. "Everybody thinks we're just dumb country folk. But actually, a lot of us out here are smarter than a lot of people give us credit for. We work hard. We support our families. And we don't let nobody step in between that. People out here will bend over backward to help you. They'll give you the shirt off their back—as long as you don't make 'em mad or cross 'em." He paused again. "Out here, a man's word and his handshake are his bond."

I told him I was heading east, planning to cruise up a few of the hollers before crossing into Kentucky, where a friend had put me in touch with a fifth-generation coal miner.

"You be careful out there, bud," he said.

I thanked him and drove off. In the rearview mirror, he was already back under the hood. Just another day, another oil change, another shift at the coal mines ahead of him Monday at 5:00 a.m. Another man in a long line of men who'd risked their lives doing dangerous and unhealthy work to build this country. To build the grand skyscrapers of the American skyline that propelled our economy ahead of the rest of the world, the skyscrapers that men in suits made all their money and dreams come true in.

Appalachia may be the nation's most iconic underdog region, but it's far from alone. So many millions of men and women performed unsung hourly labor to help make this country what it is today, only for whole industries to collapse around them as modernity took hold. Up until the 1960s, 95 percent of our grandparents' and great-grandparents' clothes and household textiles were made domestically, in places like North Carolina, where 40 percent of the industry's jobs were. When that production was outsourced overseas, six hundred plants shut down. Now, only 2–3 percent of textile products are manufactured here in the United States.

It's the same story for the lumber mills that built the Pacific Northwest, or the sharecropping undertaken after the abolition of slavery by souls who were the very definition of grit and perseverance . . . only for industrialized agriculture to come on in. And even that's now threatened by an increase in wealthy investors and foreign interests buying up American farmland.

A few generations back, the people working in these industries could be proud of their contributions to the success of the country—proud of feeding, clothing, housing, and warming their fellow Americans. They could look at something tangible—a bridge or a shirt—and say to their kids, "This is what I made." They felt needed, past tense. Since coal has turned into a pejorative in recent years, I got the hint that many of the people here felt lesser than. That they understood the country had stopped noticing them, even though they were an essential part of giving their countrymen the modern world they desired.

* * *

Some interesting town names spread out in front of me as I left Welch and twisted up the valley: Coalwood, War, Paynesville. I was about as deep into Appalachia as you could get. It's one of those parts of the country where you can use Street View on Google Maps, zoom out, and still see a lot of space in between blue lines—large tracts of green separating old coal towns from one another. I'd pass a closed gas station and some vacant storefronts being slowly eaten by rust next to a cheerfully painted home, a broken-down trailer, and then a neat garden full of zinnias. It didn't make sense in any linear way. Broken poverty and high pride lived side by side out here, often behind the same front door. And yet how was it that the roads in a place this remote and poor were in better shape than the main highway from the Fiumicino Airport coming into Rome?

I decided to take a left after a house with half its roof caving in and entered my first holler. The road turned into one lane, the houses almost touching. It felt somehow like I had passed into a different dimension. Things slowed down. Driving twelve miles per hour felt too fast. My speedometer read in the single digits.

I crept by some old homes with junked cars in the lawns. Up in the distance, a man had his head down, walking slowly in a swerving pattern, clothes dirty and torn. I heard the deep bass of some loud barking dogs in the distance. To my left sat what looked like a meth house: windows blown out, sheets hanging in their place. Something tightened in my gut. It felt like a place where things could turn bad quickly, like the narrow road could be closed off behind me. As NO TRESPASSING and BEWARE OF DOG signs became more frequent than American flags, I realized it was time for me to leave.

Back on the main road, I felt like I was in my country again. Back to the rules of the USA, where I'd have due process if something went wrong. Still, feeling that I didn't get the best holler experience, I decided to make another go at it.

I turned onto a narrow road that carried me through a long tunnel beneath the train tracks. When I emerged on the other side, the road began to climb—winding up through the valley to a house painted a bright blue, like someone had taken a piece of the sky and placed it on the hillside. A porch stretched along the front, a crucifix hanging beside the door.

Two people sat back in the shade: an older man in a plain white tee and jeans, and a woman in a turquoise tank top dress, gently rocking on a wooden swing. She was barefoot. At first, she looked half asleep from the heat. But then they saw me, and their faces lit up. They waved me in.

The woman's name was Maye. Jay, whose accent was as thick as the kudzu vines shrouding the forest, had stopped by for a visit. He was married to her oldest son's ex-wife, which made him family.

The three of us sat for a while, chatting about the heat, the hills, and the internet that out here can be down for weeks at a time. The swing creaked gently. Maye disappeared into the house at one point and came back with a red book, the edges worn soft from use. The cover read *They Died in the Darkness.*

"I thought you might be interested in looking at this," she said, placing it on the railing in front of me and opening to the page she had in mind. It was filled with names in columns: the ninety-one men who'd died in the Bartley Mine.

Maye pointed at a photo of a man and his young son. "Both of them were killed down here." The father looked proud, his posture straight. The son looked solemn, older than his years, a face you'd see in old class photos or church directories, from an era when smiles in pictures were frowned upon.

She paused, her voice thinner now. "My dad was killed down in these mines. He was killed in March, and I was born in August."

"I'm sorry," I said, and we grew quiet for a while. A breeze drifted through the holler, rustling the screen door. The butterfly wind chime above the door spun once and fell still again.

"That's the only thing that keeps us going, though, you know?" Jay finally said.

We got to talking politics for a bit. Whichever party is perceived as more supportive of the coal industry tends to win here. In 1992, McDowell County voted more strongly for Bill Clinton than New York City. But the county has been red for more than two decades now.

"When I worked every day in the mine, it was just like being at home," Jay said, looking off toward the tree line. "But once, I told a buddy of mine, I said, 'Hey, the miner cut too far against the wall.'"

He shifted in his seat. "We got water in the man trip we was riding. And that water has twelve breaks of water, backed up. And it just blowed that coal out, just like an explosion." His hands motioned outward—quick, sharp.

"Had about eight of us working on the evening shift there," Jay said.

"You saved eight people?" I asked.

"Yeah, when that water was blowed out there."

He said it matter-of-factly, but the way he looked away told me it had landed deeper than he let on. Coal mining was an inheritance, passed down like land, or DNA, and it came with serious costs. Families who waited by radios or on doorsteps. Whole towns built on top of dark tunnels.

Somewhere down the holler, a woodpecker let out a wild, echoing laugh—sharp and sudden—snapping my attention back to the hills. The sun had shifted while we sat there, catching the tops of the trees now and casting long shadows that reached across the yard. I told them I needed to keep moving. I still had ground to cover before sundown.

Maye was already inside again, returning with a cold bottle of water. "It's a hot one today." She handed it to me like a grandmother sending me on my way to school.

* * *

The road twisted and wound beside a river, lowering in elevation. Right on the Virginia state line, the lawns started getting bigger, the houses grander. With West Virginia in the rearview mirror, I missed the place already. The authenticity of the people I met there, the raw beauty, the simplicity. The feeling of being removed from everything.

We'd be missing the whole truth of the United States if we only talked about the places with fairy-tale making-it stories. The ones everyone used to dream of, cities like Los Angeles or New York. Because as exciting as these places are, most of the country isn't living their stories (including most people actually in New York or LA). People are doing what they can to make rent or their mortgage, to keep the lights on, to grab on to stability and feel a little love in the middle of all that grind. Like the Chicano man trying to hold on to his roots in a place where gentrification is inching in. Like the Amish farmer working to keep his culture thriving in a world that increasingly lives online and bases its reality on what's there. Like the young man in the long Alaskan winter, dreaming at once of a place that's warmer than the tundra and the whale he'll hunt to feed his village. Old and new. Tradition and modernity. The heart versus the head. Relinquish or reinvent.

It's hard to know what balance to strike, but just thinking about it gave me a strange kind of optimism. I thought back to that old high school in Welch, sitting quiet on the hill—windows half-smashed, half-replaced. *Maybe*, I thought, *it'll get another shot. Some young families will move in nearby, kids in tow. Maybe someone will see the bones of the place and decide it's worth rebuilding for the sake of educating a new generation.*

After decades of people flocking from rural areas to cities, the tide does seem to be turning the other way, in some places, anyway. Even here in McDowell County—one of the poorest corners of the country—the population has ticked up ever so slightly in recent years. But hope, like everything else out here, comes layered, and even good change often arrives with some friction. I'd learn that just a few days later in North Carolina, when I'd meet a woman who would tell me she had become ashamed of her accent.

"Folks come down here because they love the *place*—but they never really learn to love the *people*," she said. "Often they come here because they don't like what's happened where they're from, and they try to change our ways to be more like what they're getting away from."

It seemed like so many of the locals I was meeting felt invaded by *and* isolated from their own countrymen.

* * *

By this point, I'd been driving for what felt like days. Like so much of America, the scale of the place was easy to underestimate. Central Appalachia is massive—at almost thirty thousand square miles, it's nearly twice the size of the Netherlands or Denmark or Switzerland.

Crossing the state line into Virginia, the road led me to a small town called Grundy. Although nearly a quarter of the eight hundred people living here were below the poverty line, the road curved past a few surprisingly grand homes set back behind wide lawns and old brick gateposts. I'd later learn that in Grundy, a nice house didn't necessarily signal wealth, just a brief alignment of good wages and cheap land, when ordinary work could still buy something that looked, from the outside, like prosperity. But jobs were scarce, and even those available weren't always being filled.

How wild, I thought, that all this was just hours from suburban Fairfax County—one of the wealthiest parts of the country, where people commute into DC. People in these two places were living in entirely different worlds, and I suspected that, for the most part, neither really understood the other. That woman I'd speak with in North Carolina would tell me she'd stopped playing her banjo, too worried about what her new neighbors might think . . . when maybe they'd have thought it was the coolest thing to have a folk musician next door.

But in spite of these misunderstandings, the reality is that rural and urban America depend on one another. Urban areas need coal miners and farmers and water reservoirs, while rural communities depend on new technologies and efficient supply chains to move resources out to the middle of nowhere. No part of this country would be better off without the rest—which, I suppose, is one of the things I hope people can see in my videos.

My stomach began to rumble, and I pulled into one of the only places in town serving food—a chain pizza spot with plastic booths and wall art that hadn't changed in decades. The place was empty except for me. After finishing a pepperoni pizza with extra cheese (greasy, perfect), I got to talking with the manager, who was probably around my age. He had that half-tired, half-kind look some people get when they've seen too much but still show up no matter what. He was going on a smoke break, asked me if I wanted to join.

Outside, the air had cooled just enough to notice, with a light breeze pushing through the forest behind the dumpster. He lit up his Marlboro Blue.

I asked him what it was like running the place these days.

"It's tough finding young people to work," he said. "We have very few kids who are eighteen to twenty-four that actually get out and try to produce at a job."

Just then, one of his employees came out—a young woman in her early twenties, with an open, curious smile. The manager hollered her over, and she jumped right into the conversation.

"What about the generation you came out of high school with, Shay?" he asked. "What percentage would you say are actually working-class Americans at this point?" As opposed to not working at all.

She hesitated. "I would say maybe fifty percent."

"Fifty percent?" I asked, surprised.

"If that." She nodded. "Because, I'm gonna be honest with you—my best friend from high school is currently locked up in prison for drugs."

The manager lifted his hand in a loose shrug, like *See what I mean?*

"What's it right now?" I asked. "Fentanyl?"

"Yes," he said. "Bad."

"Very bad," Shay added.

The manager flicked some ash off the end of his cigarette. "I give people a second chance. Always have. We have a girl here right now, she finished fourteen hundred hours of community service—from a drug situation. She's really straightened herself out. She's a role model employee."

"Fourteen hundred hours?" The number shocked me, being equivalent to thirty-five (forty-hour) workweeks.

"Fourteen hundred," he repeated.

"She would go to the courthouse and work nine to five," Shay said. "Then come straight here and work five to eleven. Then drive almost an hour home."

I asked Shay if it had been hard to avoid getting into drugs in high school.

"It wasn't as easy to get your hands on something, you

know?" She shrugged. "I was one of those people that nobody really talked to. I just stayed to myself. I was an A student . . . and I worked here"—she motioned to the restaurant behind us—"from the time I was sixteen."

She hesitated for a few seconds and then continued.

"I come from a long line of drug users. I'll be the first in my family to hold a college degree. I'm actually getting ready to graduate with my associate's in criminal justice."

"Congrats," I said, my smile wide.

"Thank you." She smiled back.

A young man in a pizza-logo hat parked his car and walked over to say hi before starting his evening shift. The manager took the opening to quiz him about stats. He'd just gotten out of high school, and his guess was that as few as 25 percent of his classmates were working.

"The majority of them are either on checks or living with their parents," he said, maybe with some particular friends in mind. "They don't really care to work. I've tried getting them into an engineering program to tell them, 'You need to do something. Mom and Dad ain't gonna be able to take care of you forever. You're not gonna always have people in your life to support you. You have to actually try to make a name for yourself.'"

"How do nineteen-year-olds get checks?" I asked.

"Disability. Anxiety."

Shay nodded. "When they put me on the anxiety and depression medicine, it was just irritation all the time. I'm cool-tempered, not an angry person at all. But it made me so irritated, like every little thing would just piss me off. Once I quit taking it, I had a couple days where I just didn't want to get outta bed at all. It was horrible. But after about a week of not taking it, I felt normal. And then I figured out different coping mechanisms. Meditation, I do that. I go on hikes with my son. We walk the dog. And we have a whole farm full of animals—lizards, snakes, everything. So we kinda keep ourselves occupied, you know."

"How many people do you think are on medicine, roughly?" I asked.

The manager blew out a cloud of thick smoke. "Sixty-five percent of the people in this area would be on some kind of medicine, some form. And as far as depression meds, I'd say well over half."

Here in Central Appalachia, the farther in I went, the deeper conversations ran, and the more tangled things around something as "simple" as solving poverty in America became. What we'd been talking about went beyond drugs or unemployment. It was about exhaustion, about how much effort one was willing to put in, day after day, just to survive. Some made their way well, working for a local hospital or a school or in the few other jobs that could give a good quality of living. But how many folks stayed simply because they were too tired or fearful to leave? Not unwilling, but unable to muster the energy that leaving requires. It takes momentum to uproot a life. To leave family and friends. It takes confidence. It takes the belief that something better exists, and that you're capable of reaching it.

And I knew some of that *stuckness* came down to money. First month's rent, last month's rent, moving costs . . . poverty traps you in place as firmly as any affection for home ever could. By now, whatever optimism I'd started with was wearing thin. But places like this have a way of surprising you when you least expect it.

* * *

The road ran alongside a creek now, with hills rising on both banks, trees swallowed up in more kudzu. The sun lowered, blurring the greens into one monotone shade. Up ahead, I spotted a group of young guys hanging around a low bridge, fishing.

I hit the brakes and eased into the gravel off the road.

"Ah, you should have been here ten minutes ago, man," said a teen with a curly mullet straight out of the hair metal days of the '80s. "I had one that was bending my pole up under the bridge."

I asked if I could film him fishing.

"I don't think you'll be able to get down in here. It's all mud." He started crawling under the bridge, boots and hi-vis striped pants sliding through the weeds, his sleeveless orange safety shirt darkened in sweat. A diesel mechanic. He was going to school for it.

Two of his friends were visiting from Indiana. They both wore cutoff tees with cross necklaces, trucker hats, and bootcut jeans paired with cowboy boots. One of them worked at the Dairy Queen as a manager.

"A manager?" I asked, surprised. "How old are you?"

He laughed. "Sixteen."

"You're probably the youngest manager in Dairy Queen history."

The fourth teen wore a beautifully crafted leather bracelet on his wrist; tinted aviators hung from the collar of his black T-shirt over what looked like a Thor's hammer pendant.

"I wanna go to college to get my degree in history and archeology," he said as his deep voice softened under the echo off the creek. "I got a grant along with the university—four years up in Farmville. And two years of it will be spent in London."

"London, UK?" I asked.

"Yes, sir. What really got me into it was my grandma telling me stories about my third great-grandfather, who was her papaw. He was half Native, and he signed up for the 34th Battalion. He fought Gettysburg, Sharpsburg, all that. Private Andrew Cole, Company C, 34th Virginia Cavalry, Witcher's Battalion."

The Indiana kids watched us quietly, neither of them jockeying to speak or fighting for attention. The whole group seemed mature beyond their years. I got the sense they were friends who didn't need to fill the air to feel close.

"My fourth great-grandfather on my dad's side was a Black man who fought in the Confederate army," the young historian went on, lighting a cigarette and drawing in slowly. "His name was Private Nathaniel Hawthorne. He was a sharpshooter for the 37th Virginia Infantry from Russell County. Me and my camp—the Lieutenant Colonel Vincent Witcher Camp of the Sons of Confederate Veterans—we put up the first Confederate statue in Buchanan County last year, at my family's cemetery. It was at the grave of my fourth great-grandmother, Elizabeth Jackson Cole, and her husband, who died during the Battle of McDowell in Highland County, Virginia." He said it all with pride.

I was astounded by his memory and the quick cadence of his delivery, and the last thing I wanted to do was take away his thunder. But part of my job, when making videos, is to dig deeper—to understand more and ask questions that I suspect people watching my videos might be wondering about, even when the answers aren't easy. Still, I felt like an ass asking it.

"For many people, when they hear *Confederate*, all they think of is racism immediately," I said. "What are your thoughts on that?"

"I don't have a problem with anybody," he replied confidently.

"Like I said, my fourth great-grandfather on my dad's side was a Black man who fought in the Confederate army, so a little bit of him is in me. Racism confuses me. It really does. Simply because of the fact that we all come from the same place. First evidence of humanity popped up in Africa about two million years ago. That's where humanity comes from. We are all humans. That's why racism, I think, is—excuse my French—kind of bullshit. It's made to divide people. It's made to tear people down."

He stopped and leaned against the railing, the creek quieter now. The diesel mechanic had moved farther down the stream, cracking a joke about there being no fish in sight.

"When you're a bored kid in Appalachia," the young historian said, "you get into anything that's interesting."

And then I blurted out what I'd been hearing. "So you either get into anything interesting, or you get into drugs, right?"

He didn't flinch.

"Pretty much. It is an epidemic here. And it's not so much marijuana—it's meth, heroin, fentanyl, stuff like that. I've seen my family destroyed by it. I've seen other people's families destroyed by it. My stepfather was on meth real bad. He's no longer with us."

"I'm sorry, man."

He stood up, straightened his spine.

"But I want to show people that Appalachia is not . . ." He paused, searching for the words. "We're more than just drugs and coal mining. We have history here. We have so much more to offer: the culture, the music, the people. The people are just great."

"I agree."

"Folks here will help anyone. It doesn't matter who you are. That's what I love about it. No matter your background, no matter where you come from—if you're a good person, if you have respect—they will help you. And yeah, sometimes we get a little rowdy, a little reckless. But at the end of the day, we're just good-hearted people."

"So what do you think is needed in Appalachia?" I asked. I thought he might say something like more job opportunities.

He let out an extended breath after a long drag of his cig. "Better leadership, I think. Pride. Not a lot of folks are proud of who they are."

"They're not proud here? I thought Appalachian people were very proud."

"Well, the older generation is. But a lot of the younger generation . . . they've kind of lost their way. People never taught them where they come from, how resilient they actually are, you know?"

We stood in silence for a minute.

"Sing for him," the diesel mechanic shouted up from the creek.

The young historian chuckled. "Of course, these boys had to bring it up." He looked at his friends. "What do you want me to sing?"

"'Follow You to Virgie.'"

He broke out in a beautiful, deep voice, his eyes half-closed, singing about loss, family, and friendship. It was one of those strange, perfect moments you don't expect to experience on the side of the road. Something that can never be planned but just happens when you're open to it. A stranger singing to me in the middle of nowhere.

"Argh! I lost him!" the diesel mechanic shouted from under the bridge. "I just hooked into a giant and lost him again!" It was the last fish any of us saw that day.

We walked slowly down the empty road, where the diesel mechanic's truck was pulled off into the grass. It was a single-cab red Ford Ranger from the mid-2000s, clean and well-kept, the only signs it wasn't fresh off a dealer's lot were the muddy tires and the silver diamond-plate toolbox bolted to the bed his friends climbed onto one by one.

"Nice truck, man," I said, knowing that's one of the best compliments you can give to a guy with a truck like that.

"Thanks. I've probably had forty vehicles."

"Forty?" I asked, not hiding the disbelief. "Four-zero?" He was eighteen.

"Yep. Just trading up. I could take this truck right here, take the motor and transmission out of it tonight, and tomorrow day, have everything put back together. I got a dirt bike one time, messed the wheel up on it. Had to get a whole new chain, a carburetor, everything. Dad looked at me—and I knew I had to figure it out myself. He wanted me to have responsibility, to work for what I got, because I'd appreciate it more. So I went out, I weeded—" He paused. "It was hay time. We mowed, tedded, raked all the hay. I threw hay bales since I was eight years old. And I fixed my motorcycle with the money I made."

Maybe this kid's hair wasn't the only thing stuck in the '80s. I'd thought this kind of hard, physical work for young people had faded away with the times.

"So, you guys were brought up to know how to make something out of yourselves?"

"I watched this man," he said, pointing to the historian. "I watched this boy right here with his mama. They completely redone the inside of a house that was from, what, the early 1900s? This man can build anything out of wood, make you tables, make you chairs, anything you want. But I'm not gonna lie to you. Schooling? You put a book in front of me, I'm an idiot. I'm in college for six months right now. Welding classes. I get my diesel, I get my Class A CDL, and as soon as I'm done with that, I go straight to work."

"And you're really set," I added, "because fewer people your age are doing that now, right?" Though that trend might be starting to change.

"Right. I think I'm doing it because, in a way, it's the only thing I know."

He was so humble. And yet the life he was building for himself was one where the work was hands-on and creative and gritty—fixing things, making things, solving practical everyday problems in ways that let you feel smart and capable, like you are doing a bit of good in the world. A life of steady friendships and neighbors who knew your kids' names. A life where interesting people crossed your path in the most ordinary places. I could understand why a young person would choose that over a chance at whatever opportunities *might* be waiting somewhere else.

* * *

Crossing into Harlan County, Kentucky, the next morning, the rolling hills of Virginia gave way to the rugged Cumberland Plateau. It had poured rain through the night. The forests looked newly washed—oak and hickory trunks darkened to near black, like they'd been freshly stained. Everything felt sharper, the colors dialed up. The air carried the scent of damp earth.

I'd come in search of a guy who was five generations deep in the mines. A friend of mine who sells and hauls draft horses all over the states had told me about him. "You gotta meet Wes," he'd said. "He's the real deal."

We'd agreed to meet outside a low-slung diner just off the

road. Wes told me there was no easy way into where he lived. "You'll get lost," he said. "Guaranteed."

So I followed behind his blue Harley, his hands to the sky on his ape hanger handlebars, riding slowly through a maze of back roads and switchbacks until the pavement narrowed and a small valley opened up ahead. We pulled up to a modest one-story house with a couple of rocking chairs on the porch, flowerpots that lined the steps, and black wrought-iron columns twisted in a scrollwork pattern.

"When you've got a COAL MINER mat," I said, pointing to the doormat that spelled it out in all caps, "it's official."

Wes grinned. He looked to be in his mid-fifties, with long gray hair pulled back in a low ponytail. A long beard was looped through a few hair ties, ending in a white tassel that appeared almost ceremonial. He wore mirrored sunglasses, a heavy chain, and a shirt with a rifle across the chest that read: WHEN TYRANNY BECOMES LAW, REBELLION BECOMES DUTY.

Wes started pointing out his neighbors up the road. "My dad's place is right there, uncle's just up around that bend. Cousin's down the hill."

He swept his hand toward a line of solid-looking homes with trimmed hedges. This, he told me, was the ridge. Around here, that meant the high ground. The backbone of the mountain where the land leveled just enough to build. Unlike a holler, which dropped low between slopes and held everything close—the fog, the cold, the quiet—the ridge was open. Breezier. More sun.

"These are all retired coal miners," he said. "Ninety-five percent of the men you meet here, they all went to coal mines at eighteen years old, some of them younger."

I asked about his grandfather.

"Got killed in the mines in '57. I started in '89. Back then, just in this little community—Cawood, not all of Harlan County, just Cawood—there were probably over a hundred coal mines. Now there's none."

He paused.

"They say mining started here in 1903, but it was actually before then, because they hand-dug. Back in the day, everybody had their own little mine. They'd just dig out the bank and dig the coal out for heat, cooking . . . you know, whatever. And then when coal finally picked up, the companies came in here. Some of the guys got rich, some got ripped off."

He didn't have to say which side his family landed on.

"When Dad's dad got killed in '57, three years later, his brother got killed. They had all these kids. Back then, it was normal for a family to have eight, ten kids, whatever. So, they all had to chip in—raise gardens, kill hogs, just take care of each other, you know?"

He led me around the side of the house to an old wooden shed filled with memorabilia. The roof sagged slightly, and the door creaked open like it hadn't been touched in a while. Inside, the air smelled like old wood and oxidized metal. Wes pulled a phone from the back pocket of his weathered jeans and tapped on the flashlight, its beam cutting through the dust. The place was packed, shelves and tables lined with rusted hand tools, vintage appliances, old bottles, dented mine helmets, coffee cans full of bolts and nails.

"My great-granddad bought this property in 1942," he said. "Most of this stuff here came out of the camp houses or outta the ground, collected over time." The light swung upward, catching the edge of a strange metal tool hanging just under the ceiling—long and curved, with a wide grip and a blunt ridged bit at the end.

"They call these breast augers in the mines. Some of 'em were a lot longer than this. Two men would run it. One would brace it right here"—he pressed his palm flat to his chest—"and the other one would crank it, drill down into the coal. Then they'd put a shot off in it."

"So drill," I said, "then stick in the dynamite?"

"Exactly."

Something else caught my eye: an old metal toy car, palm-size, wedged between a chunk of petrified wood and a battered meat tenderizer. I asked if I could pick it up. It was heavier than I expected, maybe four pounds, and simple in its beauty: boxy and plainly crafted, with cut-out windows, a hollow interior, and iron wheels mounted on straight axles. Solid in the hand, like it was built to outlive its owner *and* the next few generations.

Wes reached for something near the door and stepped outside, holding it up in the light. A Davy lamp—the kind miners used before gas detectors—tall and cylindrical, with a steel bonnet and a fine wire mesh where the glass chamber used to be. "It's got a striker on the bottom," he said. "You ignite it, then take it in with you underground. If the flame goes out, that means there ain't enough oxygen." He turned it slightly in his hand. "And if the flame burns blue, that means methane. That's how the miner know'd to back out."

I asked if there were any spots where you could still look into old mines to actually see what it was like down there.

Wes gave a small nod. "Yeah. I'll take you to one."

We got in his side-by-side and drove for a while—long enough that I lost track—winding past fields and spaced-out houses, then climbing into a patch of forest that grew denser the farther we went. The road turned rough, the side-by-side jolting over ruts, tires spraying mud from the puddles left behind by last night's rain.

Eventually, we pulled off at what looked like nothing, just a shoulder of hard dirt, the tree line slipping downward. We got out and started on foot, single file. The trail was overgrown—thorny brush to duck under, more to push through.

And then we saw it. The mine. Or what was left of it, anyway: a gaping hole at the base of the mountain, like a five-foot-tall groundhog burrow.

I followed Wes in, rocks crunching under our feet. It was cold.

"Wow," I said. "That's like a twenty-degree difference right here."

Wes knelt beside the wall, where the ceiling dropped gradually as the tunnel narrowed, and traced a finger across the rock.

"See that line?" he said. "That's your seam."

I'd thought of mining as something slightly more vertical, a shaft down into the earth. But in this part of Appalachia, miners go in horizontally, following a coal seam—a thick, dark stripe inside the rock that might stretch for miles. That's where they dig, bolting the ceiling as they go to hold the overhead rock in place. Some seams are tall enough to crouch through; some are only twenty-four inches. You'd lie on your side with a pick in one hand and a light strapped to your head, crawling inch by inch. One of the seams Wes worked ran nearly four miles. Just the description of it made me feel claustrophobic. "Like crawling through a four-mile-long CT scan machine," he said.

I looked back toward the light at the mine's mouth.

"Five generations down here," I said. "Does it stop with you?"

He nodded. "I got four kids—two boys, two girls. I'm a single dad with my youngest. He's twelve. I don't want him in the mines. His education comes first . . . just starting sixth grade and already got awards hanging at home."

Five generations in, and he was fine with it ending.

"My oldest son did go into mining for a while," he said. "But when I decided to come out in 2017, when I knew I had black lung, I talked to him. Told him he needed to look at something else. Just like my dad told me. I didn't listen."

Wes told me that black lung used to be the number one killer of miners. Well, for those who didn't die in the darkness from cave-ins, explosions, suffocation, machinery accidents . . . the list went long.

"What it does is scar your lungs," he said. "The rock dust, it's like breathing in tiny shards of glass. It just cuts and cuts. I watched every one of Dad's brothers die from it. There were six boys."

His oldest son was with one of the electrical line companies now, making almost $200,000 a year. Most parents here seemed to want their kids to do something different—anything other than coal. But I could see why it'd be hard to let go of the only life you've ever known. Coal put food on the table. Built the house. Paid the church tithe. Walking away from that feels like losing a piece of yourself. What happens to your people, your land, your stories?

* * *

The side-by-side kept climbing the old mine road, the path twisting up the ridge, until we popped out at the top and the view opened wide. Wes pointed across the valley, his house far below. "This might not be nothing to nobody," he said. "But to me . . . look at it. It's beautiful."

The hills stretched out in every direction, lit unevenly by

the afternoon sun: dark green up close, fading to softer blues the farther they went. A few clearings broke up the forested slopes, thin roads cutting through them with houses along the way. But mostly, it was just a whole lot of space.

We walked a little more along the hilltop, just to see the drop better.

"I could knock on any door out there," Wes said, "and I guarantee they'd feed you. You . . ." He pointed at me, a little fire in his voice. "You're not even from around here. I guarantee you could go to any door around and say, 'I'm thirsty. I need a bite to eat.' Ninety-nine point nine percent of 'em would take you in, set you down, and feed you a meal. Give you something to drink. You know what I'm saying?"

I nodded. "I think that's what doesn't go out to the world about Appalachia. Deep Appalachia, like this."

"And family ties are everything," Wes said. "Everything. I'd die for anybody in my family."

I thought of all the conversations I'd had over the past few days. "So either you're born into a good family here, where they're tight, or you're born into one that's drugged-out," I said. "And that's gotta be—"

I didn't finish the sentence. Wes had already lowered his head and let out a sigh. He rubbed his jaw slowly. "Buddy, I'll just be honest with you . . ."

He looked me in the eyes. "I got hurt in the mines back in '94. I was one of the first people in this county ever put on OxyContin."

I had a hunch where this was going.

"My family stood beside me through every bit of it. Seen that I got clean and got straight. Stayed right with me—they never pushed me away."

It wasn't just *his* story, it was *the* story. One that played out across towns like this again and again. You probably know the outline, even if you haven't followed closely. The pill mills. The Sacklers. Purdue Pharma. Doctors overprescribing OxyContin to anybody who hurt just to get them patched up and back on the line—and to get their kickback from Big Pharma.

"Doctors kept me on 'em about six years," he went on, eyes fixed somewhere below the ridge. It was hard not to see how the opioid crisis in places like this was tied to something deeper, a depression that was both economic and psychological.

"They started me on forty milligrams. Within a month, I was up to three eighty-milligram pills a day. Three Xanax a day."

"Did the doctors go to jail or anything for that?" I asked.

"Yeah. My doctor got seventeen years in prison."

"No way."

"Yeah. I got twenty."

I blinked, thinking I'd misheard.

"You've been in prison for twenty years?"

"I didn't do twenty. I done nine and a half."

I hesitated, trying to find the right way in.

"For doing . . . can I ask?"

"When they cut me off . . . you're so sick, you know?" He paused. "A guy asked me for a pill. I hooked him up, and next thing I know, they got me in court, got me in jail. And nine and a half years later . . ." He shook his head.

"The whole pill epidemic . . . it destroyed the region in a way, huh?"

"It hurt it really bad. And then it had gained its way back, and everybody was doing good. Everyone got sober, it seemed like. And then this shit hits around here, fentanyl." He looked off into the distance with a disappointed look. "It's the younger people, man, and that's what's so sad. You see all these young people dying. I mean, it's really sad."

He waved toward the valley. "The schoolhouse—you actually can't see it through the trees, just across the street—they had four die in one house there."

On our way back down to the valley, I tried to shake off some of the weight from earlier. Wes must've felt it too, because somewhere between the ruts and the dirt, he cracked a dry grin and told me an old local joke: "'You a miner?' 'No, I'm fifty-two. Why?'"

Back at the house, he disappeared into a side room and came back out holding a mason jar filled with clear liquid and a beautifully carved wooden cane. "Little souvenirs for you," he said, and winked. "The best moonshine you'll find around here, straight out of Smith, Kentucky. About 140 proof."

"Homemade?"

"Of course." He laughed. "I won't say too much more on record about that."

Then he held out the cane. "But be careful, or you'll need this. Buddy of mine made it."

"Thank you, Wes." I didn't have the heart to tell him I hadn't been drinking in eight years.

We shook hands—firm, then a full-on bear hug. Swapped numbers. Promised to keep in touch. Later in the trip, I passed that jar on to another thirsty traveler.

A few weeks went by, and then a small package showed up in the mail. Inside was a heavy cast-iron toy car—the one I'd seen in Wes's shed. There was a note folded beneath it.

My granddad was born in '29. This was the only toy he ever remembered getting as a child to share with his brothers. One doll for the girls, one car for the boys. It's old. Pap passed a few years ago. He'd want it somewhere appreciated. Glad it's in a good home.

Wes died not long after in a motorcycle accident, a sad ending to a storied life. When I think of him these days, I think about the many people in that region of the world who carry something fierce inside them. Resilience. Grit. The ability to start over after being knocked flat.

Because the people I spoke with in McDowell, Buchanan, and Harlan Counties remind me more than anyone I've ever met before or since of the men and women who made this country. As scrappy colonies, we fought a war against a far stronger, richer military . . . and won. This underdog spirit is baked into our DNA. It shows up in the movies we watch, the sports teams we root for, the challenges we dare to overcome. It's why we believe in fights against the odds.

In days of cynicism and division, this universal love of the underdog is in all of us.

And I wonder sometimes what would happen if we came together as Americans and rooted for these underdog places. Not just Appalachia, but the onetime manufacturing hubs of the Rust Belt, the small farming communities dotted across the Great Plains, the struggling "south sides" and "east sides" of so many of our big cities. America is full of these places, these stories. And I think we love an underdog story not just because we want the underdog to win, but because they remind us that we still live in a country that's a place of possibility.

I'm not here to be any sort of authority; I don't like telling people what to do or what to think. I feel like my job is to listen and understand and try to be a conduit, to transmit what I see to people who might not ever be able to meet someone like Wes. But as I drove through the maze of back roads that led me away from Wes's house, I remember hoping that some of the people who'd watch my Appalachia videos might come out the other side feeling and thinking something different from when they'd pressed play. Not pitying these people. I wanted viewers to respect them, to understand where they're coming from, even if the truth of *here* made them feel a little discomfort.

I've heard people say that what Appalachia—or the hood, or any other forgotten place—needs is more resources. More money. And money helps, sure, but I've seen how, without addressing the underlying problems, flooding an area with temporary "help" often just turns into more drugs and nicer cars. The same destructive cycles with shinier packaging.

The hard truth to swallow is that turning things around for places that aren't doing well requires a lot of things that work slowly and aren't great for photo-ops: self-confidence built by self-agency, education that actually works, leadership that doesn't disappear when the cameras do, and accountability that applies to everyone, including the people trying to help. That's a tall order.

In the past decade, America has started noticing Appalachia again. Opioid addiction, rural collapse, generational poverty . . . they've become part of the national conversation. Books like *Demon Copperhead* and *Hillbilly Elegy* sold millions of copies, won awards. And yet I've driven through these towns. It's hard to point to what's actually changed in many of them.

Look, I don't have the answers. Changing how we think about underdog places isn't going to magically solve problems people have been wrestling with for generations. I know that. But I also know that we're never going to see an end to these cycles if we keep treating the people living through them as a burden to the rest of us, even as they're responsible for so much of America's prosperity. These are people, or the descendants of people, who kept lights on, coal moving, factories running, families fed. They're people with dignity, people who deserve our country's attention.

And if we can start there and actually *stay* there, then maybe something better could have a chance.

CHAPTER 5

The Mississippi Delta

I landed in Memphis on a cold, damp January evening and drove the seventy-five miles south to Clarksdale. By the time I reached town, the streets were empty, the expansive Mississippi Delta horizon flattened under night.

Months earlier, a woman had written to me. "You ought to come see the Deep South," she'd said. "And if you do, you need to meet my uncle, Booker T. Beckum—a true legend. He knows what's up."

"Yep, Peeeter, you come up here to Mississippi, and I'll show ya round, show ya a tour like no people never see," he'd said when I called.

This was a man I had to meet.

Booker T lived in the countryside east of the Mississippi Delta, a flat sweep of land between the Mississippi and Yazoo Rivers that's long been one of the poorest regions in America—and one of the most storied. Slavery marked the land; blues music came out of the struggle. And yet the place remained, to me at least, one of the most mysterious parts of the country. I'd come a day early to see it for myself, to get a feel for the Delta before Booker T gave it a voice.

At the edge of Clarksdale, my headlights swept across a

long brick driveway and stopped at the shape of a guesthouse. Two stories tall, white against the dark, its large windows threw rectangles of light across the dead grass out front. The Colonial Revival facade stood square and symmetrical like a courthouse, slender columns holding up the porch. The house was like a fishbowl, its oversized paintings and otherwise bare walls visible from the street for all to see. But there were no signs of life, no cars in the parking lot. I stepped onto the creaking porch and pulled out an envelope wedged in the jamb. Inside was a key and a note: "Your room is the second door on the left, towels are on the bed. Enjoy your stay."

The key made a soft click, and I stepped into a hall that smelled faintly of polish and old pine. Wide golden floorboards ran beneath thick patterned rugs, their reds and browns fractured into a kaleidoscope by the light of a chandelier overhead. At the center of the foyer stood a round table with a vase of extravagant purple orchids tangled among bare brown branches. A walnut staircase rose toward the second floor, its banister hand-worn to a gloss. I passed the dining room and a painting of a fisherman—a full moon rising behind a face that seemed from another age, one of those portraits where eyes follow you around from every angle.

I entered my room, each step sinking into thick carpet. I'd thought the Deep South would be warmer in winter, but this place felt like an icebox. The fireplace in the bedroom was sealed, its iron plate embossed with a decorative ornate crest. The rest of the room had the same heavy grandeur, the crown moldings on the ceiling like icing on a cake.

Maybe it was the weight of the old furniture, or just the strangeness of a house lit up with no one else inside, but it felt like someone else was there. There was a heaviness . . . perhaps from some dark past? I learned later that the mansion once belonged to John Clark, the founder of the town. A lumber magnate, he stood out in the region for refusing to participate in slavery—not as an abolitionist crusader, just a wealthy man in 1800s Mississippi who'd chosen differently. Perhaps that resistance was what seemed to linger in the walls, as if the house carried its own conflicted memories. I fell asleep to the tired heater's rumble coming through the vents.

By morning, the past had given way to the present. I opened the door to a crisp, sunny day, though a thin, smoky haze lay in the air. Delta Avenue was quiet; a few cars drifted past as I walked toward town.

Brick storefronts lined the street, their windows warped and sun-bleached—doors that had once opened to carry blues through town. I could almost hear the guitar strings pulled tight enough to ache before musicians, long gone, eased them back into something tender.

A banner hung from a lamppost, bearing the face of Early Wright, the "Soul Man" of the radio. In 1947, he'd become Mississippi's first Black announcer, spinning gospel and blues on WROX, pulling in church families and restless kids alike. B. B. King, Ike Turner, Muddy Waters—so many legends passed through his studio before they were known. His show ran for four hours nightly, and Wright always asked Clarksdale locals to honk their horns outside the studio if they liked what they heard. Time passed, as did the great Early Wright, but I wondered if anyone ever still cruised by the old studio and honked, just for the sake of memory.

The avenue kept offering up pieces of old stories: a quiet clapboard church with its tall steeple; white columns of a former bank, a monument to the cotton money that once filled the Delta; a pawn shop window displaying battered guitars and harmonicas recycled through generations. Between old concert posters curling in cloudy windows and the bold sign rising from a cracked parking lot—USE THE POWER OF YOUR HOME'S EQUITY!—there was still some hope sprinkled into a few cheerful storefronts. But mostly, I felt the stillness, like all the oxygen had left.

Appalachia had been the first stop on my mission to look under the hood of those large swaths of land—away from the prosperous coasts and thriving parts of the interior—that are facing real economic challenges in America today. But the Mississippi Delta was another underdog region: smaller at roughly seven thousand square miles (about the size of New Jersey) but still getting left behind. Different regions, different histories, the same story of twenty-first-century economic decline that I was curious to learn more about. Plus, to a guy born and raised in Vermont, the Deep South felt more culturally foreign than anywhere else in America. I wasn't sure why I'd held off on this experience for so long.

I found a restaurant open and stepped into the smell of burnt hash browns. Plastic tablecloths clung to nearly empty tables, photographs of longtime patrons watching over them from the walls. I took a seat at a counter worn smooth by decades of elbows and spilled coffee, the vinyl stool sighing under me. When the waitress came by, I ordered a short stack with eggs, over easy—her favorite, she said.

Two seats down, an older woman sipped at a coffee mug. Her hair was set in tight gray curls, her brown hands veined and ringed. She didn't look at me at first—just caught my reflection in the mirror, then turned slowly, eyes narrowing.

"You ain't from here," she said.

I smiled, shook my head. "Just passing through the Delta for the day, ma'am." I'd made a habit of using *sir* and *ma'am* in the South; locals respected that.

Her lips pressed into something between a smirk and a frown. "Figures. Don't nobody come here to eat from out of town unless they on their way to somewhere else." She tapped her spoon against the mug, eyes still on me. "Where you headin'?"

"I thought I'd take my time until something caught me, get a feel for the real Deep South."

That earned a small laugh, dry as the smoke in the room. "You'll be drivin' a long time waitin' on somethin' to catch you. You want Delta, you go off the path south through Alligator."

"Alligator?"

"Mmm." She nodded slowly. "Ain't much goin' on there, but worth stoppin' to see what's gone. Or you might could make a stop in Greenville. That's a pretty one. 'Course, I ain't been round there in a good while. Last time I went, I went with some o' my girlfriends. Lord, we thought we was somethin' then. Must've been late eighties. I 'member clear as day, 'cause that was the mornin' I opened the paper an' read 'bout that poor girl got killed joggin' up in Tupelo, way east of here. Lord, I never could forget that. An' my hickory coffee tasted all wrong that mornin'. I always had me hickory coffee on a Saturday, an' that day it soured the whole taste of it, you know?"

I nodded, mesmerized. She was like a character out of a Faulkner novel come to life.

"Poor girl had a sock stuffed in her mouth—what a animal. But we went on anyhow, all of us done up with big hair an' painted lips. I felt strange most the whole day, but we still managed to have us a time on our girls' trip, laughin' like fools, ridin' down the highway. Greenville was hoppin' back then, cars lined up two streets over. An' that diner we pulled into was so crowded, line at the do', we had to park in the back by the oil-stained delivery bay."

She cracked a laugh, short and sharp. "Funny the things you remember. How we was all dolled up an' still walkin' past trash cans like it didn't matter a bit. Lord, I can see it just like yesterday."

She took a long sip of her coffee. I thanked her, but she waved it off like I was wasting words. The waitress slid my breakfast down the counter, egg yolks dripping over the pancakes, and with that, my route was set.

* * *

Alligator turned out to be a small community of just over a hundred people, south of Clarksdale. I took a roundabout way and came in through East New Africa Road, which carried me past open fields that were flat and exposed, broken only by bare trees and the occasional fencerow. The land was drained of color—winter did that here. As town approached, redbrick mansions with wide porches alternated with rusted trailers and boarded storefronts. The streets were frozen, empty but for a lone man pushing a walker, its rattle echoing through the silence.

"How are you doing, sir?" I called out, rolling down my window.

He slowed to a stop, glanced up at me, and gave a small nod. He looked to be around his late fifties.

"Is this downtown Alligator?"

He smiled, shaking his head as if the question amused him. "This the whole Alligator. The guy that used to own the liquor store, Mr. Bruno, and Mr. Brem Bremly. They dead and gone, but they put alligators in the lake. That's why they started calling it Alligator."

It was "a nice-going town," he told me, except for a few noses trying to get in your business. "Sometimes you might have to hit 'em in the nose 'round here."

"That's how you defeat alligators too," I said. "Hit 'em in the nose. That's what I heard."

He fixed me with a steady look. "No, take my advice. Do 'em like I do 'em. I stay the hell away from them."

"Mutual respect," I said, raising my hand in farewell. "Take care, sir."

I rolled through to the edge of town, which came up fast, then back again down the same empty block. The post office seemed the only place still in business. A sticker on the door read: LOBBY HOURS: 7:15 A.M. TO 9:15 A.M. Another taped notice inside warned, in bold letters, PLEASE DO NOT LEAVE TRASHS OR MAILS ON THE TABLE OR FLOOR. WE NEED TO KEEP THE POST OFFICE CLEAN AT ALL TIME. It made me reflect on the strange rules of English grammar and why we insist, illogically, on not putting an *s* at the end of *trash* and *mail*, when the crunch of gravel made me turn.

A silver Chevy pickup pulled into the post office lot alongside me, a waterline of dust marking the doors like a ship run aground. Its engine settled into a low idle. The driver, a thin older guy in a camouflage jumpsuit, leaned out, studying me for a moment before offering a hello. From there, the talk came easy. He told me he was a farmer, the only kind of job most people here still leaned on.

"At one time, there were three different gins here," he said, working a cigarette from a soft pack with two fingers. "The current one's right 'round the corner."

"Oh, cotton gins?"

"Yeah," he said, sparking his lighter, the flame catching quick.

"So when did those dry up?"

He took a long drag before answering. "Prob'ly 'bout the eighties. There were tenant houses all over the place. I mean, every road you'd go out had a line of houses on it. All this innovation in farmin' did away with all that labor"—new machinery increasing yields and novel crop varieties now resistant to pests. "One man farms a thousand acres now, where it used to take ten men, you know?"

He squinted at the low row of buildings across the street. "All the farmers usually went there for lunches and stuff," he said, gesturing to one on the corner, the name above the door already half-erased. It'd closed after the owner died the previous January. "There was six convenience stores here at one time," he said and began pointing them out one by one. "Chinaman had a store . . . and then there was a Jewish guy had a store. Then there was a Black guy that had a store."

A low hum of a car engine drifted in from down the road, clear in the thin winter air.

"You guys get along pretty well out here?"

"Oh yeah. We don't have no problem," he said.

"You have police out here?"

"Nope." He tipped his chin up slightly with a bit of pride.

A red minivan reached us, both of us turning our heads to watch it roll past. In these parts, I was realizing, something like a car going past was an event.

"That's the mayor, Tommie 'Tomaso' Brown," the farmer said, with the same tone he might've used to announce the mail truck. He flicked his ash and started in on crop dusters, but I excused myself and hurried on foot to see where the mayor had gone.

By the time I reached Tommie, the car door was open and he was climbing out, tall rubber boots thudding on the road. Mud streaked up his washed-out blue jeans. He had on an orange Henley, a black pistol at his belt. It looked like Tommie doubled as the local law enforcement.

Up close, he seemed about my age. His eyes caught mine with a baffled look—somewhere between *Who are you?* and *Do you need help?* When I told him I was here to document the region, his expression shifted only slightly. He said he'd been mayor of Alligator since 2009, the town's first Black mayor. Obama's presidential victory had pushed him to run for the local seat against a thirty-year incumbent. Proof, he said, that America wasn't *just for the few.*

He told me Alligator was once home to more than one thousand people, its economic backbone mostly the labor of Blacks, Chinese, and Italians, who came to work the plantations in the fertile Mississippi Delta. In the 1920s, the Yazoo and Mississippi Valley railroad ran eight trains a day that stopped in town, dropping off and picking up salesmen who would gamble all day in the Gibson Hotel. Other visitors would arrive on boats that plied the Mississippi River from Memphis to New Orleans, transporting timber and grain.

You could hear the blues in those days on Front Street, which seemed fitting for a place where even the earth itself felt heavy, the rich soil born out of floods that brought as much tragedy as treasure. Tommie pointed to the ALLIGATOR BLUES plaque planted proudly upright, the street sign beside it leaning toward the ground at forty-five degrees. George "G. P." Jackson, Robert "Bilbo" Walker, Johnny Drummer, the Kelly Brothers, Robert Johnson—all had lived in or around town.

In its heyday, Alligator had two schools, two churches, sixteen brick storefronts, two blacksmith shops, two lumber yards, and two doctors' offices. The trains that carried both cotton and songs north quit running in the 1950s; soon after, the hotel closed and was torn down, replaced in time by trailer homes and what looked to be Section 8 housing. As industry took over the fields producing cotton and corn, and the Great Migration kept carrying people away to cities like Cleveland and Detroit for factory work, much of the region emptied out. These days, there were just over a hundred people left in town. Some of the surrounding fields still grow cash crops including soybeans.

"Right now it's pretty quiet," Tommie said. "I'm trying to keep the peace, but we suffering for business right now because we just had Gator's Grocery close on us, and Mary Ann Grocery closed." He looked out at the empty intersection with the weary patience of a farmer watching a field yield less and less each season. "It's called a convenience store because it's convenient." Now locals had to drive thirteen miles for the closest groceries. And "some people don't have transportation. And it's hard on 'em, you know what I mean?" He kept taking his hands out of his pockets and putting them back in. "I'm trying to get a Dollar General or something going on around here—"

"Dollar General?"

"Yes, we want Dollar General." He widened his arms in an easy shrug, a quick chuckle escaping as if that were all there was to say, like he knew something in the soul of a small town gets sold to self-checkouts under the gaze of a security camera at the register under bright neon lights. I grew up near a creaky-floored general store where charges were written down on paper and paid off once a month, and where the owner knew my name and kept an eye on what we kids were up to, another set of parental eyes. It was more than a place to buy the basics; it was the center of the community. That store's long gone now, of course. I'd hoped that if there were any old-school general stores left in America, I'd find them in a place like Alligator, a place that could really use profits staying in town instead of heading off to corporate headquarters. But I understood why it'd be hard to make a living running a general store when you'd have all of a hundred local customers with an average income of just $11,000 a year.

We walked the block along the roadside, Tommie's rubber boots dragging through the stiff winter grass with a dry rasp, each step shredding the brittle stalks where a sidewalk should have been. He asked where I'd come in from and, like the few others I'd spoken with in the Delta, where I was heading next. The question seemed less about me than about a habit of mind, as if people here always measured things by the leaving part of the story.

"Who knows," I said. "Maybe I'll stay here in Alligator forever."

Tommie burst out laughing, a deep contagious sound.

"Over there," I said, nodding toward an empty lot with a hand-painted LOT 4 SALE sign. "How much are they asking?"

"They want five thousand."

"For this little lot?" I don't think I was able to hide my disbelief. "You think it's gonna happen?"

"Not in my lifetime." He laughed again and cleared his throat, then paused for a moment to let time formulate his thoughts before he spoke. In these parts, there was no competition with time; it felt like an endless resource. And maybe here it was. Time is often a state of mind, dependent on the environment it's operating in.

"I can tell you one thing," he said. "It's best to be in a small town, what's going on and the situation we in. If you had a war, what you think the first thing they gonna hit? The big cities. You ain't waste your missiles trying to find Alligator. A lot of us get prepared for it, and we can live off the grid. You know—with power outages, gettin' your own food."

He was right. Cities would be chaos during any sort of disaster. All you need is for the grid to go down for three days, and it's mayhem.

"Will you guys let my wife and me move here?" I asked, grinning.

He laughed again. "Yeah man, we'll be more than happy to have you. I'm always welcoming the people to the community. We are not just stabilized, we're trying to grow now."

From the outside, economic downturns can look awfully sudden. But I'd noticed that when residents of these towns speak about their decline, it comes with a softness, almost a tenderness, as if the love for what's left smooths the edges of the loss. They speak about places as though they're elderly family members and the slowdown is the natural progression of time, age, or nature, or simply a mirror of society's attitude toward the elderly in general. The sort of places you can love for their ruins, even when you know they're never coming back, not the way they were before.

Which reminded me: There were some ruins ahead of me.

* * *

An hour later, the road carried me through a country stretched so flat it seemed *pressed by the hand of God himself*, as the woman I met during breakfast might have said. I drove, watching the smoke from ditch fires rise in slow ribbons that bent and wandered before vanishing. It seemed like the farmhouses leaned back from the highway, as though shy to be the focus of those driving by. Occasionally, there'd be what seemed like an oasis, with a massive, well-kept front porch and beautiful landscaping. At last, I came to the flat-topped hills breaking the horizon's line.

The Winterville Mounds rose from land that once looked nothing like the bare expanse around me. This was once one of the most important Native American settlements in the Delta, a place where hunters, fishermen, and farmers lived long before the fields were cleared for cotton.

The mounds weren't built quickly. Beginning around AD 1100, the earth was dug and carried in baskets, poured out and stamped flat, with the motion repeated over and over until whole platforms of soil rose against the horizon. When the buildings on top grew old, they were burned, their ashes buried beneath fresh dirt, and the mound was raised higher. The work was relentless. By the thirteenth century, Winterville had become a city—twenty-three man-made hills arranged around two broad plazas. The civilization had everything: chiefs, shamans, and farmers who grew corn, beans, and squash in the black Delta soil. The mounds formed a type of community center, a place for religious festivals, games, and ceremonies.

The largest of the mounds, fifty-five feet high, was the tallest point (if tracing the Mississippi River) between here and Cahokia, a capital of the great Mississippian culture and the largest pre-Columbian city north of Mexico. Cahokia's ruins can be seen today in Illinois. A temple rose from the mound's summit, visible for miles across the Delta, its smoke marking the reach of Winterville's influence. It was a city of earth made to last. And it did, for some 450 years, longer than Boston or Philadelphia has been around. The people living in the surrounding countryside probably didn't think they were going anywhere, any more than we do.

But permanence was an illusion. In the 1540s, Hernando de Soto's expedition cut through the Southeast. Along with steel and horses, the Spaniards brought disease, and with no immunity, the people of Winterville sickened and died. Those who survived scattered, later forming tribes like the Choctaws and Chickasaws. Only the mounds remained, grass-covered, settling slowly back into the Delta.

Today twelve still stand, the rest lost to highways, erosion, or plows. Archaeologists have pulled from them bones, pottery, and worked stone—fragments of a time left unwritten, a reminder of what people can build and how easily it can vanish. Not just from the earth but from memory.

Growing up in Vermont, the only thing we really learned about Mississippi in school was its history of slavery. It sounds a bit silly to admit, but I knew nothing about the ancient cultures that existed here until I saw a sign for the Winterville Mounds on the side of the highway. Then again, I'm sure they don't teach much in Mississippi about the Battle of Lake Champlain or the Green Mountain Boys. It was another testament to the constant discovery this country offers if you're willing to explore it. Though it was humbling to realize that even if I do ever manage to visit every mile of this place, there is still over twenty thousand years of human history to explore.

* * *

Close to a millennium after work began on the Winterville Mounds, we're still reaching toward the heavens. Approaching Greenville, the first thing that stood out from the flatness was a towering Gothic Revival church: pointed-arch windows, carved stone trim, and a steep slate roof climbing to a spire that stretched confidently into the sky. I climbed the stone steps and peeked through the cracked front door, where a paper sign read PLEASE RESPECT—WEDDING IN SESSION. Inside, the bride stood beneath a long white veil that fell over her face, her hand joined with the groom's at the altar, while the priest's voice carried through the high rafters: " . . . if either of them falls, one can help the other up. But pity anyone who falls and has no one to help them up. Though one may be overpowered, two can defend themselves."

It felt almost uncanny, as though the priest were speaking about the life cycles of the towns I was traveling through: "Yes, there is a time for everything under heaven: a time to plant, a time to harvest, a time to weep, and a time to laugh, a time to mourn, and a time to dance. In every season of your life together—the joyful ones and the difficult ones—God will be faithful. His mercy will be new each morning for you."

The long horn of a ship sounded in the distance, and I let the door fall shut. Out on the Mississippi, river barges hauled their loads past the Tropicana Casino, its parking lot busier than I'd expected for a midweek afternoon. The river looked endless, a band of steel running level with the land, a towboat pushing its barges along like toys set adrift. The far bank across from me was Arkansas—a five-mile loop of Arkansas land left behind when the river changed its course and poked deep into the state. The Mississippi River is forever shifting yet forever constant, carrying on its back more commerce than any other waterway—grain and soybeans, corn and ore, steel and fuel drifting south in long tows that could stretch a quarter mile. According to the US Army Corps of Engineers, roughly nine out of ten tons of America's bulk agricultural exports move through the Mississippi River and its connected inland waterways on their way to global markets.

Greenville felt like the other towns I'd been passing through, like the past hadn't quite let go and the future hadn't yet taken hold. But it was a cheerful place. A dead ringer for Chester Bennington of Linkin Park told me about the joys of marrying a Delta girl and then chuckled, cautious and a little embarrassed, him and a buddy suddenly like teenagers trying not to say the wrong thing as their voices tumbled over each other in search of what made Delta girls so special. ("If they cook good cornbread, they can be my wife," his buddy decided.) Chester told me his wife worked at a nonprofit, helping with local housing restoration. It was nice to think people were marrying here, fixing up old homes, starting families.

I thought back to the reading I'd just heard from Ecclesiastes: "But pity anyone who falls and has no one to help them up." One housing nonprofit wasn't going to get a whole town back on its feet. But it was a start. It was a start.

* * *

The following morning, after a quiet night in a roadside hotel, I set out with Booker T's directions in hand. The sun shone bright and cold, the road stretched out smooth as glass, and I wondered, not for the first time, why it so often seems to be wealthier counties where the asphalt's cracked to pieces.

In this part of Mississippi, the flat started giving way to low hills, and before long I turned onto the gravel road climbing to Booker T's place, which was perched on a rise above a pond. The house was huge, with six parking spots marked off by yellow lines like you'd see in a commercial lot. Three cars were already parked there, and I checked the address again to make sure I was at a house and not a dentist's office.

Booker T told me on the phone that he was sixty-four, though the Motown cap squared on his head and braids falling over his shoulders made him seem younger, and a Bluetooth piece clipped in his ear gave the impression he was always on call. His clothes were sharp, all in black-and-white: a checkered shirt, pressed pants, white shoes. A heavy gold Cadillac emblem swung from a golden chain across his chest.

"This is my baby," Booker T said, pointing at the champagne-colored Escalade EXT pickup gleaming in the parking lot. "I been had it for twenty-two years." The rims flashed like they'd been polished that morning. Through the glass I could see the wood-grain steering wheel and smooth beige leather seats.

"Get in," he said. "Let's go."

Soon trees were rushing past my window. Out here, the plots of land opened wide, rolling fields with big brick houses, roofs pitched high, driveways stretching out like they had all the space in the world.

"The closer you get to the Delta, where you just came from, the poorer it gets," Booker T was telling me. "'Specially you still got peoples in them li'l houses don't even have restrooms an' stuff like that. They prob'ly still pullin' water from wells an' all, you know?"

"Did you grow up with well water?"

He nodded. "I was fifteen 'fore I had a bathroom. My

brother, the one got me into weldin', worked with the water folks when they come out here, put the first water line through this way."

He was an easy one to talk to. One simple question was all it took to get him sharing a lifetime of adventures.

"When I left Mississippi, I didn't even have a GED," he was saying, "but I went an' took that first weldin' test an' come out a welder. Later I went on to college, studied up to be a maintenance supervisor, an' after that I got sent to work in plants from Abu Dhabi to Alaska. Spent over forty-two years doin' that work out in Wyoming. People out there were good to us, an' quite often we were the only Blacks around, but that didn't matter. They took us in like family—me, my wife Lodine, an' the kids. She spent near four decades workin' as a nurse."

"But you came back to Mississippi?" I asked, chuckling to myself at how fitting it seemed for this striver to share a name with Booker T. Washington.

"Wasn't no need stayin' in Wyoming no longer. Me an' my wife's family is here, might as well enjoy it for the rest of our lives an' be back 'round 'em some."

He started pointing out the neighbors. "Now, all of these are Berrys." He waved toward the Berry Circle street sign flashing by. "All those houses that way is 'em. The old preacher used to live over there on the left. . . . Now, that's our church straight ahead, Sweet Home AME Church. An' right in this corner here is my mom's first li'l schoolhouse."

"Oh, this wooden one?"

It was the size of a storage shed: rough plank walls leaning under a pitched roof, a thin sheet of tin laid across the top, a single square window cut into the front. It sat like a dollhouse at the bend of the T-road, woods crowding in behind it. Inside, there were still desks and toy dolls on the ground, like one of those schools in Chernobyl where everyone had to get up and flee and everything stayed behind.

"They had the schools uptown, but my mom and 'em were just out here in the country. They didn't have no buses or nothin' then."

"What about your school?"

"My ol' school was all White before. We knew of White kids an' stuff, but not to be learnin' and sittin' with 'em every day, you know?" He smirked.

"How did it go?"

"Well, we were just kids, seventh or eighth grade. The Black kind of stayed to theyself, the White would stay to theyself. But we knew it was integrating time, an' we just accepted it and just went along. An' when we started gettin' more into learnin' each other is when things started gettin' a li'l better, you know?"

On the other side of the street stood a long house with an adjacent shed, both graffitied over with names and hearts.

"This used to be our store." He pointed through my window as the truck rolled on. "Open on Wednesdays, Saturdays, and Sundays. When my daddy and 'em first come here"—from nearby Starkville—"his cousin Miss Rosie used to live in that old house by the shed. My daddy's cousins set up a lumber mill here, and they built homes—helped build a home for everybody. An' my daddy, after he got out the army, an' my cousin too, they come in here," and his father's first cousin, Mr. Centry "Babe" Magee, bought up two hundred acres of land.

"We're gonna run through here just a minute an' show you my folks," Booker T said.

He turned the car off the road, bumping across a field toward rows of headstones. "This here's our family cemetery.

My brother"—he nodded toward a bucket of bright flowers set at the base of a new marker—"Willie Earl Jackson, 'Dynamite.' He just died a few months back, right before my birthday. And that's my parents right next to him—Mattie Lue Beckum an' Booker T. Beckum. My daddy, he lived to get a hundred years old."

* * *

"Our house used to sit right back there in them trees," Booker T said, pointing through the windshield as the Cadillac eased down a narrow forested road, the sun cutting through bare branches, the taller pines still holding all the green. "And we used to walk right over here down the road to our godmother's."

A low house with white siding trimmed in dark blue paint sat in a field, a pair of sheds standing in close on either side. I asked who lived here now.

"My sister, Berta Beckum."

We got out, passing a rust-colored Chevy slumped on its tires in the yellow grass. Booker T's voice lowered.

"That there, that was my brother's that died. I'm gonna fix that up one day. An' my mom built all these." He nodded toward the sheds with a faint smile, as if the memory hurt and softened him at the same time. "My brother used to live out in this first one. He drank quite a little bit, so my mom put him out the house and built him a shed out here so he wouldn't bother them comin' in at night."

The front door cracked open and a woman stepped out onto the porch, sunlight catching her short dark hair and turning it almost purple, like the sheen of a grackle's wing.

"That's my sister, Berta Beckum. Don't she look like me?"

"You guys are twins."

Booker T threw back his head, laughing. "She's cookin' a coon for dinner, and my older sister Rita an' her daughter Pam cooked some greens and peas."

"So we're having a raccoon for dinner tonight?" I tried not to let the surprise carry too far in my voice.

"Yeah," Berta answered plain. "An' cornbread."

"An' pork chop and fried chicken." Booker T smiled wide.

Inside, the ceiling hung low enough that the bare bulb seemed to hover just above our heads, casting a soft sepia haze across the room. The air was thick with the smell of fried meat, vinegar, and spices. Every surface seemed to hold something—pickles, bottled sauces, seasonings. Pots and pans leaned into one another beside a polished stack of plates and tin-foil trays, ready for carrying food across town come dinnertime. It was a kitchen that had served a high purpose, feeding a sprawling family for generations.

Rita and Pam were there too, stepping out of Berta's way as she peeled back foil and paper towels to reveal rounds of cornbread, their edges browned and centers glowing golden red, like the light of a setting sun through the pink curtains of the lone kitchen window.

"What's the secret recipe?" I asked.

"Jus' fry it on top the stove," Rita said, like it was obvious.

"With meal and flour," Berta added.

"Eggs and buttermilk," said Pam.

The crust had a toasty crunch, the middle still soft. It tasted rich and earthy, the balance of sweet and salt making you want another bite before you'd finished the first.

"Oh yeah," I mumbled.

Berta laughed, already moving through the kitchen with a rag, wiping the table and straightening chairs.

The house had four small rooms, a bed in each taking up most of the space, the walls so crowded with photographs they looked pieced together like a patchwork quilt: black-and-white portraits of ancestors in stiff collars beside Polaroids of children in bright Easter pastels, grandkids' ultrasounds, school pictures with crooked bangs and toothy smiles, young men in uniform, women in graduation gowns, cousins posed proud in front of new cars, all layered in with calendars from years gone by, military honors, funeral programs, wedding invitations, and certificates of achievement, with Mardi Gras beads and strings of costume pearls tacked up like garlands.

"What'd your parents do for work?" I asked Booker T.

"Pickin' cotton," Rita cut in from behind us. "Choppin' cotton, choppin' corn."

"Did you pick cotton?" I asked.

"Did I?" Rita shot back, her tone edged with disbelief. "I'm one of the first ones! I started when I was six years o'd with a seven-foot sack. When I got twelve, I got the twelve-foot sack."

"Twelve-foot sack?"

"A sack to put the picked cotton in." Booker T turned back to me with a smile. "You get different size sacks dependin' on how old you are."

"When we was six years old, it was like a croker sack," Rita went on. "When we got twelve, we got the long one—"

"Long sack that dragged behind you," Booker T chimed in. He glanced at his wristwatch. "I'ma take him to a little plantation over here and ride around the town a bit, so we'll see y'all at the dinner, okay?"

Soon, the Cadillac was easing onto a road barely wide enough for two vehicles, no painted line down the middle for guidance. Gray sweetgums, oaks, and pines climbed high on either side, their branches tangled with brown kudzu that drooped like uncombed hair, giving the woods a heavy, unkempt look.

"What do the people do for work out here?" I asked.

"Well . . ." Booker T slowed around a blind curve. "We got the paper mill here, some factories . . . now they be up at that new Milwaukee plant too, so that's gon' help a lotta folks."

"Milwaukee Tools?"

"Uh-huh. And we still gotta lotta farmin', more cotton bein' raised now than I ever seen."

"Oh, really?" I realized I'd sort of just assumed those days were over.

"Yeah, 'cause it used to be a lotta soybeans in my years growin' up. We used to eat soybean burgers. Here—" He cut his hand from the wheel and pointed through the windshield at the clearing ahead. Beyond the trees, the land opened wide, pale grasses running to the horizon. "This was a cotton plantation. Rich guy bought it out now, an' he's just got cows and all on it. . . . I was comin' up usin' mules an' stuff. They never would give us no big loans to buy a tractor or nothin'."

I glanced at Booker T to make sure he wasn't ninety years old.

He kept on talking as we drove past what looked like hundreds of acres stretching over stubbled earth. "With the farmin' we did, it was jus' for ourselves—our co'n an' soybeans. We raised our molasses, sold it for six dollars a gallon, an' that's how we made our little money." And then there was the cotton, of course.

"We'd get maybe three, four hundred dollars a bale then, if that. My daddy an' my cousin, 'em were sharecroppin' with Mr. Centry Magee. But then once he died, they lost the land, see?" Mr. Magee's brothers came down from Chicago and sold it off.

He started explaining how the economics of sharecropping worked. "So, my cousin, Mr. Babe—by him lettin' us farm on the land, we would get two bales of cotton, he would get one. Same thing is co'n—we'd get two loads, an' we'd take him a load to his crib for his animals."

"So it's his land, and you do all the work?"

"That's right. But it was like eight of us in the house, ten with my mom an' dad. It took more food an' stuff. But we had hogs an' a few cows, goats—and that's what we kind of lived off. Chickens. Raccoons. Possums." He shook his head, like he could hardly believe that had once been his reality. "You can see some cotton out there. I should get you a stalk."

He eased on the brakes and pulled over to the side of the road. The late-season cotton crunched under our feet—brown leaves and stubble with white tufts popping here and there. I reached down and tugged at a boll, surprised by how soft the fibers were against my fingers, even as the husk pricked at my skin.

"Cotton ball by cotton ball, is that how you do it?" I asked.

"Yeah, jus' pick it by hand." Booker T pinched with his thumb and two fingers, showing me the motion. His hands moved quick, almost automatic. He plucked a husk tangled in the fluff and held it up, grinning wide. "We used to play with 'em like little animals, you see?" He dangled it for a second, smiling like a kid with a toy, then flicked it aside and slipped right back into the steady pace of plucking. "Then you just keep pickin', row after row, puttin' it in the sack behind your back."

"So that was the time when having more kids made you better off financially?" I asked.

"Was good, yes." He rolled the cotton slowly between his fingers, absent-mindedly, like the feel of it had a way of calming the hands even if the work itself never did. "See, it wasn't no problem with my mom. When my dad met her, she already had six kids—but two of 'em died—so it wasn't no problem for him to marry my mom with four kids already. 'Cause he was comin' in on a farm, you know?"

He started reminiscing about holidays growing up in a family that big. "You keep your shoebox for Christmas where you could put your stuff in it—the little oranges, an' apples, an' the nuts. An' every year I'd get a paper cap pistol, a paper gun." He gave a low laugh, almost to himself. "That's what it looked like every year—you got your paper cap gun, you know?"

"So . . . literally in one generation," I said, trying to square it in my mind, "it went from have as many kids as possible—'cause it's gonna make you better off as a family—to don't have many kids 'cause they're expensive."

"Yep. An' then that's why you see now, like a lotta the womens have a lotta kids now—they pretty well on welfare or somethin', you see? 'Cause ain't nothin' for her to do." He leaned over and snapped off a stem, then another, cotton balls clinging white against the brown stalks.

It made me think of Central Appalachia and how in just one or two generations the switch had been made from even little kids being put to work to government dependence.

By the time Booker T had three stems in his hand, he gave a soft *uh-huh*, straightened up, and worked them into a neat little bundle. Satisfied, he stretched it out to me. "You can take that back with you."

* * *

So many of my trips end up being journeys of the mind and soul as much as of miles. As Booker T drove on, I got to thinking about the things we romanticize about the past. I got the sense he enjoyed sharing his story of where he came from and where he is now. Just one generation before him, this journey would have been much more difficult, and a few generations before that, impossible. I could tell he was proud that he made it—that this life was no longer a dream, but his reality. The truth is, a place like the Mississippi Delta can be noble, admirable, and still pretty dang rough and troubling, all at once.

Just down the road we stopped at a wide white house set back on the land, a deep porch running across the front. Christmas garland still hung from the railings, bright against the winter-brown grass. Twin chimneys rose above the roofline.

"So, this was the big mano' house there," Booker T said. "The big plantation home."

"So, the business model was"—I swept a hand toward the fields behind it—"get a bunch of land, get a bunch of slaves, make a bunch of money?"

"That's right." Booker T paused a moment, thinking. "I knew my mom an' her forefathers—like my granddaddy's daddy an' 'em—was into this slavery, prob'ly. We were just so much out of it by the time we come up, but . . . I just kind of feel for 'em, you know? The work, the torture an' stuff they went through."

After slavery came a century of sharecropping, some folks picking cotton for the sons and daughters of the people who'd enslaved their parents. But Booker T also told me proudly about this one Black guy who "wouldn't be no farmer for someone. He bought his own land, and had the Blacks to help him, you get me? He ended up prob'ly like the plantation guy. But he paid 'em better, an' he gave 'em stuff, you know? An' that's why a lotta the Blacks ended up doin' better."

In 1870, there were just 1,600 Black farm owners in Mississippi. By 1950, Blacks owned 23,293 farms and were invested in over 5,000 more, totaling over 2 million acres, although that was still only 10 percent of all farmland in the state.

We started driving again. Downtown Grenada slid past the windows. A white gazebo in the middle of the courthouse square, the ring of flower beds around it gone dry. Leafless oaks and maples throwing patches of light across sidewalk benches. Two-story commercial fronts circling the square, their pressed-tin cornices and tall glass windows that once showed off hardware and dry goods now holding boutiques and cafés. Empty spaces were clawed out here and there, like something had come along and excavated the block. Past the square came rows of old houses, Queen Anne gables rising at odd angles, Colonial Revival porches stretching wide for sitting out in the evening air.

We'd reached the outskirts lined with shotgun houses when Booker T said, "I'm tryin' to look at when I do turn sixty-five, I wanna do a little somethin' more, you know?" He was talking almost to himself now. "If I could set up a weldin' shop or somethin', a weldin' business. I wanna do more, but I don't really wanna do more, you get me? 'Cause I'm retired—I wanna just enjoy my life. But I don't wanna leave this world an' not share the knowledge I got."

I did get him. Booker T's ability to excel as an individual enabled him to benefit whole communities; so many people relied on his work in their daily lives, most without ever even knowing. And now here he was, thinking about how to maybe keep on helping others in this new chapter of life.

"I'd like to pass more of it on, even with my kids an' grandkids," he said. "But you know, they already got their thing—basketball playin'—an' that's all they interested in nowadays . . ."

We passed a vacant corner.

"This used to be the old thee-ay-ter," Booker T said, easing the car in near a crumbling facade, its white paint filthy and peeling, wires dangling down the wall. "I went in there a few times when I was a kid. An' a barber was right next to it. Li'l Pinky Café used to sit right here." He pointed to yet another empty lot. "Had the best chicken sandwiches."

A crow cawed overhead.

He let the Cadillac idle in front of a tiny house set back from the street—shed-size, the front step busted loose. "My sister used to live right here in this li'l house," he said. "This where we used to par'y. That's where me an' my wife . . . kinda met." He smiled shyly, almost boyishly. "It was nice back then. When I'd come up here in '78, '79, it was all nice. Couple more clubs in here too."

Then came meth and fentanyl. That classic tale, again.

He motioned around the empty streets. "All the gangsters asleep right now, see?" His laughter rocked loud inside the car as we crept past a two-story brick box, grates welded over every window.

"Did anyone have bars like this on their windows back in the day?" I asked.

He shook his head. "Not as much as now. Cause people break in 'em, you know?"

We drove on a little farther.

"That was the church where Martin Luther King came to years ago."

We turned the corner and the sun hit us square. The church's front wall was split and gaping, the cross hanging stubbornly in the wreck. A new church was going up beside it: Decay and renewal, standing side by side.

In so many places I've traveled through, once I started looking, I found people who, like Booker T, lived by the belief that tomorrow could still be better. Who were already at work, already lifting, already adding to their communities in unremarkable yet remarkable ways. Welders, carpenters, social workers, church leaders, men who rebuilt transmissions in their driveways, women organizing free meal programs out of VA halls. So many places in America aren't waiting to be rescued; they're helping themselves through local hands that know the land, through people who love these places enough to stay, enough to keep giving, and enough to believe that what's broken doesn't have to *stay* broken.

From what I'd seen here, though, I wasn't sure there were enough of these types in Grenada to outweigh those bringing the place down.

Booker T's little welding shop sounded awesome. And yet I found myself wondering if people really would show up to learn from him. I've seen big money go into things like the most beautiful Boys & Girls Club (of the Flathead Reservation in Montana), which had some excellent leaders but couldn't find enough employees to run the place at full capacity. Some local youths showed up, excited, but I was told too many would rather just play video games at home. I'm an optimist by nature, but it's hard sometimes to see how to get to a future that's different from today. If the problem were just money, it'd be easier, but often money isn't even the solution. It's good role models, a stable home, education, less crime.

Like so many places I'd been to lately, I was finding Mississippi gave me more questions than answers.

* * *

The afternoon was leaning toward supper, the sun laying its weight across the pond until the water turned gold and still. *Heaven on earth*, Booker T said, looking up at his house on the rise—and I could see why.

Two white hearts rose from a garden bed, BTB JR. and LODINE cut in red through the middle. "Here was my first weldin' when I learned how to cut in school," Booker T told me.

"You're a true romantic," I said, shaking my head with a smile. The air carried the faint smell of grease and something savory from the kitchen.

Inside, the house was set up for comfort, as if life here had been arranged to be enjoyed: leather recliners, a wide TV, family photos looking down from the walls. I stepped onto a black-and-gold rug, silky underfoot. "With this carpet, you could dance in here."

"Yeah," he said, grinning. "Watch this."

He dropped into a little line step right there on the rug, hips swinging, knees bouncing loose. "Ah-uh, uh-uh," he called, snapping his fingers. "Da-da-da!" A quick shuffle forward, then a jump. He spun half a turn, one arm raised, Bluetooth piece flashing in his ear, and let out a sharp "And *uh*!" before finishing with a kick and a shake of the hips, laughing so hard he nearly doubled over.

"Your hips are a little tight, Booker T," I joked. I twisted mine like I was working a Hula-Hoop.

He slapped his thigh, laughing. "One of my friends in Wyoming said, 'Booker, you'd do pretty good if you sprayed a li'l WD-40 on dem hips.'"

He kept shuffling, shoulders bouncing, while his wife, Lodine, her long braids falling down her back, dressed the table in holiday place mats and teal plates. Berta followed with the steaming centerpiece: a silver pan of raccoon sunk in its own gravy like a Thanksgiving turkey, ribs poking through, ringed with soft orange yams. Rita brought out the platters of batter-dipped fried chicken and crappie, coatings browned and crackling at the edges. Cornbread, black-eyed peas, okra slick and green, mashed potatoes piled up white beside turnip greens cooked down dark—we had it all.

Chairs slid, a shuffle of legs under the table, napkins came open in laps. Booker T cleared his throat. "This a nice li'l meal, an' I'm gon' say a verse for us . . ." His eyes moved slowly across the faces around him. "Here we are after sixty-four years o' my life. I thank God for my wife—I been with her forty-five years—and three wonderful kids. . . ." He thanked God for his sisters and brothers, for food like this, for watching over us always.

"I told Peter on the drive I'd like to see more ambition in kids now than what they are doin'," he said, after we'd all joined him in "*Amen.*" "Far as workin'. Get a craft or somethin'. Not jus' bein' sorry an' don't wanna do nothin'. You want the money, but you don't want the labor—an' it takes labor to make money."

"It's an evil town," Rita said, her voice flat. "It's an evil state. They don't want you to have anything. If you get anything, you get it on yo' own—ain't nobody gon' help you get it." A low *mm-hmm* rolled across the table.

"Who's 'they'?" I asked.

"There's still a Black-and-White thing down here in the South," Lodine said. "It's moved since way back in the time, but this particular town here is still kinda stuck in the ways it was years and years ago. So Blacks had to strive and struggle to get everything that they wanted, and Whites have always had it easy, because that's generational wealth."

I mentioned I'd seen White folks in trailers who didn't look like they'd been handed much of anything either.

Lodine nodded. "Back in the old days, Blacks sharecropped, and you sharecropped with some Whites too. Those Whites were just as poor as you were, but you were working together, trying to obtain something. And you had some Whites that had to work on the plantation too, to make a survival."

"But the ones that really control Mississippi," I asked, "those are the families with generational wealth?"

"Definitely," Lodine said. "You just have to get in where you fit in, you know?"

Plates started moving again, forks tapping, voices rising over one another. Bowls of peas and greens and okra made their way around, arms stretching, people leaning, everyone helping everyone else fill a plate. I carved off a strip of raccoon, its gravy spilling into the sweet orange yams.

"This is my first run-in with raccoon, so thank you for that," I said, looking at it on my plate. "Ever since I kicked them out of my house after they destroyed it, I've had a bad relationship with them. This might be my revenge."

The table broke into laughter.

"Just like a nice roast." Booker T smiled.

I took a bite, and the table hushed, forks hanging midair, waiting for my reaction. The meat was lean and falling off the bone, the flavor rich, close to turkey thigh but with a faint sweetness and a touch gamey.

"That's actually really good," I said, surprised.

"My buddy Lance in Wyoming, he loves it now," Booker T said, chewing. "C'mon, fix you a nice plate up, Peter. You at home now."

The talk eased from food to the question of staying or leaving, following the Mississippi dream to Chicago or St. Louis or wherever life took you. And then, suddenly, the meal was over—plates carried off, water running, towels snapping dry.

Booker T led me over to his home bar to show off the wine he'd made. He lifted a half-gallon whiskey bottle, raspberry red liquid gleaming through the glass. "Bought a whole case of muscadine at the market, and 'hen I put 'em all in the five-gallon bucket, let 'em set for about a month or two," he said, patting the glass like a football. "Then I strain it out, put sugar, yeast with it, and let it set for about two months."

"What do you ladies think of Booker T's wine?" I asked.

"Well, he make it just like my mom used to make it," Rita said, drying dishes.

"It just ain't good as my mama's," Berta cut in.

As the chores wound down, we returned to the table for drinking and joking.

"I got 'nother one for you," Booker T said, after a couple. Berta glanced over, lips clamped shut, like she knew which one was coming and had sat through it a thousand times but still couldn't keep a straight face.

"So one Kool mo'nin'," Booker T started off, dead serious, spacing out every word, "Ms. Pall Mall headed down Chesterfield Lane in Winston-Salem . . ." The corners of his lips twitched as he looked around the table to see if we were starting to catch on. " . . . where she run up on Philip Morris, an' he took her to the Raleigh Motel in Newpo't. An' right away, he put her in the king-size bed an' stuck his king-size L&M in her flip-top box, an' if she don't look like a Camel in nine months, it's a dam' Lucky Strike. But he wasn't worried, because he used a filter tip."

The table fell out laughing. Booker T slapped the place mat, laughing at his own joke.

Sitting there at Booker T's table, as the laughter faded around me, I found my mind wandering to the way places change with time, and how that's just about unavoidable. Fields go empty, towns fade. Machines replace hands. But what doesn't change are the things that make people who they are—kindness and pride and humor and the stubborn will to keep (or start) living good lives. I could tell that time had weathered the Mississippi Delta, but like so many other places I'd been on my travels, time hadn't taken the heart from the people.

I thought back to the young historian I'd met by a creek on my drive through Appalachia six months before. In a way, he was about to follow Booker T's path, chasing the opportunities beyond the horizon. Sometimes, I think the biggest crime is telling kids they can't achieve anything because the system will just keep them down, when that chance to chase your dreams—maybe not to ever quite find them, but to chase them nevertheless—is one of the greatest gifts this country offers. The ability to take risks and fail and go at it again is one of the most beautiful traits in American life.

I hadn't forgotten that young man's comment about how maybe the thing his peers needed most was to learn how resilient they were. Maybe it wasn't even just them, I'd thought sometimes in the months since. Maybe we all do. Maybe we all needed to rediscover that pioneering spirit this country was once famous for, to amp up our excitement and ambition, to forget the forces against us and just go for whatever makes us tick.

It was a thought I kept in mind as I hit the road again in search of places that had endured across generations, coming back again and again from hard times, to find the people there who knew how to play the long game.

PART III

THE LONG GAME

CHAPTER 6

The Land of the Redwoods

In Humboldt County, California begins to unspool. Drive up past wine country, deep into the northern reaches, almost to the border with Oregon, until the Golden State sheds its aura as the home of the *next big thing*: gold rushes, silver screen dreams, startups, AI. . . . The Pacific crashes hard against this edge of America, always heaving, always returning. It throws up salt air across the Lost Coast, where mountains meet the sea and fog rises inland like a tide. It often arrives early evening—sliding between branches, draping over the roads—and then, depending on the day, pulls back to the water and burns off over the horizon.

From the mist, the giant redwoods emerge like memorials—some taller than the Statue of Liberty, some with roots that reach back centuries before Christianity, before the Roman Empire.

Even in the seeming stillness, banana slugs stretch like molten gold across cedar bark. Moss creeps up the sides of trees, and ferns crowd the bases like offerings, keeping the forest damp. In some groves, you can hear your own heartbeat louder than your footsteps in the muffled silence.

Keep driving—inland now—and the land changes from

minute to minute: orchards laid out in narrow fields, steep hills suddenly giving way to pastures rimmed with wild fennel and cattle fencing, greenhouses shimmering in open fields. Somewhere out there, towns barely blink on and off the map. We forget sometimes that for all its population, the majority of California is still rural.

Humboldt County will probably never be considered an easy place to live. The land has a way of reminding people who's in charge: earthquakes rolling in from the subduction zone offshore, forest fires, winter storms snapping power lines, rivers jumping their banks and swallowing whole acres of bottomland. Here, towns have been built, washed out, and rebuilt. The people who stay learn to adapt to the land, to live on Mother Nature's terms.

They've gotten a lot of practice over the years. As the old-growth logging era slowly collapsed—from overcutting in the 1960s, environmental regulation in the '80s, then global market shifts in the 2000s, when the housing market crash tanked demand—whole communities faced the hollowing-out that comes when a single industry declines rapidly. Mill towns lost their mills. Paychecks dried up. Families left. Those who remained had to reinvent themselves, as the Pacific Lumber Company declared bankruptcy and fishing fleets shrank with the salmon runs and crab seasons. The cannabis economy rose in the shadows and became something huge, then crashed hard as legalization collapsed prices. It would have been enough to undo a weaker place.

But Humboldt has a long history of getting back up.

You'll see it in Arcata's food co-ops and maker spaces. Former mill sites have become trailheads, university satellites, and places to develop new environmental careers. Communities put their energy into restoration—restoring salmon habitats, restoring forests, restoring Native land stewardship in collaboration with tribes like the Hoopa, whose presence here predates memory. The cannabis downturn, while rough, has pushed people to diversify to survive: to experiment with agriculture, tourism, creating new products for local markets or to sell online. . . . But the forests stayed key to Humboldt County's identity, now through conservation, recreation, research, and a more deliberate relationship with the land.

For towns still struggling, still searching for a way forward, Humboldt County offers proof that recovery is possible, even as it's still trying to figure out its own transition right now. Because a community can lose its old story and still write a new one.

* * *

I first came across Brett through a song. In his raspy country voice, he sang about redwoods and rebels, hippies and rednecks, moonshiners and mystics, blood in the soil and weed in them hills. It felt personal, like he'd lived all of it.

I dropped him a message. He wrote back not long after, and we agreed to meet up the next time I was in California. It was late fall by the time I got there.

Brett came out of his barn in a battered tank top and worn brown suspenders, work pants rolled slightly at the hem, walking barefoot over the rough driveway. He was tall and lean, with a full dark beard and a black cowboy hat that cast his face in shadow.

"This is Crazy River Ranch," he said, shaking my hand.

We were a dozen miles from the coast. A layer of mountains rose into a cloud-streaked sky east of the farm, a large pond to my right, cows off in the distance grazing in a field. In front of us stood a twenty-six-foot-tall barn, made from finely milled redwood boards.

"We built this," Brett said. "Community effort. All round pole construction. Harvested every one of these trees ourselves.

"I even had a pole stripping party to get it started," he added.

I smiled. "That brought people in?"

"Actually, it almost turned them off." He laughed. "'Cause people were like, 'What?!'"

He ran his hand across the wood's wavy texture. It made a sound almost like a heavy wind. "Old-growth redwood," he said. "My neighbor Herschel found it. He just had a feeling. Walked out into what looked like plain pasture, jumped on the ground, and said, 'There's a log there.' I kinda laughed. But sure enough, there was a perfect old-growth redwood log buried right beneath him."

Out front of the barn stood an antique red New Champion cider press from Trenton, New Jersey. "It was making juice before Prohibition," Brett said, placing a hand gently on the side like it was an elderly relative. "I saw one just like it in a barn as a kid. Never thought I'd end up with one."

The machine clattered to life, apples rattling up the chute, getting ground to pulp and then squeezed through. Brett handed me a small cup of unfiltered juice—raw, cloudy, fresh.

"Cheers," he said.

Outside, crates of apples waited their turn. Brett reached into one and held up a rough, golden fruit. "Ashmead's Kernel," he said. "It's from the 1700s. Old English apple. Take a bite."

The apple was cold from the previous evening, the flesh dense, crisp, tart. A living time capsule. Perhaps the best-tasting apple of my life.

"So good, people have continued to grow it," Brett said, like he had a family tree of this apple going all the way back to the Enlightenment.

I nodded, still chewing. I've always loved this part of California for its rugged nature, its crisp, fresh air. Somehow the food tastes better here; the colors are sharper. The vastness of untouched land makes you feel very present. Small . . . but also part of something larger, in the way that nature allows.

"Most people don't picture this when they think of California," I said.

Brett followed my gaze. "I leave Humboldt, and I'm still shocked."

There's some pretty big country up there. The Trinity Alps, then the Marble Mountains, then the Russian Wilderness. They just run into each other. The Trinity Alps alone stretch over half a million acres, with granite cirques, sapphire lakes, and entire drainages where you can walk for days and not see another soul. The Marbles, with their knife-ridged limestone spines, are close cousins. Light-colored marble runs in seams through the darker rock, catching sunlight in flashes that feel alien. Some days it doesn't even look like stone, more like something scorched and left to harden. The Russian Wilderness is more remote still. The name dates back to the early 1800s, when Russian fur traders pushed south from Alaska, hunting sea otters along the coast and, some believe, scouting inland in search of game. A name from the years before it was certain whether Northern California would be Russian or British or Spanish or American.

Out in the wilderness, locals will tell you things get strange. Stories of compasses spinning. Trails vanishing. People vanish too from time to time. Sometimes for real, other times there are just stories—passed around in bars, over woodstoves, or said with a dry shrug. People say Bigfoot lives out there. That the famous footage from the '60s was filmed just a few ridges away.

Brett led me onto a felled log stretched out over a still green pond, the surface glassy as a mirror, like throwing in a rock would shatter it. A lonely cloud drifted across, brushing past reflections of trees that didn't seem entirely rooted to this world. The log flexed under our weight. He asked if I felt it. I did. The water was nine feet deep here, he said. Fourteen near the middle. "Once you go, you're in there. All in." He said it with a grin. I wasn't sure if he meant the pond or the place itself. Either way, it felt true.

* * *

Brett started his first farm at nineteen back in South Dakota, where he is from. "Three acres of organic row crop vegetables," he told me. "My brother and I made about a buck fifteen an hour. It was hard work, but I loved it. Still do."

We were following a narrow path skirting the edge of a field, the grass still damp with dew. Brett picked a sun-gold tomato from the vine. "End of the season," he said, handing it to me. "Still good, though."

I took a bite. It exploded with bright, sweet-sour flavor. "How do you eat a regular tomato after this?" I asked.

"You don't," he said, smiling. "You can pick as many as you want. Take 'em home. And remind me when we come back here, I'll get you some ground beef too."

The tall grass bent under our steps, Brett still barefoot, as we made our way toward the edge of the orchard.

"I love being outside when it's gonna rain," he said. "And it's really vulnerable because your whole livelihood could get wiped out—storm, or frost like it was in my case back in South Dakota." He paused for a moment, looking ahead toward the fence line. "Over the years, after I moved to California, I did the same thing. Started an organic vegetable farm. I didn't know about the other crops people were growing here. I had customers come to my vegetable stand, pull out big wads of cash, skim off a couple small bills, and pay me for my lettuce. I was curious, so I asked them, 'What do you do?'" He laughed as if it was a long story that he'd get back to. "We're gonna go through this gate. We're gonna go see my neighbor Ken."

We stepped off the grass and onto a narrow path. The gate leaned slightly in its frame, crooked on old hinges. On either side, red cedars hung low, their boughs heavy with moisture, filtering the light like stained glass.

"When Julia, my wife, and I first moved to Humboldt," Brett said as we walked through a wide open pasture, "our friend came over, saw a painting on the wall, and said, 'You have a Jarvela?' and I'm like, 'What are you talking about?' She said, 'The painting—Ken Jarvela. He's a famous artist.' And I just laughed: 'Ken? He lives in a trailer right over there.'"

"There's a lot of talent out here," I said, thinking of Brett's music. "Is it the nature that inspires it?"

"I think that's part of it." But maybe this was also just a place that's always drawn people full of yearning, the sort of yearning that sometimes has to express itself in art.

First, it was fur and then gold that lured people in. While most prospectors swarmed the Sierra Foothills, explorers from the Sacramento Valley discovered that the rivers cutting through the Trinity Alps held rich deposits too. Getting there, however, was nearly impossible. In the winter of 1849, a stranded group of miners led by Josiah Gregg set out in search of an easier route from the coast. Their brutal journey ended at Humboldt Bay—and Gregg did not survive—but the news of their discovery carried back to San Francisco. Prospectors poured in from across the world. Soon, pack trains were leaving from Humboldt Bay, Trinidad, and Rohnerville, carrying hopeful miners and their gear into the interior. When more traces of gold were found in the black sands of Gold Bluffs Beach, companies spent decades trying everything to get to it, from dredging to questionable chemical extractions, even a short-lived attempt at underwater mining. Ultimately, the cost of recovery outweighed the yield, and the dream of gold in Humboldt County faded.

But not before a population boom reshaped the region. Newcomers arrived from nearly every state and European nation; Chinese settlers formed small Chinatowns; and increasing pressure on Native hunting and fishing grounds fueled violent conflicts that led to the creation of military posts. Businesses sprang up almost overnight: farms, dairies, blacksmith shops, banks—anything that could support the influx of people. Many who failed to find fortune in the mountains settled on the coast, including William Carson, who made his wealth not from gold but from the "red gold" of the redwood forests.

By the 1860s, newcomers realized that the true wealth of the region rose above them: vast stands of old-growth redwood, some of the tallest and oldest trees on the planet. As the population increased across the West, the demand for lumber soared, and Humboldt's deepwater bays made it possible to ship cut timber to San Francisco and beyond. Sawmills multiplied along the waterfronts, and towns like Eureka, Arcata, and Scotia grew up around the mills. Companies like the Pacific Lumber Company became the region's economic anchors, offering stable employment and, in some cases, worker housing and civic infrastructure. For a century, the work was consistent . . . and the forests seemed endless.

Then in 1967 came the Summer of Love down in Haight-Ashbury, San Francisco. Streets filled with long-haired kids and runaways, incense and protest signs, music in the air. There was this convergence of counterculture folks disenfranchised with the way the country was going: the Vietnam War, big corporations, corruption in government. They came to San Francisco, but there was so much energy, it couldn't just stay there. The wave broke north. They scattered—up the coast, into the mountains. Especially here in the Emerald Triangle counties: Humboldt, Trinity, Mendocino.

"And that's where it got interesting," Brett told me. "Back in the sixties, these communities had a lot of logging and fishing and ranching. Very salt-of-the-earth people. Also very conservative in their values. And then came the back-to-the-landers. The hippies. Pot-smokin', free-lovin', a lot of artists. People who wanted to live off-grid, grow their own food, raise kids close to the land. Different clothes, different politics—but in a lot of ways, they were after the same thing."

He sang a line for me from a song he'd written: "*And that's when a redneck made love to a hippie, they had themselves a child and they named her Gypsy.*"

He looked at me and shrugged. "And somehow, it worked. That's made the whole Emerald Triangle sort of a cultural melting pot. Where you have people that have very different values living close to each other and working together. That's what I think's really beautiful." He paused for a moment, collecting his thoughts. "Because I see so much of the country is so polarized."

I agreed, and I didn't. This *was* a special place, absolutely.

But in my years of traveling around the country, I'd found that people with different values living close to each other and working together wasn't actually all that unusual. Nobody really cares if the UPS driver delivering your package voted blue or red, as long as he gets your package to your door. But I smiled and kept the thought to myself.

"I take my dad hunting," Brett went on. "He's a disabled veteran, and we go hunting in Wyoming. If I tell people I'm from California, they're like, 'What the heck are you doing there? That place sucks.'"

I started to say something about who profits by making us think we're more divided than we really are.

"Watch the bullshit," Brett cut in teasingly, tugging my arm just before I stepped in a steaming cow pie.

I laughed, although I didn't know if he really meant it as a joke.

"I feel like it's so important to be curious," he said. "Out here, you can't really get away from difference. You have to accept it because it's more diverse."

We walked farther into the field, where the light felt thinner, low clouds gathering heavy overhead. The pasture ended in a wide stony wash, the river flowing through it so quietly that I'd mistaken its sound for wind. A massive tree lay half submerged at the bend, its roots twisted skyward.

An old green truck with smoky windows was parked in the grass, its tailgate hanging open. A man—mid-sixties maybe, his gray hair and beard spun in soft chaos, pants freckled with old paint—stood in front of a wooden easel with a canvas rested on its frame. The painting showed the same log, same mountains, but cast in a sunlit palette: greens too green, shadows tinged with lavender, bark patched up with ashy blue, as if nature only allowed the artist to see its true colors.

"Whatcha workin' on, Ken?" Brett called out, reaching to hug him.

"Ohhh . . . umm." Ken gave a small shrug, trailing off like the answer was too long to explain. "You must be Peter," he said, offering a handshake. In his other hand, he still held a long brush covered in paint.

"This is beautiful," I said, nodding toward his work. "How long have you been painting for?"

"Forty-five years, maybe." He looked at the canvas like he could see through it. "Not long enough."

Brett smiled. "He paints the full moon. Keeps himself up all night. Hikes into the redwoods with his gear. Paints in the dark, by moonlight, by himself. And he does it all times of year," Brett continued. "He's born and raised in Humboldt County."

"Just over the hill," Ken said, pointing into the distance. "I'll tell ya, it has a hold on me. I've lived away a couple times. Oregon, Arkansas. About a year or two apiece. And man . . . you just stand there, looking back to the West, and think, 'Damn, that's my home. It's way over there.'" He laughed. Then in a more hushed voice: "It draws you back, for whatever reason. Why fight it? I mean, look at the light. Listen to the soundtrack here."

As Brett and I caught our breath, the quiet grew somehow louder. You could hear things now: the subtle, layered noise of the land. The faint tick of wind pressing through dry grass. The river running over the smoothed rocks. A few birds flickering in and out of the scrub, their wings making that soft-paper sound.

"You think about what was it like, oh, a thousand years

ago?" Ken went on. "Man, it was all like this. Hundred thousand years ago, million years ago—the skies were like this. The sunlight was just like this. So this, I was thinking today, this is history repeating itself. Usually that sounds like a bad thing. But here? This is showing you what it looked like three hundred years ago. Four hundred twenty-five years ago, there was a day just like this."

He waved a hand toward the field. "And that's when you start to see the here today, gone tomorrow aspect of it. And all summer long, if you come here every day, oh man, you'd be familiar with all the bushes, and the rocks. Then winter comes: What the hell happened? Everything is different.

"Like this here," he bent and brushed his hand across the grass. "You start looking at it close, there's all kinds of nice detail here and there. But you look at that tree." He motioned toward a tall pine standing alone in the field. "What does it look like in your peripheral vision? It's a blur of nothing."

Ken paused for a moment, watching the light shift along the tree's high limbs. "Our brain fills in the rest as we scan around. But to get it in a painting, what it actually looks like to have human vision . . ."

He smiled slightly, like it was a thought he'd circled many times before. "That's the key. Someday."

* * *

Back at Brett's ranch, his wife was moving crates of apples, their young daughter following close behind. Brett loaded the back of the old Chevy with boxes of fruit and plastic bins of capped cider bottles, then rolled us out onto the gravel road. Not five minutes later, as we crossed an old metal cattle grate with a hollow clank, a large white pickup crested the opposite hill.

Brett tapped the brakes and leaned out his open window. "What's up, neighbors?" he called out. "I got some juice for ya." Without waiting for an answer, he swung open the door and hopped out. "Got the good stuff."

The window rolled down, and an older couple smiled. "Thank you, neighbor!" the man said. "Moonshiners right in the middle of nowhere."

"This is Fred and Rose," Brett said, handing over two jugs of Humboldt's gold. "They sold us the ranch. We pretty much would not have been able to survive if it wasn't for 'em. They've helped us since day one. Helped with the cattle. Fred showed me how to pretty much do all kinds of stuff."

Fred smirked. "I was gonna sell out to them cheese makers, them goat farmers. But I couldn't beat this guy, you know?"

"I think we provided a lot more entertainment for you," Brett answered, a mysterious smile playing along the corners of his mouth.

As it turned out, Brett had a story for me, one that sounded more anxiety-producing than entertaining. As we eased back onto the road, he started in. "When we first moved out here, I'd only been here about six months," he said. "There were federal police coming and raiding my home in town. And it was all over the news." He gave a dry laugh that didn't quite reach his eyes. "I wasn't arrested at the time, but it was stressful."

I stayed quiet, letting the story unfold.

"What really got to me was worrying how this could impact my relationship with Fred and Rose, 'cause they were amazing. It was like having adopted grandparents, and now I'm wondering, oh man . . . it's all over the news." He glanced at the road ahead. "And then I got this message from Freddie: 'Hey there, neighbor. I figure you had a rough week, so I just went ahead and took care of them chores over there.' Turns out Freddie called up his buddy Elmer, who at that time was in his eighties, and Fred was still in his seventies. And they went over to my place and hauled off anything worth keeping. The loader, the tractor, boat, my trailer . . . every piece of equipment. Moved it all over to Freddie's house," in case the feds came looking to confiscate things.

He shook his head, still a little stunned by it. "When I found out, I said, 'Freddie, oh my God. Thank you.' He just looked at me and he goes, 'Brett, the feds have been comin' to Humboldt for a long time, makin' a big deal outta nothin.'"

We pulled onto the paved road, no other cars in sight. Thick brush reached in from both sides, wide canopies of eucalyptus blurring slightly as Brett shifted gears.

"Why were the feds there, if you don't mind me asking?"

He rested his elbow outside of the open window, keeping his eyes on the road. "Somebody got busted with some weed back east, and they gave a list of thirty names—people they'd ever gotten weed from or knew. This one person said I'd sold them three to four pounds two years prior to their bust. . . . I didn't have any weed growing out here, but I ended up getting a five-year prison sentence."

"Everyone was growing" in this part of California, a local guy told me a few days afterward. "The postmaster, the police. At the very least, a plant or two for Christmas." Even before legalization, growing weed was pretty tolerated. You had kids learning to grow from their parents by age ten. Plants tucked under trees or hauled up into the canopies of makeshift wooden platforms. Some called it criminal; others called it outlaw farming. Either way, during trim season, whole towns would flood with strangers; a town of three thousand might see thousands more come through. Backpackers from Argentina, France,

Chile. Ninety-day visas, cash under the table—*trimmigrants*, the locals called them. It was chaotic. It was normal. It was just what people did. But then the feds would come through.

Brett paused to roll the window back up; the silence that followed felt sealed.

"They wanted me to snitch," he said. "They've had this thing called mandatory minimum sentencing laws—a lot of them came in under Clinton. Part of the drug war. And mandatory minimums give all the power to prosecutors. Judges don't have power anymore," to decide how long a prison term the circumstances might merit. "What they tell you is, the only way to get under the sentence is by snitching. And I say that 'cause they use hearsay as the only evidence. They don't need a wiretap, drug bust—"

"Really?!"

"Nothing. Just people's words. And you can imagine how often it's not the whole truth, or it ain't even true at all. In fact, it's so common there's a name for it in prison: ghost dope."

The highway straightened out in front of us. A green sign flashed past the window: ARCATA, POPULATION 15,700, an outdated number from the '90s. The population has grown to almost nineteen thousand. But who knows. Did the census count those hiding far off in the hills?

"Five years," I said. "Can you talk about it at all?"

Brett glanced out the window, like he might find the words out there somewhere.

"Well, it's been a little bit of time now, so it's easier to talk about. I've been working a lot on my own healing from some of the parts that were traumatic." When he wouldn't plead guilty, they threatened him with ten years, when they'd originally been saying five.

"Oh, geez," I said.

His fingers tightened on the wheel. "So I get this call from my attorney—this had been going on for a year and a half. Just anxiety, stress, fear ongoing. Finally, I said, 'Ask them if I sign, will they drop that ten-year mandatory minimum back to five?' He called, and they said yes. So I pled guilty, and I got five years for growing cannabis." Brett could have avoided those five years if he'd snitched, but he didn't.

The town of Arcata felt pleasantly busy: an old Chevy truck in front of us hauling a load of root vegetables; students weaving past on bikes, headphones in. Mixed-age crowds ambled in and out of a brick-lined plaza surrounded by brightly painted buildings (purples, yellows) with a bit of a Western frontier feel. The road had been blocked off for a farmers market: folding tables stacked with fruit, bread, jars, meat. Music buzzed from different corners, local bands overlapping in a warm, uncoordinated hum.

Brett hopped out of the truck to trade some cider for shiitake mushrooms, introduce me to the ladies who he said ran the only oxen farm west of the Mississippi, chat with a man whose husband was a sixth-generation dairy farmer. Then we got back on the road.

"Fred and Rose asked me and Julia to come over for breakfast," Brett said, picking back the story up where he'd left off. "We were living in a little travel trailer on the ranch back then. They said, 'Julia, if you wanna come stay with us . . . it's kinda lonely to be on that land all by yourself at nighttime, in the dark.' We didn't have electricity at the time. So basically, Fred and Rose invited Julia to live with them in while I was in prison. She didn't take 'em up on it—but it meant a lot, to have that kind of community support."

"What year did you get out?"

"In 2017. California was going through a big old legalization celebration." He laughed softly. "It was like a big green rush right here in Humboldt. I mean, there were people from all over the country and the world investing in farms. It was massive." What had cost him years of his life was suddenly a new boom of entrepreneurial promise, the outlaw economy rebranding into an industry of flashy dispensaries where professional salespeople connected customers with whatever strain of weed they wanted.

"I'd ask people what the long line was for in front of these new stores. And they'd tell me, 'Oh, weed's legal now. A new dispensary just opened.' And we're all standing there in line for what I'd just gotten out of prison for. And in some ways, it's really beautiful," Brett went on. "It's beautiful because I know the persecution for people is finally on the downward trend. But on the other hand, it sort of underscores what a bunch of bullshit the whole thing was."

With legalization came pricey permits and endless red tape. The small farms couldn't keep up; mom-and-pop grow culture thinned out like smoke. California did make an effort with programs to help growers transition into the legal business, an attempt to undo some of the damages of prohibition. But in practice, barriers remained that were just too hard to overcome.

The cartels kept going in the meantime. There'd been remote grows staked deep in the backcountry going back decades. Camps guarded by tough guys with weapons. Booby traps. Chemicals in the water supply. The cartels often grew on other people's land and kept their costs low. They didn't need trimmigrants; they just needed to get their workforce over the border illegally, pay them half nothing, and threaten anyone who tried to leave. There wasn't a care about the health of the plant or the soil, just pure profit. Those were operations that could survive through legalization.

Inside the cab, Brett was silent. The windshield had that faint shimmer of saltwater film and Pacific sky golden light. I found myself wondering how he'd handled being inside, but he spoke before I could ask.

"There's a saying in prison: 'You can either do your time, or it's gonna do you.' You can be a victim and powerless, or you can use the time and do the best you can with it. When I first went in, I was bitter. I was angry. I was mad at the government. I was *so* mad at those snitches. Thought, 'Man, you sold my freedom to keep yours.'" He rolled his jaw once before continuing. "So I had all this anger and resentment in me. But I had all this time to do, and I figured out pretty early on: If I stay here, I will die. I will become bitter, and I will wither away."

He looked out the window. "For me, the big thing has been learning how to heal. And that's about forgiveness. Which is just a word. It's easy to say, but it's something to explore. And it changed the whole trajectory of my life."

* * *

In nearby Eureka, Queen Anne and Eastlake Victorians lined the streets—elaborate with intricate spindle work, sun-faded turrets, and pastel facades. The streets narrowed as we passed through Old Town, where restored brick storefronts stood shoulder to shoulder, their bay windows catching glints of the bay beyond. A few blocks inland, the Carson Mansion seemed to preside over the surrounding houses, its ornate spires and gables a testament to the city's lumber baron past. Even the smaller homes wore their history proudly: gingerbread trims, stained glass transoms, and hand-turned balusters, many crafted just down the road at Blue Ox Millworks, where Brett said we were heading.

We turned onto a gravel lot, dust kicking up behind us, stopping at a porch that looked like a whimsical old Western outpost, all done up in ornate white woodwork with a rustic metal smokestack off to one side. White-railed steps rose to a sky-blue building through a burst of color: mossy succulents, red flowers. A Monterey pine leaned dramatically over the porch, and in the garden a carved lumberjack towered eight feet tall, cheerful in a red shirt and blue pants. He stood with arms crossed and boots planted, like some enchanted sentry left behind by a fairy-tale woodsman.

The stairs creaked as a woman stepped outside to meet us, her silver hair curled gently at the shoulders, eyes sharp behind thick glasses. A black cat stretched on the steps behind her, entirely unimpressed.

"That's Viviana Hollenbeck," Brett said. "We're gonna go see her husband, Eric. He made the barn doors for us. Good people, great community members."

"You're bringing the goods?" Viviana smiled with the relaxed good humor of someone who'd greeted a thousand guests but still meant her welcome.

"Isn't the first time," Brett chuckled, lifting a crate of apples from the truck bed. "I wish you could try the pie she makes out of these."

Viviana gave a little mock bow. "Only if you bring the right apples."

I nodded toward the statue. "Who made this?"

"That was made by one of the most renowned timber fallers in the world," she said, opening the door with a faint squeak. Inside, the scent hit first: wood dust, old books, a trace of tobacco smoke. A stained glass panel in the window caught the afternoon light, throwing red and cobalt across the wide-planked floor.

"Is that a true art-craft here, timber felling?" I asked, eyeing the delicate wooden fretwork above the window, like lace made out of lumber. Every specialty has its legends.

"It *is* an art," she said. "You really gotta know what you're doing."

Eric, dressed in a red-and-black flannel that matched the checkered enamel mug in his hand, looked like a character who might not appear again if you blinked. His hair was combed back in a tidy wave, gray-blond and theatrical—part Paul Bunyan, part Walt Whitman, with a touch of circus ringmaster. He struck a match with a dry rasp, and his pipe caught with a tiny flare. A curl of smoke wandered upward.

We followed him into his workshop, sectioned off into rooms that were labeled with carved signs: LATHE ROOM, FABRICATION ROOM, BLUE OX VETERANS PROGRAM.

"Eric, what about timber fellers?" I asked, walking around a low workbench stacked with split boards labeled with students' names in careful pencil. "Are there many of those guys around still?"

"Not the old-growth, no," he said, his voice whiskey-smooth. Old-growth redwood trees were the region's wooden gold. "We haven't cut any old growth in this county in fifteen, twenty years. There's still second-growth fallers, and they're good. No slouches by any stretch of the imagination." Second-growth forests could still get to a hundred feet. "But old growth, that was a different bag of puppies."

I grinned at the phrase.

A nearby display showed delicately carved torch motifs, winged brackets and ornamental spindles pinned to a board like specimens, each one a reproduced detail from Abraham Lincoln's hearse.

"So the old-growth value must be very high now?"

"Exactly. But that's why we work for the historic trust only. Because that's where this—what's left—should go. Viv and I started this business fifty-one years ago. We just got done with 220 feet of wooden rain gutter for Emily Dickinson's house in Massachusetts."

He paused, pointing to a photo on the wall: a butter-yellow brick house with forest green shutters and fluted white columns, topped with a cupola.

"Now that's Emily Dickinson's house. You can't be putting a metal gutter up. It has to match what the original was. That's why we're a very, very niche market, and we're the only ones doing it with original equipment."

Brett stepped closer, pointing at a cast-iron scroll saw with a large flywheel and a foot pedal beneath a curved seat. "That's a pedal-powered jigsaw right there. Still in operation."

To an untrained eye like mine, it looked part bicycle, part sewing machine, almost as if the Old Order Amish had come up with the contraption.

Eric nodded. "That's from 1870. I like to say that we don't make reproductions, we make reissuances."

Like so many of his fellow woodworkers, Eric bore his profession physically. His hands showed scars from chisels and planers, and I imagined that his forearms were always covered in a fine, pale layer of sawdust. A subtle cedar-and-linseed-oil scent hung on him, the warm smell that emanated from wood as it was cut. His back was stiff. He joked that his gigantic

Great Pyrenees was the perfect height for petting, tall enough that he didn't need to bend. But he was still sharp mentally, agile, blessed with a patience that comes from decades of measuring twice and cutting once.

He led us out back, where instead of a yard like I'd expected, we stepped into what looked like a small village. A narrow road ran between a row of weathered cabins, all shaded under a tangle of western hemlock and alder. Everything was made of wood: sidewalks, benches, fences squeezed into the narrow space between buildings. NO CAULK BOOTS IN THEATER read a sign outside one.

It was an old skid camp from the 1800s, back when they were using misery whips and hand tools and oxen to harvest redwoods. They'd log a hundred acres in a year or two, Eric said, then "tore the wooden sidewalks out, backed two oxen up to every building, and away they'd go to the next logging site. Set the whole thing up all over again."

"Were they paid in scrip, like the coal miners in West Virginia?" I asked.

"We had company towns that they couldn't get out of, you know?" Eric said. "I mean, they could, but it was a two-day trek. And they got paid in vouchers that were only good at the company store."

"And where were these workers from?"

"In this county, mostly Danes, Swedes, and Norwegians, I think."

We walked a little farther, the trees parting just enough to reveal what looked at first like a small chapel made of barn wood. REDWOOD SHRINE was carved above the entrance. There was a massive redwood cross-section just inside, its rings dark and wide, the edges flared like the cap of a giant mushroom. Eric stepped beside it, barely reaching halfway up its height.

"This era and this logging was very, very technical," he said. "It took a lot of skill, and people working with these trees were not laborers."

He placed his hand on the slab like he was gently shaking it awake. "So, this cross-section is a foot thick. It was taken out of the Fieldbrook Giant, seventy feet off the ground. The tree was fifteen feet in diameter at that height. The base was thirty-five feet. You could park a bus on it," and still have room to walk around.

"Wow . . ." was all I could say.

"It was one of the huge, huge trees in this area. Cut down in 1901." Eric paused. "Here's what I want to tell you about this. You see, the loggers have gotten a bad rap. Really bad rap. But think about it: The dudes and dudettes who came here all of a sudden were dealing with trees like this."

He gave a small wave toward the slab.

"First off, how you gonna get it on the ground? How you gonna do that? Okay, the wizard comes along, and magically you got it on the ground. Now, how you gonna buck it in the lengths that you can move? Okay, the wizard helps again. Now how you gonna move it? All you got's oxen. You gotta figure out how to move these things. Okay, you get 'em to move, where you gonna move it to? There have never been sawmills in the entire world in all of history to deal with something like this."

He lowered his voice. "Those guys and gals had to solve every one of those problems to build this country. Once they did solve it, the United States said, 'We need cheap building material. We need it now.' And those guys and gals stepped up to the plate and did that."

"So you think they don't get the respect they deserve?" I asked.

"Correct," Eric said. "You know the railroad coming across the US, where they met in the middle and drove the spike?" The first transcontinental railroad, the tracks from east and west meeting up at Promontory Summit, Utah, in May 1869, where railroad baron Leland Stanford drove a ceremonial 17-karat gold spike into the ground. "In fifteen years, the loggers, who were not engineers, they weren't railroad people. They built narrow-gauge railroad in Oregon, Washington, and Northern California. In some of the toughest land there is. They built enough railroad in twenty years to span the continental United States three times. And they did it with their hands. Just using their brains, solving problems as they came up."

He let the silence hang for a beat. "And that's what we are in this county. Problem solvers."

Brett stepped closer to the slab. "Eric," he said, pointing to the line of tiny metal dots sunk into the grain near its center. "These little . . . what are they? Every ten, or every hundred?"

"The pins?" Eric said. "Every twenty-five."

I felt my eyebrows raise. "So this tree is how old?"

"One thousand four hundred fifty years old," Eric said.

I stepped in, squinting at the rings up close, following the timeline of pins across the surface. "So the Constitution was written right . . . here?" I pointed near one of the outer rows.

"Here, I'll give you an idea." Eric crouched a little, dragging his finger gently along the grain. "Right there, the United States of America became a country. That's the signing of the Declaration of Independence." It was practically on the edge of the tree.

He stood back again and looked toward the darker center of the slab.

"Whole lotta stuff happened back that way."

* * *

Archaeologists believe the Hupa moved into California about one thousand years ago. But that's not how the Hoopa Valley Tribe frames their history. They believe that their people didn't come from anywhere else but the very spot where they still live. That they've been there since the world began.

In the Hoopa timeline, they were here watching the Fieldbrook Giant grow as a sapling. What was the Pacific Coast like in the year 575, I caught myself wondering? Was it like Ken said, days just like this one?

By the time we left the mill, the air had turned cold, thick with fog off the Pacific. Brett pulled on a jacket, glanced toward the ridgeline, and said, "You want to see where the old ones still grow before dark?"

About an hour later, we were headed into the forest, just the two of us, our steps soft on damp mossy earth. Brett was still barefoot. The fog settled in thicker, draping over the trees and curling low into the ferns. We walked single file, our voices swallowed as soon as we spoke.

"Wanna walk into the tree?" I heard Brett's voice ahead.

I laughed.

"I try to go in whenever given the opportunity," he said.

One of the royal giants stood in front of us, its base dark and cavernous, the trunk open like a doorway to another world. The top stretched so far above, it looked like it belonged to a different forest altogether. Branches the size of full-grown trees jutted out high above our heads.

Inside, the air felt older, heavier. The space was wide enough for both of us to move around without ducking, roomy in a way that didn't seem possible from the outside. Brett pulled out his phone and lit the space with a soft glow.

"Been through fire," he said, nodding. "Look." Soot coated the walls, but you could see patches of green growing through it here and there, soft moss threading through the black.

"Burned up from the inside, and yet it's still alive," Brett said. "They can live for hundreds of years in a state like this."

I stood still a moment, trying to imagine what that meant. To be partially hollowed out but still standing, the ash bringing needed nutrients to saplings on the forest floor.

"So good for the soul in here, huh?" I finally said.

Brett nodded. "Remember I told you I learned in prison the importance of forgiveness? Well, I also learned the power of personal growth and development. Those things seem at odds, but . . . I ended up going to this mystery school, led by inmates."

We were walking again, past ferns just shy of our height.

"They started talking about manifestation and limitless thinking. I thought, 'What are you talking about? We're literally in prison.'" He chuckled. "But I had nothing to lose, so I stayed. We made drawings. Mind maps. We'd talk about our future goals in the present tense."

"We'd even have these parties," he said, smiling at the memory. "Future-now parties. We'd sit around and say things like, 'I'm so grateful for my family.' 'I'm so grateful for abundance on the farm.' 'My business is thriving, I don't know what to do with all the money. Mind you—we were in prison and broke saying that stuff." He laughed.

"I drew all that out. Just little stick-figure sketches. A barn. Me singing on a stage, playing my future. A child. And none of it existed back then. Our life was in shambles. We were almost gonna lose everything. I was in prison. My wife was struggling. But they said, just keep going. You have to see it in your mind and say it, even if you feel like you're a liar."

He shook his head, softly. "When I came back, it wasn't all that rosy. It was a grind. It was painful. Sometimes it seemed like it was never gonna happen. But the other day I pulled those drawings out of the box."

He looked over at me. "Everything you saw today—our farm, my family, the music that led me to you—that was all drawn in a prison. I made those drawings in 2014."

I didn't know what to say.

A soft rain fell without urgency. All around us, trunks rose from the floor like pillars, their crowns lost high above, scattered fragments of sky peeking through the canopy.

"So those are all old growth?" I asked. "Never been logged?"

"Maybe fifteen hundred years old or older," he said. "And if you look at the grain, if you see a felled one, you can read it. When you have a bigger grain, it's because they had a lot of rain, or a tree fell over next to it and it got a little more sun. Tight grain? It was a drought, or it got buried under the canopy and it had to wait another hundred years until its time was to come."

He glanced around. "All those trees in the forest . . . they were born in the shade. Grew up in it."

"How do they grow without sun?" I asked.

"Slowly, with patience." He laughed. "That's the magic." They'd only ever catch the sun for a few minutes, when the angle's right and it finds a way through.

I thought about all the places I'd passed through over the years—towns suffocating because of shuttered mills, closed-down mines, boarded storefronts, and the invisible prisons people build from dangerous habits or a simple lack of options. Places where resurrection feels out of reach. Here I was standing in a countryside that had survived its own cycles of boom-and-collapse, and had, like these ancient redwoods, risen again from what had burned, stronger for it. Talking to a man whose own life story echoed those same rhythms: near ruin, and then a slow, patient rebuilding.

I remembered something I'd heard a few days earlier about how even the Hupa, who were never conquered by either the Spanish or the Americans, had, just the year before, regained another ten thousand acres of their ancestral land, some of the most beautiful land in this country. Everyone in Humboldt County, playing the long game.

Standing beside Brett in that living cathedral of a tree, I thought I maybe finally understood the lesson of this place. Maybe survival isn't just endurance, but believing that there's more for you if you keep going. That reinvention is possible even when the world has given you every reason to believe otherwise.

That it's not too much longer now before your turn in the sun.

CHAPTER 7

A Bit of Old England in the Chesapeake Bay

For a while there was nothing but sea and sky. The American flag atop the *Captain Jason II* snapped in the breeze—tossing a mist of bay water into the sunlight, with each droplet flashing for a split second before vanishing into the air. Then the horizon broke, low and pale, a thin strip of land almost melting into the water. Smith Island, one of Maryland's last inhabited islands, a holdout community of roughly two hundred souls. As the little passenger boat edged closer, the shape began to take hold: long stretches of flat green marsh, a row of two-story houses, a radio tower, a lone church steeple. White workboats sat tied side by side along a pier, their decks cluttered with traps and rope.

The distance from the mainland might not look like much on a map—ten miles, twenty miles—but back in history, storms and tides meant it wasn't always a given that you could cross. Residents might not leave a place for weeks, months, years, and everything moved more slowly as a result: commerce, mechanization, migration. Traditions passed almost unchanged from one generation to the next, so an island's sense of self could remain more old-world than new, even into the twenty-first century.

I'd been told the island was like that, with some locals' accents still carrying the traces of Elizabethan England. Smith Island remained so isolated for so long, the speech here seemed to freeze in place even as English kept evolving on the mainland. Listening to some of the old-timers, you could close your eyes and imagine yourself on the rocky shores of Cornwall or Devon or Wales.

Smith Island is one piece of a scattered archipelago, a constellation of marshy lands that rise just barely above the Chesapeake. They were never all that solid to begin with, mounds of ancient river sediments and skeletons of drowned forests. Some thirty-five million years ago, a meteor struck Earth here, leaving a vast crater beneath the bay. When the glaciers that once covered North America melted and the seas rose, the impact site slowly filled in, until what remained were these fragile, shifting platforms.

The islands have been shrinking for centuries now. Smith Island alone has lost thousands of acres since Colonial times, and it may slip under the Chesapeake for good by the end of this century. It's a place that's physically eroding but had, I'd heard, managed to keep its culture remarkably intact. Which is what drew me here. I wanted to see a community in the process of adapting to loss, even while facing a future it could no longer hope to find a way out from. Where the best they could do, it seemed, was to live in the moment.

* * *

The man I'd come to Smith Island to speak with greeted me at the pier as I disembarked alongside a few locals and a whole lot of Amazon delivery boxes. A salty specimen from the sea, his white rubber boots were streaked with mud, black overalls clipped to a faded *Jaws* T-shirt—the shark surging toward a tiny oblivious swimmer. He wore a camouflage cap, aviator sunglasses, and a thick blond mustache that flared wide over his lip like a pair of gull wings. Jerry was sixty, his skin sunbrowned and textured like he'd lived most of his life outdoors.

"Ya must be Peter," he said.

"That's me."

He smiled. "Well, welcome to Smith Island. Don't worry, we don't get many sharks out here."

Like all the men in his family going back ten generations, Jerry was a crabber—a waterman as he called it, using the Old English word for men who worked the bay. So far as he knew, his first ancestor was born on Smith Island in 1650. If that was correct, his family had been on this island continuously for 374 years, his son the latest iteration of that DNA. He told me all this in an accent that was more of a Carolina brogue, a briny blend of Old English and Southern twang. It was the vowels that sounded different, mostly—deep and wide, stretching out syllables: *down* becoming *dane*, *house* becoming *heh-uss*, *calm* becoming *calam*. He told me folks *dane* in Tangier Island, just seven miles south, sounded totally different.

Jerry stood next to his Chevy pickup with a rusty bumper that looked oversized parked on a sand-and-shell road barely a lane and a half wide. We hopped in and moseyed past fishing nets and buoys hung from fences to dry in the breeze, the smell of salt and marsh grass carrying through the air. Jerry told me we were in Ewell, the main town on the island, which he referred to as the "capital." The island seemed to grow its houses at random, roofs scattered through the open space like mushrooms after rain, large patches of grass in between. Most sat pretty close to the tight roads, tall and narrow nineteenth-century artifacts with steep gables and clapboard gone gray, or plain postwar boxes from the 1950s. Kayaks lay on their sides by porch steps, crab pots and buckets stacked against sheds, everything looking used and left where it was last needed. Open grass ran from front yards to the ditch alongside the road, with the occasional CHICKEN CROSSING sign or low metal fence to keep barking dogs in line. There were no traffic lights to slow things down or speed things up. We were the rare car in a place where most people seemed to get around by golf cart or bicycle.

"That one looks abandoned, huh?" I said, pointing at a two-story house with a half-white, half-yellow facade, the upper windows boarded with plywood.

Jerry looked over. "Somebody lives there. They're remodeling it." He nodded toward another house, almost hidden behind a tangle of shrubs, its wooden siding gray and splintered like old decking. It looked a little haunted. "That one—nobody's ever lived in that house as long as I've been here on the island. When I was a kid, every house except that one had somebody in it," he told me. "The population was around six hundred in those days. But then things started changing. I'd say about a hundred people left one year," he said.

"What year was that?"

"Maybe '95, '96, somewhere in there. Crabbing got really bad, and a prison opened," on the mainland. "I mean I don't blame 'em," he went on. "It was health care, a steady job, and steady money."

He turned onto a narrow dirt road, the truck's mirrors nearly brushing the power poles, and nodded toward a small white building ahead. A flag hung over the roof, barely moving in the lazy wind.

"This post office," he said, "used to fly a British flag until the late sixties. Because we were Tories until the revolution was over."

"Till the late what?"

"Nineteen-sixties," he clarified. "Used to fly just under the American flag."

During the American Revolutionary War, a whole lot of people living in the colonies—around 15–20 percent, historians believe—were loyalists who didn't want to break away from Britain at all. But it was crazy to think that folks here had clung to that divided loyalty for two hundred years.

"So, you have a lot of affinity toward the Brits here?" I asked.

"Yeah, back then they did, because they were pretty much left out here to dry. They had to side with the British—they had no defense."

It made sense as a survival mechanism. If the well-armed British navy was occupying your nine-square-mile island, were you really going to mess with their tea?

Jerry started telling me about finding a cannonball not too long ago, half of a chain shot: two cannonballs linked in the middle by a piece of chain, engineered to take out the rigging of a sailing ship. He figured it was left over from a skirmish in 1782.

I couldn't quite wrap my mind around how recent the American Revolution seemed here. This place really was somewhat stuck in time.

More streets went by in a blur of houses and small businesses: a bakery, an inn, a red shingle-sided building that looked like it had survived a dozen storms, still promising milkshakes and seafood. Before long, we were at the edge of Ewell. The road widened into a pale strip of crushed shell stretching straight through the marsh. A narrow tide channel shouldered the road, flashes of pale blue breaking through the reeds in the distance. The truck drummed over the ruts, and for a few minutes it felt like we were driving on a causeway built on water, one narrow strip of sand and shells keeping the marsh apart.

Jerry pointed toward a distant stand of trees. "Probably ten or so homes used to be there before I was born. There was a doctor there. And there was a church." But the land kept sinking—partly on its own and partly from pumping groundwater, which slowly compacted the earth below. And "the ocean was rising, and rising, and all this land that used to be farm land turned into marsh," Jerry said.

One silver lining was that the wetlands were great for preserving history in little treasure troves of artifacts, like time capsules. He'd tell me later about Little Thorofare, a stretch of marsh that used to be a Native American village—home of the Aquintica, he figured, one of the tribes that settled the Eastern Shore of Maryland. As a boy, he'd sat on a mound of oyster shells there, digging with his hands until he found fourteen arrowheads in two hours. *Chesapeake* means *great shellfish bay* in Algonquian, and the marsh had still been covered in burnt shells from bonfires centuries before. He had whole cases of arrowheads at home—flints and grays and browns, each shaped by a hand long gone. The oldest were twelve thousand years old, others eight thousand, the most recent ones seven hundred. You could see the evolution of the weaponry: Clovis points with fluted channels slowly replaced by parallel-flaked points.

Back in the present, Jerry nodded toward a tall smoking mound of ash and debris. "Here is what's called the burn pile. They put leaves and old wood and stuff like that." There was another pile next to it. "This is all weight goods," he said, "'frigerators, washing machines. All the metal gets loaded on a boat and took off of here. And speaking of, see that little green hill poking out in the distance? A house used to stand there. I was told it burned down twice—kids playing with matches. The parents built the house, the kids burned it down, then rebuilt it. And later on it happened again." His mustache twitched with a quick smile. "Same thing. Kids playing with matches."

I caught myself wondering if the story was a metaphor for this place: washed-out, storm after storm, only to be built back up again afterward.

Up ahead, the flat of the marsh began to change, patches of white and red appearing where the grass thinned, houses rising out of the landscape as the road bent toward them. We were approaching Rhodes Point, where Jerry lived, what he jokingly called "the hood."

"This is where the pirates used to live," he told me. "Used to be called Rogue's Point."

"The pirates?"

"We talk about pirates, we think jewels and gold," he said. But the Chesapeake's pirates were "more like river pirates. They were stealing your cargo. They would bring in a boat they captured, take everything useful off of it, and then just use it for firewood."

Out here, the land became an accomplice. The Chesapeake has thousands of coves and marsh tunnels that are easy to disappear into. It was a maze of brigand routes, a kind of a maritime no-man's-land where smugglers and privateers could avoid the British customs officials who patrolled the deeper waters of the Atlantic. Pirates could unload cargo, repair ships in quiet inlets, barter with sympathetic locals, and vanish again before the authorities could get within cannon range. Some of the

Chesapeake's pirates were famous, men like Marmaduke Mister and his nephew Stephen, whose descendants still gathered up for pirate family reunions. Others were just locals, watermen who knew every bend of every creek and sometimes took to piracy as a sort of side hustle.

Looking at Jerry, I thought I saw some pirate in him. Not that he got up to anything criminal, but he seemed something of a storybook, a larger-than-life type.

"You don't need license plates here, huh?" I asked as we idled past a tagless SUV caked with dried mud.

"Eh, technically I think you do," he said. But there weren't any cops on the island to write you up. Jerry told me they'd had a sheriff a long time ago, but without one now, the place more or less ran itself. The only crime he'd heard about recently was somebody stealing gas. On an island this size, you couldn't exactly make off with much more than that—everything had its place, and if something went missing, everyone already knew where it'd ended up.

Each spot along the drive had a story to it. His aunt's house where a tornado had come through as she was lying in bed, the whole building blowing down around her. "Didn't get a scratch on her," Jerry said. What used to be a nice restaurant back when tour boats came through in the '80s. "And then somewhere right around here"—Jerry motioned to the road ahead, where three Methodist churches lined up, one after the other—"this road is over three hundred and something years old, probably one of the oldest roads in the whole country."

In the graveyard between the churches, Jerry said, "you'll see Tyler, Evans, Marsh, Bradshaw," all original English families who'd settled Smith Island.

"What's your last name, Jerry?" I asked.

"My name's Smith," he said, with some pride.

There were a lot of Smiths in Smith Island's history. This part of the Chesapeake was charted by Captain John Smith in 1608, while he was living in Jamestown, a hundred miles south of here. Seventy years later, the island was named after Henry Smith when he was granted land here by the king. "They're called hundreds," Jerry explained. "A hundred people could live on a tract of land. This would probably been called Rogue's Hundred or something like that, Bradshaw's Hundred."

Some of the newer homes were built up on tall wooden pilings, the space beneath them open for the tide to pass through. "This is my wreck in progress," he said, easing the truck to a stop and climbing out. It had been beautiful once: built around 1880, with large windows framed with wooden shutters the color of seaweed, though the roof now had a gaping hole in the shingles—two feet across, at least—the work of Hurricane Sandy a dozen years earlier. He didn't go in that part of the house anymore, he said. He and his son just lived in the back.

Right at the shoreline, cement blocks and big chunks of limestone formed an improvised defense against the bay. "Is this what you guys are doing to create a barrier from the high tide?" I asked.

"Up until a point," he said. He tapped his knee, said the water could get that high, easy, in a storm.

"So what about your house? You're not on stilts."

"It'll come in it." He smiled. "It comes in when we have storms. That's usually about once every two years."

"So the water comes over your floor?"

"Oh yeah. I have a foot of water in the house." He said it casually, told me that when that happened, he'd just "walk around in boots. Hit the recliner and watch TV until the tide goes back down. Watch it come in, watch it go out."

I had a really hard time picturing it.

"See the minnows swimming all around," Jerry went on, without a trace of irony, like it was the most ordinary thing in the world.

"The minnows in your house?"

"Yes," he said.

"Jerry, you have such a good attitude."

"Why not?" he laughed. "You can take your life any way you want. You can blame every little thing happens on you and make it the worst possible life, or you can take what you have got and make it the best possible life."

I'd have thought a man with Jerry's circumstances would have been mucking around in the glory days of the past. And yet here he was: nonchalant, totally unbothered by the future. It was that old-fashioned all-American instinct: *We'll figure it out. We'll make this work.* Only without the swaggering frontier bravado. In a culture forever chasing the next horizon, Smith Island was showing me what it looked like to drop anchor and take whatever might come.

* * *

We headed off again to check out Tylerton—the island's third town, this one accessible only by boat. Jerry had borrowed one from a friend, something to cruise around in while his own crabber was getting fixed. The boat was plain and open: just a flat deck, some coolers, a fuel tank, and a pair of white folding chairs that looked like they'd come straight out of a schoolroom. We eased away from the shore. A couple of seagulls cut across the bow with a flash of white wings and rasping calls.

The waterway widened ahead, full of light, the surface flickering like a thousand broken mirrors. Jerry adjusted his sunglasses against the glare.

"You got no glasses, so you probably won't see it, but there's patches of grass out there under the surface—that's where the crabs are. My favorite spot's just half an hour from here."

He started telling me about the daily life of a crabber.

"All the work's in the back and arms. You're hunched over for hours, pulling and pulling. When I'm working, I drag two big nets behind me—metal frames with mesh bags on them. They call 'em scrapes. Each one's got a smooth bar along the front so it can ride right over the grass, and as it moves, it makes a pressure wave that pushes the peelers, grass, shells, or whatever else straight into the bag. Every few minutes, you haul 'em up, dump everything on the culling board, pick out the crabs, and throw the grass back. Then you drop the scrapes again and keep moving."

"What time do you start working?" I asked.

"I get up at four every morning. Now . . . see that one down there?" Jerry pointed toward a small bump of land covered in puffy green trees. "That's called Hog Neck. It was a preacher from a long time ago, his name was Joshua Thomas. They called him the parson of the island. He used to sail from Deal Island down through here and preach to all the islands, and he preached to the British just before they invaded DC in the War of 1812, and he told them they were gonna lose, and they lost." He let out a rocking laugh, then waved something off his forehead. "God 'mighty, these bugs!"

A cloud of gnats flew straight into us, so thick I could feel them on my lips and in my eyes. I tried to blink them away, swatting the air uselessly as they swarmed my face.

"Let's get out of here." Jerry laughed, pushing the throttle forward. "These things will eat you alive." The boat picked up speed, the wind finally starting to scatter the bugs.

In no time, I could already make out the shape of Tylerton's dock. Long and narrow, stretching out over the water with its greenish pilings. A few elegant Cape Cod–style homes with wide porches and dormer windows faced the bay, alongside cottage bungalows and tall skinny houses with steep roofs. Jerry told me this settlement was named after his tenth great-grandfather, John Tyler. *Tyler-town.* The way Jerry said it, any *w* was muffled and what was left just a flat, quick *uhn* sound, almost like he closed his mouth before finishing the word.

"Like for the mountains, we say *meh-unt'n*," he explained. "Oh, and we talk backward too! If I see a real pretty girl, I'll say, 'Damn, she ain't purty none.' That means she is."

I smiled. "And everyone understands, including her?"

"Well, yeah. You don't want to say that to a strange girl." We both laughed.

He taught me some other phrases as we walked along the waterfront. "Ain't hardly a little one," which you'd say when you pulled in a big crab. Or "I ain't done that never," meaning you definitely have. Some local words too: *yarney* for a friend, *yarneyin'* for chatting, *nary* for none, *pokin'* for moving slow.

"Hey," Jerry said, surprised. "That's one of my best friends in the world!"

In the shade of a tree sat a golf cart with a small wagon hitched behind. The driver looked like a copy of Jerry—similar cap and aviator glasses and a similar mustache, just a tad more pruned up. Beside him sat a woman whose face I couldn't quite see in the shade.

"What are you doing, Danny?" Jerry called out.

"What are you doing, Jerry?" the man hollered back.

It was the intro to a conversation that'd been going for close to four hundred years, I figured, as normal as air.

"I thought that was you, but I weren't sure, Jerry," Danny said, his drawl so thick he rolled the vowels together until the whole sentence sounded like one long word. Jerry had warned me that as close as Smith Island's towns were, folks from each had a slightly different way of talking.

"Hello, ma'am," I said. The woman seated beside Danny wore glasses, her gray hair pulled back, her posture small but lively.

"That's Ida," Danny started to say, when she cut him off with mock sternness.

"Don't call me ma'am!"

"She ain't purty none," I offered quickly, and the men broke into laughter. "That's better, right?" I added.

"He's learning!" She giggled.

"Ida, you're waiting for the freighter boat to come in?" Jerry asked.

"Uh-huh." She nodded, then turned toward me. "I deliver the medicines and packages here on Tylerton. Pick 'em up at the dock and drive around in the golf cart and deliver to homes." Which didn't sound all that difficult, until she added, "I'm legally blind. I can't see your face, so I couldn't tell what you look like."

"You're not missing out," I said, and she laughed.

I was starting to like this place's rogue behavior.

* * *

As Jerry and I ambled down the narrow gravel roads of Tylerton, the main street barely wider than a bike path, our conversation turned more personal.

"I'm sure single life's a little bit hard out here," I said.

"Yeah, not really." Jerry smiled, a little mysterious, some mischievous pirate energy peeking through. "They stumble around once in a while. Not very often, maybe every two years."

"Ladies from the mainland?"

His last girlfriend was from Pennsylvania, he said. She moved out to Smith Island for a few months, but her kids weren't wild about the place.

Our feet eventually brought us back to the dock, the whisper of a south wind rippling the water's surface as we motored out into the bay. The lowering sun had turned the shallows a deeper shade of jade. Jerry eased back on the throttle, then cut it completely, and we drifted along the flat, marshy banks.

"Right here, the Maryland–Virginia line cuts straight across the island," he said. Which could be convenient for shopkeepers back in the day. "They would build half the store in Maryland and half the store in Virginia. That way if there's anything illegal going on either side, they just shove it into the other state. And I've actually heard about back in a long time ago, there'd be men wanted from Maryland or Virginia, and they would coy 'em into the store. And then a bunch of men would push the wanted man over into the state that he's wanted in." Oyster thieves, mostly, he said.

Even if you've lived around the Chesapeake your whole life, the Oyster Wars, I'm sure, still sound half-mythical. From about 1865 to the late 1950s, conflicts between state authorities and oyster dredgers were common. Both Maryland and Virginia were locked in separate but overlapping conflicts with watermen: a long-running turf war over the Chesapeake Bay's oyster beds. Watermen from each state poached in the other's waters, raided reefs at night, and dredged illegally on the richest grounds. Maryland formed an armed Oyster Navy to enforce its oyster laws, while Virginia operated its own patrol boats to police harvesting in its waters, sometimes leading to tense confrontations on the bay. There were shootouts, rammings, arrests. Neighbors suddenly became trespassers.

Not that Smith Island was entirely populated by rowdy types. I'd heard it was a dry island, after all.

"People make moonshine?" I asked Jerry.

"Uh, I did once," he said, mustache curling up with a chuckle. "A little bit. But no . . . people bring alcohol from the mainland."

Jerry reached for the cooler, popped open an icy-cold can of Mountain Dew, and eased his hand onto the throttle. The boat started forward, parting the water in slow, even ripples.

"The people who came here," he said, reminiscing now. "They were poor. These people were very, *very* poor, but I believe they were willing to put up with the poverty for the freedom." Things had changed since then. "I make more money in a day than my parents made in a week."

"But still that tune carries on?" I asked. "You're not out here to get rich?"

"Nobody ever became a waterman to get rich." He laughed.

"So that's your priority in life, you want your freedom?"

"Yeah. And I think America's always worked . . ." He shook his head, started again. "Why it worked was because you had this push and pull from either side . . . and it kind of kept us centered. Not going crazy this way or that way. But now people have just . . ." He let that thought go too. "It's like football teams," he said. "It's like, 'I'm gonna overlook everything my side does just to support my side.'"

"So you're not on a side, Jerry?"

"Nope," he said. "I've voted Republican, I've voted Democrat. I vote for the person I think's got the most intelligence. I don't want 'em to tell me what I want to hear. I want 'em to do what I think they should be doing. Personally, I think we all want the same thing."

I nodded.

"We all want a nice life," he said. "We want our children to thrive, we want to thrive. That's it. We want to be left alone to do what we want to do. We don't want to be overregulated, we don't want to be overtaxed, we just want to live . . . just want to live without somebody telling you what to do every five minutes."

He bumped up the speed, shaking his head, like he was ready to get back to looking for crabs and arrowheads.

Farther out, beyond the shallows and grass beds, the water was deepening into a glassy sapphire blue. A lone pelican coasted alongside us, wingtips brushing close to the water. Another shape began to rise on the horizon—at first just a pale smudge against the blue, then the white outline of a double-decker ferry, its wake rolling behind in long, even swells. Jerry angled our boat toward it, waving energetically.

"This is the school boat!" he shouted over the engine's rumble. "This is the boat the children take to Crisfield every morning at six a.m. My son's on that boat right there. He should be about the third seat up."

"*That* is the public school bus out here?"

"That is the public school bus." His face softened into a wide smile.

"How many kids going to school?"

"Three."

"They run that boat for three kids?"

"Mm-hmm."

He didn't see his son. "Probably asleep," he said. "They all got their own pillow and blanket, and when they get on the boat, they go to sleep. They sleep for the ride over in the morning and sleep for the ride back in the evening."

"'Cause they're getting up so early?"

"Yeah."

As we followed beside the school boat making its way back toward the shoreline, I thought of all the resources—the driver, the boat, the fuel—that the Somerset County Board of Education was spending for just a few kids. What a gift to live in a country able to offer opportunities like that.

"Just be careful when the sea comes," Jerry warned, easing off the throttle as the ferry turned toward Ewell. "Okay, watch out here, gonna be a little . . ."

I braced as the bow dipped, water splashing up in the first heavy bump of the wake. Jerry steered us into a narrow channel, headed back toward Rhodes Point.

"Here's the boat I work on," he said as we glided past the docks. "*Miss Betty.*" She sat tied in a row of other crabbing boats, her white glossy hull catching our reflection.

"How many of you guys are still here on the island?" I asked.

"Altogether, there might be twenty watermen on this island."

"That's it?"

Jerry nodded. There'd been a hundred when he got his start, but, he said, "every time they make a regulation"—time of day limits, net or trap limits, even rules on what types of fishing equipment could be used—"it kind of pushes out a few crabbers, because there's always a few living on the margin." It was one of those jobs where you made your money during the season and then lived off that money when times got lean. "And when he's gone," Jerry said, "the crab buyers say, 'Oh, we lost another waterman or two. We gotta bump up the price.' But the price never gets bumped up before we lose a few more watermen."

I asked if the younger generation seemed interested in crabbing.

"There's one boy over here, he's my son's age," Jerry said. "I think he might go to the water, but that's because his dad, and his grandfather and all, are still working on the water . . . but he's the only one."

"So how are people gonna eat crabs?" I asked.

"That's a good question. But you know how that is. As soon as there's a gold rush, people come in in a hurry. If the crabs come back and the price is right, people will get back into it."

"But your son isn't following your footsteps?"

"I wouldn't think so," he said. "He's really smart, so I want him to do something with his mind."

"You don't want him crabbing?"

"It's too poor," he said. "I don't mind it, but, you know . . ."

I thought back to my time in Appalachia talking to fifth-generation coal miner families who felt the same: a pride in their ability to bring something useful to society, but also a desire for their kids to do something different, something better for the body, better for finances. That forty-five-minute ride across the bay each morning was probably the first step toward a future on the mainland. And unlike Booker T, if this island really will be underwater within seventy-five years, Jerry's son might not be coming back.

* * *

We were back at Jerry's place. Through the open door, I could hear him moving around inside—doors creaking, something clattering, the dull thud of boxes being shifted. He'd warned me his place was a mess and told me to wait out by the shanty while he got things together. The air was still and buggy, the only other sound water lapping under the dock.

The shanty was Jerry's man cave on the water, packed with years of accumulated fishing rods, coolers, and tools. He came back loaded down like he was running a one-man restaurant—a large plastic lid off a trash can in one hand, a bag of steamed crabs in the other, a roll of paper towels and a bottle of vinegar squeezed under the arm.

"Fresh-caught?" I asked, taking a quick peek into the bag.

"Fresh-caught," he said, setting the lid on two milk crates. A waterman's dining room table. He laid the bag on top and opened it to reveal a pile of large reddish crabs. "Blue crab's the best crab, just about."

We dragged a couple of seats across the floor. They looked like they'd been rescued from different lives: his an old office swivel with one arm missing, mine a car seat pulled from a van.

"The people in DC or around the country at nice restaurants are eating crabs from here?" I asked.

"Oh yeah," he said. "They go right to DC, every crab we catch."

I thought about this supply chain, like so many that keep the country going—rural and urban worlds dependent on one another for survival in indirect and unconscious ways.

Jerry got to work, pulling a crab mallet from the table beside him. He picked up a crab and held it up so I could see. "Cut the face off it, cut the dead man off, cut the legs off." He coached me with mechanical precision, dropping the scraps into a plastic bucket. "This is how my mother taught me how to do it. I watched her do that for years and years."

"You put it in vinegar?" I asked as he dropped the lump of tender meat into a bowl.

"Oh yeah, that's the way I like it."

"You mind if I go no vinegar?"

"Either way you want," he said. "There's no wrong way of doing it." Back in Colonial days, people would make crab stew, crab pudding, crab pie.

"People don't understand that we rarely eat crabs," Jerry said, the sound of breaking shells filling the pauses between words. "I might eat crabs two times a year. Oysters once or twice. Like a nephew of mine said, when he grew up, they ate crabs because that was a meal." Not a delicacy, just the only thing you could afford when you didn't have money for the store.

The meat was soft and sweet, with a hint of salt from the bay. Simple and perfect.

"See," I said, reaching for more. "I could eat this all day long."

Jerry laughed. "Ain't it good?"

"So good."

Jerry smiled, certain of it. After almost four hundred years of his family working these waters, he knew Smith Island had the best crabs and oysters around.

For the grand finale, Jerry brought out a heavy paper box.

"The cake!" I said, excited, eyeing the chocolate icing and stack of thin layers—nine, maybe ten in all. I've always loved good chocolate.

"Not just a cake," he said, lowering his voice. "The Smith Island Cake." A proud smile emerged.

He cut me a slice, the icing parting softly under the knife. "The story of this cake is, back in the probably late 1800s, early 1900s, the women would make this cake for their husbands on the dredge boats. They would go away in October and come back in December. So it was a couple months and the wives would send 'em with these cakes because they're moist and the fudge icing layers on it would hold the moisture in. That way they could keep it on the boat, something from home they could have for a few weeks. And that's how the cake started."

The chocolate was warm, dark, and a little caramelly, the soft yellow cake buttery, spongy, and faintly sweet—that perfect amount in old recipes with just enough sweetness to satisfy but not overwhelm.

I started thanking Jerry for everything he'd shared with me, everything he knew about this place.

"That's a curse," he said, laughing. "Some people forget it and they're all happy, but I don't forget anything in life. Our stories here are as long as we are."

I wondered, briefly, what would happen to those stories when Smith Island was gone. For generations, the people here had stared down disappearing shorelines, rising tides, the slow erosion of the place they called home with a stoic acceptance I'd come to see as beautiful. I didn't sense any anxiety in Jerry for what the future might bring. There was no trying to stop where things were going. That future was coming—and worrying about it wouldn't change a thing.

I thought back to what Eric at Blue Ox Millworks had told me, standing in his shrine to the redwoods, about our being a nation of problem-solvers. It's easy to take pride in that, pride in our courage to fight for a different future. But I wonder sometimes if we have a harder time as Americans finding the serenity to accept those things we cannot change. To acknowledge our powerlessness in the face of forces larger than any human.

That was what I so admired about a man like Jerry. He didn't seem hung up on what he'd lost. He'd found peace and gratitude in a time of uncertainty, knowing that all he could do—all any of us can do—is to enjoy the life he has for as long as he is able . . . and to then let the future course ever onward.

CHAPTER 8

The Hamptons

Just a few hours northeast of Manhattan, at the far eastern tip of Long Island, another set of men go out to sea before sunrise. Their boats are smaller than the luxury yachts docked a few piers over; their hands tell a different story than the ones holding Aperol spritzes in July. Most visitors will never see them, because nobody comes to the Hamptons looking for people who start their day before the after-parties end.

When people said *the Hamptons*, I used to imagine champagne, linen shirts, starched white tablecloths, the sounds of twirling blades overhead as a weekend helicopter shuttled Manhattanites to their second, third, or fourth homes. But there are men here who rise and sleep by the marine forecasts and speak the language of catch quotas and dock prices. They live in some of the wealthiest zip codes in America and yet are the spiritual kin of Smith Island's watermen. There's always been a fishing economy in the seaside communities up and down the Eastern Seaboard. But there's also another economy here in the Hamptons—the summer economy, the weekenders whose arrival turns the whole region into a different world.

The Hamptons is a place forever balancing two versions of itself, sometimes in harmony, sometimes with friction. Like so many other regions of America, this is a place of layered, diverging identities, and standing in the middle of it, you can feel the tug from both sides, each insisting it belongs here just as much as the other.

* * *

Jimmy lifted a heavy bucket of old fish into the back of his truck and slammed the tailgate shut. I was at his surfboard repair shed in Montauk, a hamlet within the larger town of East Hampton, way out at the eastern tip of Long Island's South Fork. The shed doubled as the staging ground for his fishing operation: traps, buckets, buoys, miscellaneous everything lying around in amounts that a lifetime fisherman might collect in these parts. It had been just three months since my visit to Smith Island; being around all this fishing gear made me oddly nostalgic.

Bolted to the back of Jimmy's truck was a surfboard spanning the width of the tailgate. It was chewed off on the top and side like a shark had gotten it, red paint tracing where the teeth "sank" in. DING REPAIR WHY YOU WAIT was scrawled between the two shark bites. FISH, LOBSTER 4SALE and BEST, FASTEST, SURF THEORY were written across other parts of the board.

Jimmy told me he's been surfing for a little over sixty years, starting as a kid and never drifting far from the life that came with it: lobstering, sea bass trapping, gill netting. He said we had to "hit the dumps" first, then he'd cruise me around and show me the Hamptons he knew. I laughed to myself, thinking about starting a video of one of the bougiest places in America at the dumps. We definitely wouldn't be going for a North Korea tour, the type where the government shows you only the nicest things. I was in for a real local dive.

Jimmy jumped into the truck with a youthful ease. He wore a faded Patagonia fleece over a T-shirt, ankle boots with tall socks, and shorts—standard gear for a cool and cloudy summer day. He had an unmistakably outdoorsman look: sun-tanned skin, wind-ruffled gray hair, and a short mustache that looked like a big part of his identity.

"I love the dump," he said as we pulled out onto a two-lane road, oaks tangled in thick vines crowding in from both sides. "If you ever need anything, you just come here."

He had that old-school New York accent that reminded me of my father and his Silent Generation Italian Hoboken roots. Saturday-morning *caw-fee.* Every sentence animated, delivered for maximum impact. Hand gestures all over the place, almost like, without the motions as an accessory, the language wouldn't work.

"For instance," Jimmy went on as we pulled into the recycling center, "if the cord on a lawn mower breaks, they throw it to the dumps. You know, it's a nice one, and you bring it home, you put a new cord in it, and it works great. God knows what could be in here."

He pulled up behind one of the bulk-drop sections, a smirk running through the lines on his face like he'd made a big find. "Look at these grills!"

The weather had turned wet. Raindrops slid off a polished steel six-burner Kenmore that had to be worth six hundred bucks, easy. You could see the area's wealth in the quality of its disposables. Beside the grill was a lawn mower with its cord cut clean off (just like Jimmy predicted), a couple of fridges, a washing machine, and a water heater. It was like a pound for dogs and cats, only for household objects trying to find a new owner.

"Cool, huh?" Jimmy said, eyeing the Kenmore. Then he

paused, the excitement dropping out of him. "I'm not taking it," he said, firm now. "I've taken too much crap in my life." There was an obvious internal battle going on, seeing so much high-end Hamptons "junk" but just not having the space for any more of it.

He grunted as he hauled the fish bucket out from the truck and emptied it into the open trash pit.

* * *

"You probably heard this one—'Montauk's a little drinking town with a fishing problem,'" Jimmy said as we headed out along the coast, humble mansions (built for aesthetics, not just sheer square footage) sliding past with soaked-through lawns and perfectly rounded shrubs lined up like rows of disciplined poodles. Jimmy wasn't a trim-it-up-and-keep-it-orderly type. I looked around his truck. There were notebooks stacked on his dashboard, a layer of dust left from probably the summer of '84, stuff everywhere.

"It's always been a fishing community," he told me. "And Carl Fisher"—the man behind a bunch of Florida development in the 1920s—"had visions of grandeur of making this place into another Miami Beach. I think he died broke. But my grandparents fell in love with this place, and they bought a couple homes in the early fifties, for seven grand apiece."

"Wow."

"Seven grand apiece," he repeated with a shrug, "and they'd come out here every summer. And when I was old enough, my parents shipped me out here." He'd grown up on the Upper West Side of Manhattan, back when that neighborhood was still middle-class. "They'd put me on the train in Bay Shore"—about halfway down Long Island, not far from cookie-cutter suburban developments like Levittown that'd seemed like the next big thing in those postwar years—"and tell the conductors to keep an eye on me. And when the train stopped, it was the end of the road. Loved it." His gray mustache stretched into a wide smile. "It was spectacular out here back then."

Already, this place's divisions were starting to break down a little in my mind. I'd seen this migration pattern before, people coming out for a summer and evolving into locals. In Lake Tahoe, where I'd lived for seven years, it was quite common to hear "I'm just coming out for one ski season," and the one turning into twenty or life.

Downtown Montauk came into view—a crowded stretch of surf shops, delis, breakfast joints, and bait counters. Pickup trucks nosed into angled parking spots. Sandy flip-flops scratched against the asphalt, and someone jogged across the street, hoodie up, a paper cup of coffee in hand.

"See that big building?" A seven-story brown-and-cream brick tower rose above the rooflines, fussy little decorative peaks at the top. "They call it the White Elephant. That's what Carl Fisher made. He built that and had all his investors go up to the top, and from there they'd pick out their properties." He poked at the air with his finger. "'*I want it from there to there, and here to here, and this and that.*'"

This would have been back around 1926, by which point the Hamptons had already been drawing in the moneyed for years. In the late 1800s, New York's industrial and banking families began drifting east by rail, looking for clean ocean air and a summer break from the city's crowds. The first grand shingle-style "cottages" went up in Southampton and East Hampton around the turn of the century, sprawling mansions built by families whose names would make up the table of contents of a book on America's Gilded Age. The artists came next—painters, writers, architects—people chasing space rather than status, and yet who inadvertently made the place even more desirable, bringing a certain cultural allure. By the 1920s and 1930s, the Hamptons had become a retreat for Manhattan's elite in a seasonal migration pattern so entrenched that whole social calendars were built around it.

Today, the economy of this stretch of Long Island runs on a mix of year-round work and seasonal surges. The backbone is still local: a hospital, schools, construction, small businesses, a few part-time commuters into New York City. But from Memorial Day to Labor Day, hotels, restaurants, souvenir shops, charter boats, landscapers, seasonal rentals—all swing into high gear. The Hamptons, Fire Island, and (farther up the Atlantic Coast) Martha's Vineyard and Nantucket all operate on this rhythm: slow winters, explosive summers, and a lot of people working two or three side gigs to surf the economic wave while it's there. One strong season could float the entire service-based community for the whole offseason, and those paychecks would mostly stay in town. They'd circle back into the auto shops, the supermarkets, the barbers—the places that survived on locals once the crowds disappeared. If the season held, the town held too. If it didn't—if the weather turned, or a bad economy had even the 1 percent feeling skittish—everything tightened at once, and people waited for the next wave of tourists to show up and reset the cycle.

"When did you move here full time?" I asked Jimmy. "How old were you?"

"Twenty-two, twenty-three," he said, part of a whole tribe of young'uns back in the day. "We came out for one reason and that was to surf, but we had to find a way to live."

The road ahead straightened out, revealing a mix of large homes and little beach bungalows.

"I became a fisherman. A lot of friends became carpenters. Very successful carpenters, and very successful fishermen."

He turned down a dirt road, the truck swinging as it sank into potholes and puddles. A gray stripe of the Atlantic opened up ahead, ripply and restless.

"Back in the day when it was first open, it was all just tents," he said. ("It was all dirt, and surf bums, and everybody was in free love," he'd tell me later.) "Then they got rid of the tents and put the trailers in. And back then you could buy a trailer for fifteen, seventeen thousand bucks, in the late seventies. Now they've built them up, refurbished them, did all this, and a trailer on the water in the first row sold for . . . you ready?"

Jimmy shot me a look, building the suspense. "Three million!" He burst out laughing. "You know what they use 'em for? For after they go surfing. They change out of their wetsuits, and take a shower, and leave their surfboards here. Go back to the regular home."

"Does that bum you out as a local?" I asked.

"No, no." Jimmy just shook his head. "More power to them. I don't care."

I asked if there was a divide between the folks here with serious wealth and people like him.

"There is negativity," Jimmy said. "Some people are really upset, and pissed off at this and that." He waved it off. "Who cares? These people worked hard, they made their money. If I was in that position, I'd probably do the same thing. Why not? The only difference is that the locals live here all year round. Where these people, they just come out here on the weekends or something like that. It's kind of like, 'Who's luckier? Us or them?'"

He gave a quick nod, like the question had only one possible answer. "We are."

* * *

"I used to own a house," Jimmy said as we drove north and turned onto a dirt road, the grapevine canopy acting like a living fence for oceanside manors with wide lots and cedar shingles not yet weathered silver-gray. "But I got divorced and, you know, *pfft*—lost that." His wife sold the house, and Jimmy took his share and "bought land in Costa Rica. But I'll never be able to afford a home here. Never."

He was renting now. "The rents are, like, cuckoo," he told me. "Five thousand a month can't even find a place to live." Jimmy told me he had affordable housing in Amagansett, where you could qualify with an income between $32,000 and $110,000; he was right in the middle of that range. Without affordable housing, he said, it would be impossible for him to live out here. But the town knew that and was working on it. Jimmy said they'd just built a couple more low-income developments, one with thirty-six units and another with fifty.

A moment later he slowed beside a narrow drive disappearing into a wall of green. "You know Julian Schnabel?" A painter and filmmaker. "He lives down there. He's a good friend of mine. I fix all his boards too. Real nice guy. Real down-to-earth guy." That was the thing about Montauk. "It's very low-key out here. The people want to blend in. If celebrities come out here to be recognized, you came to the wrong place. No one really gives a shit. You're a nice person, you're a nice person."

I believed it. I could see Jimmy showing up at a famous

person's home to do a ding repair on their kid's surfboard and being exactly the same guy he was everywhere else. When a wealthy-looking family walking along the side of the road waved him down because the son's shoe was falling apart, he'd produced a knife to cut off the bottom part, offered to throw it out for them, and then joked jovially that the son now had "no sole." People often get weird about class in a place like this, either intimidated by the wealth or trying to prove something. But Jimmy didn't operate that way. He had the confidence of a man living exactly the life he wanted. I've always observed that when someone is fired up about their life and honest about who they are, most people respect them, no matter how much or how little money they have.

The road narrowed under the canopy, the vine's leaves swinging in the wind like a living tunnel. A break in the brush revealed a small reed-filled pond where Jimmy used to hunt ducks as a kid. Farther along, the brush thinned and the land opened into broad fields and old wooden fence lines. Jimmy motioned toward a weathered gray barn that matched the color of the sky.

"This is the first cattle ranch in America. This ranch"—he punctuated it with a point of his finger—"right here."

"Montauk?"

"Look, it says right there." He nodded toward the tall metal gate with a DEEP HOLLOW RANCH sign hanging from its welded crossbar: OLDEST CATTLE RANCH IN THE USA ESTABLISHED 1658.

"It's still operating?"

It was. "It's really cool," Jimmy said. "America's freakin' great."

I nodded. There really wasn't a better way to say it. The more I travel the country, the more I realize it *is* freaking great, and a lot of that comes from how it keeps refusing easy labels. You peel one layer back and there's another underneath, and then another. There was something comforting in that: knowing that even a place as "obvious" from the outside as the Hamptons still had so much more to it that those of us who live elsewhere just . . . rarely get a chance to know.

"You know who commissioned that?" Jimmy snapped me out of my thoughts as we approached the Montauk Point Lighthouse, the tower striped white-and-brown, a black lantern room perched above like a small crown.

"Who?"

"George Washington."

We hopped out of the truck and walked toward the cliff's edge, shielding our faces from the whipping wind. Jimmy still managed to light a cigarette, cupping the flame with his hand.

"In World War II, they used to have gun turrets all around here," he said, the smoke blown away in a blink. "Big cannons. See the old radar?"

In the distance, a massive AN/FPS-35 steel antenna rose above the trees, a 1960s long-range radar capable of tracking aircraft more than two hundred miles out. Jimmy said that growing up, the radar sweep would catch their rabbit-ear antennas and make the TV pop a little *neep* on every pass.

There was a surprising amount of World War II history here. In June 1942, a German U-boat dropped four plainclothes saboteurs on Amagansett's shore—members of Operation Pastorius, a Nazi plan to attack American factories, railroads, and infrastructure. A coast guardsman reported the men, and all four were caught carrying explosives, cash, and forged papers. It was strange to think of something so lethal sneaking onto this serene shoreline not that long ago.

"Lot of shipwrecks along this coast," Jimmy went on. The

land dropped straight into the Atlantic in sharp ribbons, like a giant sandcastle left to harden in the wind. The ocean rolled in heavy and gray, each wave hitting the rocky shore with a dull thud.

Not all the wrecks were accidents. "That cliff over there"—he motioned to one farther out. Out there, "local pirates would pretend there was a lighthouse and have fires. It's called the False Point. Ships would come in, and run aground, and they'd loot 'em . . ."

We stood there for a moment, breathing in the cold, salty air. Jimmy took another drag on his cigarette, which burned down fast with the professionalism of his inhale and the steady breeze.

"I didn't expect to see this at all here in the Hamptons," I said, tracing the white break of the waves along the wild, empty beach. "Nature like this. I had no clue."

"It's spectacular." Jimmy squinted into the wind, his gray hair whipping around.

"Spectacular, yeah."

I pictured the Hamptons in full bloom. Low, hardy wild roses and beach plums hanging from the edges of the dunes. Small families of piping plovers running up as waves receded to peck at the wet sand, only to dart away as the water rushed back toward shore. Dolphins arcing into the air, sharks, sea turtles riding the currents underneath. If you were patient, you might even see the distant rise of migrating humpback whales, creatures who'd been passing by the Hamptons long before any human.

The place had soul, I was realizing—one of America's fanciest enclaves fitting right in with the hundreds of other pockets that make this country so interesting. In Springs, Parsons

Blacksmith Shop still rings with the renewed sounds of hammer on anvil. In East Hampton, the old Hook Windmill, built around 1800, has been restored to working order. All around us were rebel holdouts against progress: clapboard houses with weathered shingles, old cemeteries, churches where the same families have worshipped for generations. The Hamptons had a long memory, the past fading but still stubbornly holding on.

* * *

As we left the Atlantic behind, the road looped west and then north toward the opposite end of Montauk. On the way toward the harbor—the working-waterfront side of town—Jimmy slowed as we passed a grand half-timber Tudor building on the hill: Montauk Manor, its steep gables watching over us somewhat eerily.

Jimmy paused. "You believe in ghosts?"

"I believe in spirits, sure," I said. It was hard not to after Saint Lawrence Island.

"I think I see them every now and then where I live," he said. "See these—*pfft*—these things. I don't know what the eff they are." He kept driving. "You know, like Frank Zappa said, 'Mind is like a parachute, it only works if it's open.'"

Farther down the road, the humid salt air picked up the faint smell of diesel and bait. Gosman's Dock sat at the edge of an inlet, a collection of fish shacks and weather-beaten walkways. Charter boats rocked against the pilings, the commercial fleet tied up farther back. Men moved around in foul-weather gear. Seagulls hovered low, waiting for handouts.

"As long as I've been coming out here, since the fifties, this dock has been here," Jimmy said.

"So, still pulling a lot of fish?"

"Oh yeah, look at all the draggers."

We pulled up to the very edge of the wooden dock and climbed out of the truck. The dock's planks were soft and darkened with the years, each step giving a tired creak. Ropes wrapped around the pilings like old vines, slick with moss. The fishing boats rocked in place, buoys swinging against the hulls, a few American flags flapping in the wind—the whole place alive with the clink of metal and the slap of water under the boards.

"You know all these guys?" I nodded toward a hand-painted sign nailed to one of the pilings: THANK MY GRAMPA, HE CATCHES YOUR SEAFOOD. Blackfish, sea bass, porgies, tuna, mahi-mahi . . . there was a lot living in these waters. Lobster, scallops, and squid were good money too.

"Yeah. They are working their asses off," Jimmy said. "We have a saying: *What would you do if you won a million bucks?* You go, 'I'd keep fishing till all the money was gone.'"

"This guy"—he pointed at one of the working boats—"guy's named Anthony, and his friend Johnny. They fish offshore. Lobsters thirty, forty, fifty miles off the beach. And they take watches going out. One guy steers, the other guy is asleep. And see these coolers?"

I glanced at the three big boxes on the boat, meant to hold hundreds of pounds of catch.

"They had them all sacked up, and he was moving one and the handle broke, and he didn't have this transom here, and he went over the stern. Went off the boat. Boat kept on going. The other captain was asleep." Jimmy paused, his eyes wide. "He's floating, watching the boat go away. Gone . . . just gone. And he was treading water for I don't know how long. See those poly balls, those balls?"

Two oversized foam floats hung off the rails, used to mark the location of lobster traps.

"He found a lobster buoy out there and untied 'em or something and took his boots off and put 'em under his armpits. You know, with air in 'em"—Jimmy mimicked the motion, lifting his elbows like he was tucking the boots in—"and he was able to float. And they found him. It was a miracle. Finally, a good story: Somebody lived."

We hopped back in the truck and set off southbound, where in just a half hour, on the outskirts of the village of East Hampton, the landscape around us began to change. Big stretches of acreage opened up—manicured lawns laid out like football fields in front of old manors. We passed houses sealed off behind eight- or ten-foot hedges, only their rooftops poking out above the tall green walls. "There's rich and there's wealth," he'd tell me later. This was wealth: a glimpse of a tennis court through the hedges, a slate-roofed pool house that could pass for a starter home anywhere else.

"That might be, and don't quote me on this, Alec Baldwin's house," Jimmy said, nodding toward the gray shingled mansion sitting way out on the property, the grass cut into long, runway-straight lines pointing right at the porch. "He's got ten acres he's trying to sell. He was asking twenty-six; I think he's down to twenty or nineteen mil."

Down the road, Jimmy took a left into Two Mile Hollow Beach, where a parking lot that could hold a couple hundred cars easily sat mostly empty. He climbed out of the truck, a gust of wind whooshing into the cab. Sand skidded across the asphalt. There wasn't a person in sight except for an ATV that rattled by and a lifeguard who jogged up from the beach, knit hat on, shirt off, football in hand. His name was Kevin Bunce, and he told me he grew up on the island, played sports at East Hampton High. And in his twenty-one years he had seen the place change fast.

"You in college, or . . ." Jimmy asked.

"I'm a dropout. I left," Kevin said, shaking a little from the cold.

"Good man," Jimmy said, giving an approving nod. "You'll make much more money."

"Absolutely." Kevin flashed a perfect, white-toothed smile.

"To hell with it," Jimmy said like a rebelliously proud father.

"As long as I keep reading my books," Kevin added, "I'll be okay."

With nobody wanting to get into the raging ocean, he had time to kill, so he didn't mind taking a few minutes to talk about how life had been treating the young guys out here.

"Winter's pretty tough," he told me. "It's that New England humid cold air coming on to you. But the money's here to be made, and if you just show up, you go to work, you smile—things are gonna happen, you know?"

"Okay, what's happening for you?" I asked. We'd wandered down to the beach while Jimmy holed up in his truck, doing paperwork and returning calls for repairs.

"Well, one, this is the best job ever." He nodded toward the lifeguard tower, where an American flag snapped sideways in the wind. "Private lifeguarding, swim lessons, surf lessons. You get in with that, you're making a lot of money, and that's just your summer gig. In the winter, you pick up a trade." Together with a few buddies, he'd also begun a small creative project that started with a heat press in a bedroom and grew into a local collective.

Avery, one of the crew, wandered over after finishing a private surfing lesson, eager to explain the rest. They made their own shirts and hoodies in a tiny shop in Springs, printing surf breaks, old boats, horseshoe crabs, anything they felt reflected the lifestyle. They called it BIGHOUSE after a surfing spot where a modest little house once stood—the biggest around back then, long before the Hamptons became the land of actual big houses.

The two of them reminded me a bit of me. With too much energy to sit in class, I'd dropped out of college at twenty and moved to the mountains to snowboard all day and wait tables at night, the only measurement that mattered was how many runs I could get in before the slopes closed and how good I could get at the sport. I understood the appeal, especially for young people, of organizing your life around living rather than working in an office. It wasn't laziness or lack of ambition, just different priorities.

I noticed how easy Kevin and Avery were to talk to: cordial, open, solid eye contact, no phone in hand. They were curious about what I was doing and carried this relaxed vibe that felt rare these days with guys of that vintage.

"This is gonna sound silly to you guys," I started, "but a lot of people live online and see the world through their phone or computer. So they think a lot of young men are more depressed. On devices all the time, sitting in mom's basement. You guys are sort of disproving that."

"If that's your reality, you're not actually doing anything," Avery said. "You're just watching other people do stuff. It's really important to do stuff yourself, 'cause finishing goals, even if it's just like going surfing with your buddies . . ."

"Making shirts!" Kevin laughed. "Doing your thing—"

"Even that." Avery nodded, laughing. "You just feel better."

They started telling me about their friend group.

"All of our dads grew up and knew each other back in the day, so we're like the second gen, you know?" Avery said. "My dad grew up in Montauk, and my Grandpa Ray actually opened up the first surf shop in Montauk in the early seventies."

As the weather started to clear, people were gathering on the beach—kids, teens, parents—flip-flops shuffling, boards knocking together, towels tossed over shoulders, someone biting into a sandwich while a football cut back and forth across a group.

Kevin and Avery's boss, Bruce, came on over. He looked to be maybe in his late thirties.

"We want to preserve this lifestyle," he told me. "Keep it pure and keep it clean."

"Is there a problem here in the Hamptons with that?"

"Well, Georgica Pond is completely trashed."

Avery nodded. "All these very wealthy people who live around it pump their grass . . ."

"Fertilizers," Kevin added. "Herbicides, pesticides."

"It's nice to kill ticks and everything," Avery went on, "but all that seeps into the pond, and they open the cut and it goes into the ocean where we all surf."

"You can't swim," Bruce said. "It's like toxic algae blooms."

Kevin motioned toward the dunes, low mounds of sand with coarse beachgrass and scruffy patches of sedge fighting their way through. "There's wildflowers up the sides of these paths. It is so biodiverse here, and since COVID especially all those corners of land, where he lives"—he looked at Avery—"where I live, they clear-cut the whole thing."

"All these old cedars," Avery added. "All these beautiful birches . . ."

It was such a contrast to my earlier conversation with Jimmy. He'd seemed almost unfazed by the waves of outsiders rolling through the Hamptons each summer. But talking with Kevin and Avery, I heard an edge I hadn't before—a protective instinct. A tension.

"So is there a big divide between those that aren't out here full-time and those that are here full-time?" I asked.

"I feel like a lot of them are on our side," Kevin said. "They came out here 'cause they liked it."

"They like how quiet, how beautiful it is." Avery nodded. "If you look up and down the beaches here, there are no big hotels. It's not Atlantic City, you know? There are rules keeping it this way. There are no fast-food chains . . ."

"And they do respect the locals," Bruce said. "It's just they don't know. There are a few hardcore, real local jabronis, who harvest the pine needle for their testosterone and know you can eat the rosehips at a certain time of year around the beach and actually are true Long Island natives. And they actually have a relationship with the environment here. Most of the locals don't even have that relationship, but . . . it starts with those who care, and then it spreads from there."

I thought of Jimmy coming out here summers as a kid and ending up staying for life.

"And then there's kids like us who grew up here our whole life," Avery said, "and we're not gonna be able to buy property of our own unless we really do something big."

Though it was home, it sounded like they couldn't hope to claim a piece of it. Maybe eventually some of the guys in their crew would inherit a modest house from their parents. But for those without any sort of generational wealth, it'd be tough to get a foothold . . . a common story in many of the nicest zip codes across the country. I had this sudden flashback to a wealthy neighbor of mine in Tahoe, who told me that if I couldn't afford to buy a home there, then I should start making changes so that one day I could. I thought he was such an ass at the time for saying that. But in retrospect, that tough love helped me change the course of my life. I got out of a place with few opportunities outside of tourism, real estate, or construction, went back to college, and moved on.

"And we take these kids surfing," Bruce was saying, turning toward one of the boys hanging out nearby. "Charlie, is this your first time surfing today?"

"Second."

"Second time!" Bruce smiled. "He loves it. And we're healing the younger generation, because all these kids are on screens. We're structuring their unstructured time after school, weekends, summers. Getting them in the water. Building a love for the ocean. It's just a healthy lifestyle."

"Yeah, they're not anxious anymore," Kevin said.

"Once they have a love for the ocean," Bruce went on, "then they develop that desire to protect it and develop the responsibility. These kids are in junior lifeguard programs. They look up to these guys." He pointed at Kevin and Avery.

A loud rattle cut him off as a surfboard slid out of a truck bed and clattered to the ground.

"Oh, snap!" Kevin lunged toward it.

"I know a ding repair guy." I laughed, looking over at Jimmy, who was pulling a drag from a fresh cig, deep in his phone. They cracked up and moved to scoop the board up.

"Good tribe," Jimmy said, as I hopped back in his truck.

He had a bit of pride in his eye, like they were his own. Which, in a way, they were. The next generation was continuing the lifestyle, carrying the torch, and he was so happy to see it.

* * *

Easing out of Main Street traffic, bumper-to-bumper with Escalades and G-Wagons, Jimmy looked out the passenger window at the Old Colonial–style shopfronts. Gucci and Louis Vuitton were the names above the doors. He seemed like someone in a new land, trying to get his bearings. Here, the ocean salt mixed with expensive perfume—patchouli and vanilla, a warm woody cologne. Gold bracelets clicked, and oversized shopping bags rustled like soft sails.

"Some guys say, 'There's so many people . . . '" Jimmy scrunched his face and made a quick *pbpbpb* sound, mimicking the annoyed way they talk. "They don't like any of these people. I don't get it. I enjoy it all. I love looking at these people. It's the coolest freaking thing in the world. I was in the grocery store one time—packed—and I'm dressed the way I'm dressed. The lady went to me, 'You must not like it here with so many people.' I said, 'Are you kidding me? I love it.' In wintertime, it's nothing but a bunch of dirtbag fishermen here. Look at this. It's all beautiful women, nice people." He let out a short, amused breath. "What's there not to like?"

Just a few minutes north of town, the road opened onto a line of farms that felt almost too ordinary. Rows of potatoes sat in low mounds; corn rattled in the wind. Work vans and tractors were parked by the barns, mud baked onto their tires.

"All of these farmers are sitting on a gold mine," I said, rolling down the window and taking a deep breath of wet soil and green stems. "The next generation most likely won't farm and will carve it up and sell it, right?"

"Who knows? This land's worth millions," Jimmy said. "They've got these big vineyards now, and they do pretty well with that. I know this woman with a pretty damn big piece of property on the south side of the highway, and she has an apple orchard. She's young, late thirties maybe, and she keeps it going, having a wonderful life growing apples and making the best cider."

I smiled at the thought of a barefooted Brett pressing cider this close to New York City.

The farms ended just as quickly as they started, and small houses—packed in under low trees—took over both sides of the road. Weathered shingles, narrow driveways, boats propped on trailers. Yards that looked lived-in and worked in rather than landscaped, with lobster traps by the fence, coolers and bait buckets out by the sheds.

"This is a bubbyville or Bonacker area," Jimmy said. "They're fishermen. Baymen. They call 'em bubbies."

"You would never know," I said. We were still just minutes from the center of town.

"Right off the road. They call this Poseyville. Don't ask me why they named it that but . . . you notice he got his old clam rake up there?"

"Clam rake?" It was lying right on one of the roofs, a long-handled metal rake with a wide wire basket at the end, for dragging through the bay bottom to scoop up clams.

"Tong rake, they call that. The people who came here first—the Bennies, the Lessers, the Balls—they came here and they settled here. And the only way to make money was fishing and farming. Chickens and this and that. They've been here for hundreds and hundreds of years. And they got squeezed out. You know, a lot of their fishing rights have been taken away. It's sad. Very sad."

"What do you mean by their fishing rights?"

"Like see that boat right there? That's a haul seine boat. They launch them from the beach into the ocean in big surf. They used to set out these nets called haul seines." You'd throw a massive twine net in the water and then winch it back up. "They used to use horses and wagons, but now they have pickup trucks with caps on them. And the government said, 'Nope, no more haul seining. You can't haul seine.'"

This was back in the early '90s, another sorrow that hadn't lessened with time.

"There would be some fish that would die on the beach," Jimmy said, "or some skates, or some small striped bass. And people complain, 'Oh my God, you're killing the fish.' They completely freaked out, and they stopped them from doing it. They made the law no haul seining for striped bass. So they just cut out a big portion of their income. They tried to give 'em town jobs, and these guys, for the most part, aren't the most educated people around. Very sad. They're stopping a way of life."

I knew I didn't know too much about these local conflicts that stretched back decades, maybe even over a century. But I've seen what happens to pristine places with no regulation, and they usually get blown out with overdevelopment and a complete disregard for nature. Like Avery said back on Two Mile Hollow Beach, there were rules keeping the Hamptons beautiful. But regulate a place too much, and it starts to feel stifling. Like everything, there's probably a healthy balance somewhere in the middle. But the contradictions felt real here, and probably never fully resolvable. There were too many opinions, too many people vying for their own best version of the future.

* * *

As we came into Sag Harbor, the buildings around us started to rise a little higher, old trees throwing shade over two- and three-story storefronts with brick fronts or wood clapboard in soft blues and grays. Big bay windows held bookstores, antique shops, an Art Deco movie theater. Flower baskets and American flags hung off a few porches. Black cast-iron lampposts lined the streets. Beyond the roofs we could already see the masts from the marina, a forest of thin lines pointing into the sky. The air had that brackish harbor smell of seaweed and salt.

Jimmy pointed to a classic, gray-shingled house hung with bright, mismatched lobster buoys, giving it a playful, old-fishing-town feel. “I think that’s Billy Joel’s house.”

We drove through the few blocks of downtown, the traffic slow as people drifted between coffee shops and boutiques. It felt cozy, I said. “Everything is taken care of. There’s not one shabby-looking anything.”

“Not around here,” Jimmy replied.

An old whaling captain’s house sat behind a picket fence, white and stately, with tall windows, working shutters, and a front porch with columns carved in a tight spiral, like giant birthday candles. In the nineteenth century, this was one of the busiest whaling ports in the country, fortunes built on ships that sailed as far as the Pacific and Arctic seas. Jimmy told me old whaling houses used to have a widow’s watch up top, a rooftop platform where wives would look out for their husbands’ ships to come in, sometimes a year and a half after they’d left. “A lot of guys never made it home,” he said.

I thought of Saint Lawrence Island, where whaling's still a way of life—people living off the meat, the oil, even using the bones—while here, that was all a distant memory. *How cool*, I thought, *that this variation was possible*. One part of the country moving on, while the other kept these traditions alive.

When whaling collapsed, Sag Harbor became an industrial town with factories and mills along the waterfront. Later, during the Jim Crow era, it became a summer refuge for middle-class Black families who were barred from other resort communities. One small village, so many past lives.

Jimmy and I made our way down to the marina, to the gleaming white yachts: long-tiered decks, dark windows, antennas everywhere, more American flags hanging off the sterns. I was surprised to see as many American flags in the Hamptons as in many parts of rural America. The yachts looked more like floating urban condos than boats.

"Be nicer than my apartment," Jimmy joked. Walking alongside them, he looked like a counterweight to all that polish and shine, yet there wasn't a trace of envy in his voice. He could admire both the dumps and the yachts, satisfied with the life he'd built for himself.

What would the Hamptons be like in twenty years, I found myself wondering? Would guys like Jimmy be totally gone, priced out and off in Costa Rica? The Kevins and Averys leaving for a life they could more easily afford? Or would these different socioeconomic realities find some way to share the same spit of land? It's such a common question across America these days, one I only wish I knew the answer to. Whatever future takes hold here, I trusted the young guys I'd met at the beach were heading for good places, grounded in the confidence and enthusiasm they'd need to make what they wanted of their lives, come what may. Which, I suppose, was another way to play the long game.

As we walked back to Jimmy's truck, I found myself thinking fondly about some of the other people I'd met throughout this country who shared his zeal for a life lived wholly on their own terms. The modern inheritors of that all-American pioneering spirit that carried people to the outer reaches of a country big enough to hold a thousand different ways of being.

PART IV

PIONEERING SPIRIT

CHAPTER 9

The Louisiana Bayou

I'd come because I was curious about what drives someone to live in a swamp.

The flat-bottomed boat nosed through the murky water like an alligator, its motor giving off a low growl across the bayou. Massive, skeletal cypress trees rose straight out of the water beside us, their roots breaking the surface as the wake slapped against them. At the tiller, Keith steered with the confidence of a man who'd run these channels since boyhood, his camouflage style and mirrored sunglasses flashing bright red against the swamp's brown-gray, screaming *summer of '87.* Tara sat up front, cosmopolitan casual in jeans and a zip-up sweatshirt, loose strands of blond hair breaking free from her braid in the cool wind.

We were slinking through the edge of the Atchafalaya Basin, the largest river swamp in the United States. An hour and a half west of New Orleans, where the French Quarter had been restless the night before, with partying tourists and jazz bands. But I was only passing through the city. I'd heard Pierre Part (population: three thousand) was about as Cajun as you could get—and so that's where I'd headed. The most French-speaking town in the US outside a village in Maine, I'd read.

Winter in southern Louisiana is still winter. Tara told me

spring and summer would bring the real show, but I didn't mind February here—my camera gear and I both fared better without the heat and sweltering humidity. Heavy rains had fallen for days before I arrived, and water lay everywhere along the roads, filling ditches and eroding moats around homes. The farther south you got from the scattered rolling hills of northern Louisiana, the more the landscape drains into the Gulf Coast. It starts with farmland—rows of sugarcane, rice fields turned into shallow ponds for raising crawdads. Then the rivers swell, creeks twist into flooded forests, and the roads buckle into some of the worst potholes in New Orleans, until the land gives up altogether and unravels into saltwater marsh, empty but for shrimpers, crabbers, and oil crews heading to the Gulf. As I drove along I-10, it was hard not to marvel that the stretch under my wheels wasn't really a highway at all but one of two parallel bridges, each more than eighteen miles long, carrying traffic across the endless swamp.

Out here on the water, the landscape reminded me a bit of the Florida Everglades: an overgrown, labyrinthine place for die-hards and outlaws. A last frontier feeling.

I'd been to a lot of places around America by this point that lived a little differently from what most people might call "normal." But unlike the farmers I'd met in Amish country or the watermen of the Chesapeake Bay, folks carrying on the traditions of ten generations, the pioneering spirit of the people here on the Louisiana Bayou was something else. This was a place for people who wanted to chart their own course, to dance to their own tune in some downright hostile conditions. I'd come to Pierre Part to meet a couple who'd decided that their American dream was to live part-time in a one-room wooden houseboat on a swamp.

Keith motored us around town a bit, passing porches, docks, weathered houses set close to the water. Pierre Part was essentially an island—a long stretch of high ground surrounded by wetlands, with Lake Verret to the south. Tara pointed out landmarks. Her grandparents' house. The street where her stepmom grew up, and her parents before her, and their parents before them. It felt like moving through her family photo album.

"This the end of the road," Tara said as I looked at the last house on the bank. There were only cypress trees beyond, their branches tangled together as far as I could see. Everything from here was by boat.

Keith twisted his wrist on the throttle and the motorboat leaped forward, spray lifting into the wind. And just like a few minutes back when I'd first stepped aboard—the boat rocking under my weight, Keith reaching out a hand to steady me—Tara watched me with that warm, slightly mischievous look, as if she knew what was coming. Like we were going off the edge of the map.

* * *

For a stretch it was nothing but open water, brown and opaque under a patchy sky that couldn't make up its mind between storm and sun. A faint stagnant odor came off the surface: mud, decaying organic matter, fungi, mildew. It felt like a place that could either strengthen your immune system or slam it down.

Along the shore, the cypress trees blurred into a solid brown-green wall until little dark cuts began to show.

"What are those?" I called over the motor's roar.

"We call 'em a bayou run," Keith hollered back, wiping water off his mid-forties salt-and-pepper stubble. "There's a maze of 'em, just like trails in a forest." He steered left into a narrow channel, speed dropping, the swamp closing in. It felt a little mysterious, a separate ecosystem that could only be accessed through local Cajun knowledge.

Here and there houseboats appeared along the bank, tied off to trees or lashed to makeshift docks, each like a one-room wooden cabin set on a pontoon boat, porches hanging just above the swamp.

"A lot of these people only come out during hunting season," Keith said, his voice lower now as we glided past the floating neighborhood, the engine putting softly. "It's usually just us."

In the distance, I noticed a man sitting on the small porch of a gray cabin, a wide wooden deck floating off to the side.

"Who are you, and what are you doing on our houseboat?" Tara called out. She had this fantastic accent, a Southern drawl with a touch of French that carried a playful ease. Time in the South teaches you there isn't one Southern accent but dozens, each tied to its own corner of culture.

"I'm the boogie man!" The man smiled.

Tara burst out laughing. "That's my dad," she said. "He's eighty-two."

We floated closer, the boat nudging gently against the dock. The wood of the pier gave a low groan. Tara climbed up to tie the rope around the porch post, her father steadying her hand. He looked no older than sixty—lean and upright in a faded denim shirt and cap.

"How are you doing, sir?" I asked.

"I'm doing," he said, reaching out his hand for a shake.

"Peter."

"Carlis Goday." In his Cajun accent, the weight landed on the second syllables. "The man without a car, Car-less. Last name's Go-day. If you can't go nights, you go days."

Tara gave me a little tour of the house, which looked no bigger than 250 square feet. "This is the kitchen." She smiled, pointing to the propane four-burner stove in one corner, a single counter opposite, and a roll-out grill wedged between. "Keith does all the outside cooking, I do the inside. We haul this grill out onto the porch just to give us more room in here."

The rest of the room was simple: a bunk bed stacked with pillows, a futon folded into a couch, life jackets, tools. Fishing gear in organized piles. A flatscreen TV and an enclosed bathroom with a toilet were the only luxuries. A small sign nailed to the wall read BORN TO FISH, FORCED TO WORK.

"The shower's out here." Tara slid open the door to the back deck, where a hose was rigged to a small on-demand water heater, a shower curtain hooked on a rail. They showered with bayou water, she said.

"We've also got an AC," Keith added, brushing his wind-tossed dark hair into his cap. "We run off a generator or solar when it gets really hot, but most of the time we just sleep with the windows open." Come summer, he told me, the bayou turned into a playground: waterskiing, hydrosliding, wakeboarding, swimming in clear pockets before the water thickened to pea green.

"The snapping turtles you gotta be wary of, they can really bite," Tara warned. "And the water moccasins and copperheads too. We've got a swimming spot we love, even with alligators everywhere." She smiled at my wide eyes, as if living a few feet above alligators was the most natural thing in the world.

"The bigger alligators are usually shy," Keith added. "The smaller ones, you can get closer to, but they won't mess with people. They like swimming up to our dock when we're cleaning fish or frogs. But out here they don't really bother us. I think they had maybe two deaths in Louisiana since, I don't know . . . hundreds of years."

I looked out at the endless woods, roots twisting like hieroglyphs out of the dark water, and wondered skeptically if those were only the *reported* numbers. And yet the thought made me somehow even more excited to spend time with people who'd chosen to build a life in this waterlogged low country. It takes a certain taste for the untamed to look at a land that floods every spring—that's thick with mosquitoes and demands you work twice as hard against all the things nature throws at you—and still commit.

* * *

The Cajun story didn't start in Louisiana. It began along the coast of the rugged western edge of France, a Celtic stronghold of sailors and pirates who started crossing the Atlantic in the early 1600s, settling in what was then the young French colony of Acadia and is today Nova Scotia, New Brunswick, and Prince Edward Island, Canada. Here, the Acadians lived the way they always had: close to the water, close to family, close to the Catholic church. They turned salty tidal marshes into farmland, wove their own clothing from flax, and—stubbornly—made a living three thousand miles from home.

But it wasn't to be. Acadia was in turbulent territory. The Acadians wanted to remain neutral between Britain and France, but when the British defeated the French, the Acadians were pushed to swear allegiance to the British Crown. They refused: Their loyalty was to God, not to European empires. That defiance came at a cost, and in 1755, the British forced them out in what became known as the Great Expulsion. Villages were torched, families torn apart, thousands deported. Many died from disease and starvation. No documents written by Acadians during this period have ever been discovered, and so the expulsion remains as much myth as heritage to the people of Louisiana (who love both myth and heritage).

Some Acadians ended up back in France, some scattered through the British colonies, and others drifted to the Caribbean. Those who came to Louisiana—still a French colony in those days—found something familiar. The prairies and swamps reminded them of home, only warmer. Difficult enough to live on that few bothered them and fertile enough to survive, especially with the help of Native nations like the Chitimacha, Atakapa, and Houma living along the Gulf Coast. Cajun French includes many Native-derived loanwords—even the term *bayou*, from the Choctaw word *bayuk* ("small stream"). In time, the groups began to intermarry, encouraged by proximity and shared hardships, and Cajun food developed from indigenous smoking methods, ways of preservation, and seasonings. The Cajun staple filé powder, made from ground sassafras leaves, comes from the cooking traditions of the Choctaw and related Gulf Coast tribes.

The story of Black influence in the bayou runs just as deep. Many enslaved Africans sought refuge in the wilderness, forming Maroon communities hidden along the swamps. Some of them lived independently; others mingled with Native tribes and Cajun settlers. Gumbo's okra-thickened broth has African roots, a stew of cultures that's simmered for hundreds of years.

As time passed, *Acadian* slurred into *Cajun*. But the backbone of the culture stayed the same: Make your own way, stay close to your people, adapt to whatever the land throws at you.

* * *

Carlis Goday wasn't born on the bayou.

"I was raised in the French Quarter in my younger years," he was telling me as we stood around on the deck, cardinals and wrens chattering in the cypress. "It was a slow, easy life while I was a boy. Nobody had a care in the world. If we had an old bicycle, we was happy." He chuckled softly.

"I remember when we first had electricity," he went on. "My grandma used to live with us. All we had was three light bulbs." He paused, hiding a smile. "That first night, I watched her for *fifteen* minutes trying to blow the light bulb out!" He let out a deep laugh, and I couldn't help noticing how all the lines on his face—deeper now—looked to be from smiling.

"But life like this"—I gestured toward the floating houses—"other than a few conveniences, it's pretty much the same out here, right?"

Carlis nodded. "Pretty much the same. We had rainwater. Big cistern in the back. Bring a cup, open the faucet underneath. You'd have all them little bivalves swimming around in it, you know?" He laughed. "It was a good life."

His parents moved the family to Pierre Part when he was six or seven to be closer to his mother's kin. He raised Tara here, escaping to the houseboat on weekends to get away from everything so they could spend time together, just the family. These days, Tara and Keith reckoned they spent maybe a quarter of the year out on the bayou.

"What do you think it'll be like in twenty years out here?" I asked. "You think it'll stay the same?"

"No, no." Carlis said it with vehemence and without hesitation. "Things are changing too much. Too much erosion."

Hurricanes were tearing up so much that there was nothing left to hold the land together but tree roots, while they pulled in salt water that killed off grasses, hastening the decline. "Everything's going," he said. "Everything's washing away. But this"—he pointed down at the water beneath the porch—"this was built when they put in some oil rigs back here."

"Oil rigs?"

"Most of the man-made canals were from the oil companies," Tara explained, cut as inroads for drilling rigs and pipelines, as well as drainage. "That's the big industry out here, oil and gas."

Big enough to employ them both. Keith did maintenance for offshore platforms, Tara was a materials coordinator. It seemed like they had things figured out: one foot in the swamp, the other in capitalism, providing the financial security that let them live by the rhythms of the natural world. A yin and yang approach.

* * *

The motor cracked alive, and we were back on the water. They called it running lines—checking the hooks and nets they'd strung out earlier in the bayou. Keith and Carlis gunned separate boats and took off down the channel as if it were a highway . . . and in a way, it was. Carlis, almost twice Keith's age, leaned into the ride with the same wide grin, the look of a man happiest with his hand on a tiller and a bayou stretched out before him.

Herons startled up, low and heavy, their wings dragging shadows across the surface. The wakes curled behind us, setting the yellow reeds along the shore into a soft dance before breaking against the bank. When they finally cut the motors, the only thing I could hear was the ringing in my ears.

We'd stopped by a single, bare cypress skeleton. Carlis hunched over the gunwale, pulling something out of the water.

"You got it?" Tara called.

"Yep." Carlis leaned back, muscles tight, bracing as the iron trap broke the surface, its black mesh writhing with catfish. He pulled fish after fish from the sagging net, whiskers flicking, slick bodies flashing silver as he dropped them into a gray plastic tub. Ten in all.

"There's just enough space where everyone respects each other's lines," he told me. People knew what was theirs and what wasn't.

"Everyone knows everybody out here," Keith added.

We continued on, then cut the motor again as another skiff pulled alongside. Carlis hollered something in French, a quick burst of words I couldn't catch. The newcomer—in his fifties, maybe—fired back in the same, both of them breaking into laughter.

They kept yakking. "Is Pierre Part a good place to live?" Tara interjected at one point, then winked at me, waiting for the punchline she knew was coming.

"Well, mais, come on . . ." Darrin, known by his buddies as Bebop, spread his hands, puzzled at such an odd question. "Till I went out to work across the country, I didn't know they had a better place than Pierre Part." His accent was so thick—*r*s rolling, endings dropped—that I had to rewind each line in my mind to catch the meaning.

"You didn't go to Mardi Gras in New Orleans with Keith last year?" I teased, knowing how tied folks here were to rural life. Keith had told me he couldn't stand crowds.

Tara laughed as the men's expressions snapped into disbelief.

"Mais . . . not a Mardi Gras guy, never was!" he said, waving his hands as if to dismiss the whole idea. "I can count the times I stepped in New Orleans, partner, 'specially these days. You'd *never* catch me in New Orleans." He was delivering it now with a punch at Keith, as if the two of them had to prove who was less of a city boy. "The man wouldn't . . ." he began, then abandoned the thought for a better argument. "I had a bunch of friends—"

"You guys are all scared of New Orleans, huh?" I asked, continuing the trolling.

Tara was giggling breathlessly.

"We're not scared, we're just smarter!" Carlis fired back, condescension sneaking in.

"Boy, they got some people," Bebop said. "My oldest boy, he's into that stuff. But this coonass here"—he jabbed a thumb at his own chest—"ain't."

The word hit my ear. I'd heard it a few times already. It's used all over Louisiana to refer to Cajuns, although the origin's murky. One theory has it that during World War II, a French soldier called a Cajun soldier a *connasse* (an insult roughly equivalent to ignorant, swamp-dwelling), which US service members then transformed into *coonass*. Others guess it comes from older regional slang to do with raccoon skin caps. It's one of those words that some see as a badge of ethnic pride, others as offensive.

"Okay, let me ask you this," I said. "You can call each other *coonass*, but if I said it to you, that's not cool, right?"

Tara raised her hand to stop me right there. "You can call me a coonass all day long!"

Voices overlapped. *Mais, it's just our people . . . no, no . . . it's not offensive to us . . . we're all Cajun coonasses.* Carlis and Bebop switched fully into French, going at each other with rapid hand gestures and laughs.

The chatter died down, and Bebop tipped his head back toward the tree line, squinting into the distance. "Look at them bald eagles," he said. "Boy, you never used to see this many." Their sharp, high-pitched cries carried down through the open air.

"Look, that's the nest right there," Keith said, stabbing a finger at the horizon. "See it on top of that tree?"

I could barely make it out—from here it was nothing more than a heavy shadow.

"They fly from Bayou Corne, and they pass every day over. And they come into Lake Barre, they go fish," Bebop said. He started reminiscing about the time before his grandmother passed. "All of us would sit on this porch in the morning, and you could see 'em, it's like clockwork—the big eagles. They come, they scoop their fish."

As he talked, I tried to wrap my mind around the wildness of the whole scene: a man who'd grown up on a swamp, speaking French in the middle of what many would call the heart of redneck America, pointing out the national emblem wheeling in the skies above. It was the kind of juxtaposition that doesn't fit into any typical story about what "real" America is supposed to look like. And maybe that's the point. Because the truth is, foreign as it was to me, this place was just as American as any other—and beautiful in its own unique way.

* * *

The sun began to glint across the water, and for the first time I caught colors where before I'd only seen brown and the slightest bit of green. Red maples dotted the horizon. Hazy Spanish moss hung thick over the cypress, swaying like old men's beards in the wind. Cypress knees jutted out of the water, spindly fingers reaching up to grab the boat. What had first struck me as unattractive now read like something special. The way the trees split their roots wide, learned to send up knobby "knees" to stabilize themselves in shifting soils, adapting to survive, the Cajun story manifested in a tree. They were called boscoyos, Tara told me.

The motor eased to a light chug as Keith steered the boat into a narrow chute, the floating weeds so thick the water showed only in thin seams. There was no straight run here—just a slow crawl as the boat's nose parted the growth until we reached a wall of brush and fallen branches. Carlis had turned around a bit earlier, heading back to the houseboat with his catfish.

"Look, snake," Tara said suddenly. I turned just in time to catch a black tail vanish, stirring up a muddy whirl before the weeds matted over again.

"Keith is the snake guy at work," she added.

"Everybody calls me when they find one," he said. "I know how to deal with 'em. I don't like to harm 'em, so I usually find a place to put 'em out in the woods or somethin'. I don't usually grab the water moccasins by hand. Even though I have done it before, it's pretty frowned upon." He smiled. People had died from their bites, I knew, without proper treatment.

"What's frowned upon is when you don't kill 'em after," Tara said.

Keith shook his head. "Yeah, a lot of people say a good snake is a dead snake, but a good snake is a live snake to me. They have just as much right to be out here, if not more, than I do, right?" He gestured around him. "This is their place."

The bayou provided Keith with subsistence both material and, I was realizing, spiritual. I thought about the Siberian

Yupik living in the frozen tundra thousands of miles away, listening to the sea in the same way Keith and Tara listened to the muddy current, both living so inseparably from their environments for so long that they weren't just living on the land, they were part of it.

"That's the gator right there, ha?" Tara said suddenly, pointing just a few feet off the boat.

Keith laughed. "Oh, I didn't even see him."

Half-hidden in the duckweed and shadows, the little gator lay motionless, its ridged, sleek back blending into the murky water. It could've passed for driftwood that happened to have teeth, its narrow pupils fixed and unblinking.

Tara squinted, smiling. "I think he's cute."

"They are beautiful creatures," I admitted.

Keith smirked. "You know what's crazy about her? She'll catch a bullfrog this big"—he spread his hands wide—"but let one of those little peeper frogs land on her? It's over." He laughed, shaking his head, giving Tara a soft glance that said more than words. "I don't know why she's so scared of those little green frogs."

"'Cause they jump on you! A bullfrog jumps away."

I watched them laugh at each other, and it struck me how natural they were together. Two people who could ride out into the swamp and get excited over amphibians, reptiles, fish, whatever crossed their path. It reminded me of the dynamic my wife, Natalia, and I have. She puts her heart and soul into editing the footage I shoot, every bit as excited as I am about giving voice to the people in our country. Ours is a synergy that could never be designed but just happened organically, one of those mysteries of life that one feels lucky to experience every day.

"Oh, look at that little baby." Tara was leaning over the

front of the boat now, hands under her chin, watching another gator nose through the weeds like it was a kitten.

* * *

Keith trolled slowly, deeper in, scanning through tree trunks to the left of us. Things got quiet, and he looked serious for the first time, like he'd switched into survivor mode.

"Hoping to go find a big nutria rat to show you," I heard him say.

"Nutria rat?"

"Very invasive around here. They tear up a lot of these marshlands. They'll eat all the roots of the vegetation, dig holes in levee systems. A lot of people trap 'em for the tails. Certain times of the year you can trap the nutrias, and they'll give you six dollars a tail."

"It's a government program," Tara added.

"We actually shot a few last weekend—and we ate 'em."

"You eat 'em?" I said, probably failing to hide my shock. In Cambodia, I'd eaten a fried tarantula the size of my hand with long, greasy, hairy legs, but a mega rat sounded far more disgusting somehow.

"They're actually a very clean meat. They're vegetarian."

"How many pounds are they?"

"Oh, they can get five pounds to probably up to twenty."

"They're like midsize dogs?" The image in my head wasn't getting any prettier.

Keith laughed. "I'ma show you some in a few minutes—you're gonna see. New York, they don't have anything on us in rats."

"Oh my God," I muttered, half laughing.

The boat slowed, the motor humming just enough to push

us along. Water lilies floated near the banks, and green pools opened between the trees, half-submerged logs slick with algae.

"They hear the motor and take off running," Keith said, scanning the shallows. "But a lot of times if you just kind of creep up on 'em, they'll sit in the lilies or in the marsh and eat grass."

Spanish moss swung lazily overhead as the boat purred low, water sliding past in long black ribbons. The layered chorus—motor humming, frogs ticking, insects droning—was pulling me into a kind of sound-healing trance, when Keith's posture suddenly shifted. He cut the motor and reached for the rifle on the floor of the boat in one swift motion, chambered a round without taking his eyes off the forest, and raised the barrel. A click. Then the sharp crack of gunfire split the quiet, echoing through the trees.

"Oh, I heard it," Tara said. "That was a good shot."

"You got it?" I asked, half in disbelief, still not seeing what he'd fired at.

"Yeah," Keith said calmly.

"You got it in one shot?"

"He's a sharpshooter." Tara laughed.

Keith shrugged. "It's not my first time."

The motor coughed back to life, the boat gliding into the brush until it nudged softly against the bank. Tara jumped off to tie us up while Keith hopped out and slipped into the undergrowth. I followed, watching as his camouflage jacket blended into the trees. He kept going—farther than I expected. He must've been a hundred feet away from shore when he finally crouched down to the ground.

Then he straightened, pulling up a long, limp brown body by its slick ten-inch tail.

"Oh my God!" I said, the words bursting out. "Oh my God, Keith!"

He was holding a wet, shaggy nutria, fur clumped and dripping from the swamp, its long, faded orange teeth jutting like chisels. Its webbed feet dangled in the air, black claws curled tight at the ends. Something between a beaver and a rat, and ugly as sin.

"That's a small one," Keith said, raising it high for Tara to see. "My friend calls 'em swamp bunnies."

"And that's part of the dinner menu tonight, right?"

"Would you like to try?"

"I mean, if you're doing it . . . when in Rome."

"We could try frying it," Tara suggested.

"Ah . . ." Keith considered it for a moment. "I think a nutria stew would be awesome."

* * *

I've often heard people say that America has no culture, and I think that claim couldn't be more off. Sure, America doesn't have one neat, homogeneous culture—it's too mixed, too big, too complicated for that. What it does have is a whole host of cultures sprinkled across its vast and beautiful geography. That's the true gift of this country: You can choose the life you want to live, in the culture that feels right to you.

I've seen this story play out again and again. The Syrian movie producer who made his way to Hollywood. The man who headed for the mountains of North Carolina to live off the land, growing medicinal herbs and selling tinctures. The retired couples from across the country who choose the Villages (the famous retirement community) in Florida to live out their most social and active years. My brother, who lives in a small shack close to the ocean on Kauai, a private chef for some of the biggest names in business and entertainment, spending his early mornings in the surf or on his dirt bike. All living true to their own tune.

And the beauty is that so much of America still stands with its arms open. If you show up somewhere as an outsider, and take the time to respect how people live there—not trying to change them, not trying to prove that where you're from does things better—you're usually met with real warmth. Come in curious, ask questions, listen more than you talk, and try to understand where people are coming from, and wow, it's a beautiful thing.

For Keith and Tara, I was realizing that it was the unpredictability of life out here on the bayou that'd become the attraction. Keith had told me the biggest threat of living here was the storms—hurricanes blowing 160 miles an hour for hours on end, floods rising fast and rolling through without mercy. Looking out at the still water all around us—the soft wind rustling the moss in slow sways, chorus frogs peeping from the banks—it occurred to me that the risk of living here was that one moment, the place gives you peace, but the next it could strip everything away. The Acadians learned that in maritime British territory when their homes were burned. Down here, it wasn't armies but hurricanes that could erase whole towns in a night. To stay in the bayou meant accepting that bargain: life built in a land that never promised permanence. Then again, none of us are ever promised permanence anywhere.

I try my best to see things from the perspective of the people I'm meeting up with, because I'm always curious how others see the world. Out here, I could feel the comfort that comes from knowing your immediate survival doesn't depend on supply chains or policies but on your own skills and relationships. Keith and Tara were as connected to their food source as you can get. Swamp-to-table cuisine. What confidence came from that sort of self-reliance?

"So, say the grid goes down," I said. "Everything stops—no cell coverage. You guys are fine out here?"

"Yeah," Tara said, no hesitation.

"We're gonna be fantastic," Keith said, a wide smile spreading across his face.

"Fuel and clean water would be the tough ones to get, though?"

Keith leaned back against the motor and glanced at Tara, as if checking that they were on the same page. "Yeah, but there's ways to get clean water. We'd boil it all day long if we got to."

"And how many rounds of ammo at the house?" Tara asked.

"Ooh . . ." he paused, trying not to look too pleased with himself. "Eighteen thousand rounds, maybe."

"You're getting ready for something, Keith?" I asked with a grin.

"Always," Tara cut in, laughing.

Keith shrugged like it was just common sense. "Well, they had all them issues with the bullets a while back, where they were driving the prices up, and it was hard to even find bullets. So I was like, 'Well, I just got enough to last.' Because when you're doing stuff like this"—he gestured at his kill—"you'd like to have a few bullets, you know?"

Keith didn't answer me on the fuel question since, of course, without fuel, all of this stopped: the motorboat, the cooking stove, the backup generator. It's romantic to imagine making it in the wild on our own—and Keith and Tara could do better than most. But the truth is, we're all dependent on civilization; it's just a question of degree. I remember a man named Monk who owned his own isolated town in the mountains in California telling me, "People say they want to live this life to live the simple life. I tell them, living in town with everything nearby and functioning is the simple life."

"What do you guys feel about the rest of the country out here?" I asked.

Keith paused. "I mean . . . we see it, we hear stuff, but honestly . . ."

"We hear stuff from work," Tara clarified.

"I watch no news. None," Keith said. He sounded proud. Defiant.

Tara leaned forward with a small laugh. "We haven't watched the news in years."

"I used to keep up a little bit," Keith said, "and it would just upset me so much to see all the stuff going on. So I was like, 'You know what? I'm a lot happier, honestly, not keeping up with it.' 'Cause how much positive stuff do you see in the news?"

"Nothing," Tara said quickly.

"So this is what we do"—he looked around—"and we enjoy our lives doing it. And if we're not here, we're doing stuff with our families. For Christmas, you're probably looking at sixty to seventy of just my family. People like to get together here. You do a crawfish boil, and you just tell everybody, and they bring a dish, and everybody just has a great time."

When I posted this video, someone commented: "Cajuns don't have friends. We only have family."

I think we often assume fewer people means more isolation. But in these parts, it just means it takes a little more effort to get to an event. In a place without many distractions, getting together is the main attraction.

I'd heard stories of how, when hurricanes hit, people who lost a house were taken in without hesitation. During evacuations, when not everyone had a place to go, those who did opened their doors. It's hardship that brings people together, not modern conveniences.

The conversation drifted off, and for a while we rode in silence. The moss from the trees hung so low it trailed in the water, dragging along like fingers searching for something.

"You know how the north and Northwest of the United States has Bigfoot?" Tara asked suddenly. "Down here, our swamp creature is Rougarou."

"Rougarou?"

Tara lowered her voice, like she was telling a campfire story. "I think we've actually heard a Rougarou out here a couple of times at night."

It was one of the great legends of Cajun country. A man with the head of a wolf and glowing eyes, prowling through the dark swamps. The story traces back to France—*loup-garou* is French for *werewolf*—and when Acadians came to Louisiana, the old tale followed, taking on a new life out in the bayou. Here the Rougarou was keeping people in line: Break Lent or skip Mass, and you risked crossing paths with it. Some said the curse lasted 101 days; others swore it could be passed on by blood, or contracted by one look into the creature's red eyes. For generations the Rougarou worked like a warning—a boogie man for children, a way of keeping order in a wild place. Today the Rougarou shows up in parades and on sports jerseys, but out here in the swamp, far from the city, the legend lives on.

* * *

Soon the houses came back into view—a neighborhood with water as its street. I spotted Carlis sprawled on the dock napping, a fishing vest bunched beneath his head for a pillow. Afternoon sunlight warmed the wooden planks, the soft whistle of a cardinal carrying across the water—*twik-twik-twik*—as rhythmic as a lullaby.

"I got you a treat," Keith said, dropping the nutria at his father-in-law's feet. "You want some nutria stew?"

"Anytime a true Cajun sees a new animal or bird or whatever," Tara said, "what's the first thing that comes to mind?"

Her dad didn't miss a beat. "Wonder if that's good to eat?"

We all cracked up, the nutria stretched on the dock beside us like some offering to the swamp gods.

I realized I'd judged the swamp harshly—for its flatness, its tangled underbrush, its water that wasn't postcard turquoise. But the bayou was like the desert in a way. At first glance, the desert can look naked, barren, hostile. Only after spending time there do you begin to see what's special: the trickles of water in hidden ravines, the way sound carries through the air without humidity to dampen it, the sky-on-fire sunsets. The place has its own pulse that only reveals itself when you give it time. The swamp was no different. The longer I spent in it, the more beautiful it became. That's the joy of discovery—but you've got to love to be proven wrong.

Tara set a heavy iron pot on the stove, rice and onion sizzling as Keith busied himself with the day's catch. Carlis lifted a bottle, the setting sun glinting off its dark surface: homemade wine, wild muscadine from the swamp, generations of craft bottled inside, stretching all the way back to his ancestors in France.

"When'd you retire, Daddy?" Tara called out from the kitchen. "What year was it?"

"I worked till . . ." He rubbed his chin. "I was sixty-five." He looked over at me and added simply, "Ironworker."

"How was that?" I asked.

"Bridges and towers." He smiled faintly. "Ironwork's a good profession. You see what you do. We'd look at how many pieces we put in. It wasn't no standing around—we worked all day. That's what I liked about it."

I thought of the bridges I drove over to get here, the tall building in New Orleans where I'd slept the night before, my travels connecting me to the people whose craft I've relied on my whole life.

"Tara, can you bring me that gut bucket in the back?" Keith called out. "The white one we found earlier?"

Tara wrinkled her nose and looked at me. "I know, that sounds so gross, huh?"

Carlis cracked the bottle of muscadine open and tipped it forward, the deep red liquid glugging heavily into a white Styrofoam cup. He lifted it under his nose and breathed deep. "*Aah.* Tolé, ça c'est bon!"

A little Bordeaux in the bayou, I thought.

"Do you feel the Cajun culture's under threat at all?" I asked as he took a slow sip of the wine.

"We're losing it," he said. His face tightened at the thought. "Back when I was little, just this area here, I'd say a hundred percent of the kids spoke French. Nowadays, you're lucky if you get twenty-five to thirty percent. Just like my grandkids. They understand it, but they never wanted to talk it."

"But you spoke it 'cause your parents made you speak it, right?"

"They didn't make me—that's all we had. French was my first language. In school, they made us quit talking French."

"So the US school system didn't want any French being spoken at all?"

He shook his head. "And then just lately, the last few years, they started with French immersion—teaching French."

"Language is like a tidal wave," I said to Carlis. "It's hard to go against." I thought back to Saint Lawrence Island.

That was how it went, the pendulum swinging from pushing out French influence to embracing it again. Starting in the late 1800s, you could see the pressure to make Louisiana less French in all kinds of small, telling ways—French street names anglicized, public institutions phasing out the language. Catholic parishes were reorganized, some priests replaced with English-speaking clergy. And yet, for all the pressure to "Americanize," the culture held on. Children still spoke French at home, even if they were punished at school for it. Music carried the language when conversation couldn't. Recipes traveled from grandmother to grandchild. What survived did so stubbornly, underground at times, until the 1960s, when the cultural revival movements—Cajun music festivals, immersion programs, the creation of a state agency for Francophone affairs—began bringing the language and traditions back into the everyday. But the reality is that kids will speak the language that's cool with their friends, the language of the TikTok videos that they're watching.

Over in the kitchen corner, Tara lifted the black pot's lid as the stew roared, a rush of steam and bubbling, rich and heavy. She leaned into the cloud, breathing deep, satisfied.

"Looks like a piece of chicken or something right there, hmm?" She tapped the spoon on the rim, then moved to check the pots on the other burners—refried beans simmering low, rice hissing under its lid. "Last weekend they had a nutria rodeo cook-off of different recipes, trying to promote the meat. They have a lot of hungry people in the world; why not eat it if it's out there?" Her tone shifted to serious. "If the government's paying people to kill nutria 'cause they're invasive, why not have a market for the meat? Clean it, freeze it, and ship it to poor counties or where people are struggling for food."

We'd been conditioned since childhood that anything with a rat tail is gross, so I could hardly imagine anyone taking on the branding challenge. But she made a good point.

Keith's phone rang. It was his son, Drake, who'd just gotten home from school, asking what fishing rod to use. Shared custody, getting kids to school, seeing childhood friends . . . none of that could be accomplished living full-time in the bayou, even if that was the dream.

The smell of supper drifted through the doorway, as Keith stepped inside to serve, scooping white rice onto a paper plate, adding a spoonful of beans, then reaching for the pot of stew, the sauce spreading in a glossy layer. Plates in hand, we stepped outside to eat in the open air. The swamp had dimmed back into grays, a thin scatter of crickets scratching here and there.

I lifted a forkful. "All right," I announced, almost ceremonially. "My first nutria." I was on my toes. Food can be such a big part of identity that the rejection of a meal can seem like the rejection of a culture.

I took a big bite and chewed on it for a moment. It wasn't bad. Earthy, dense, close to rabbit or dark chicken meat.

"It's like nothing I've had before, to be honest," I said. "Texture's like . . ." I hesitated. "Gummy. A lot of flavor. It's got some kick to it, right?"

Keith nodded, nonverbal approval.

"Good balance of onions in there, Tara," I said.

"Mm-hmm." She nodded, chin propped on her hand, watching me eat.

"I feel like there's a lot of nutrients going on here," I said, failing to come through with anything more positive.

"It's that organic meat," Tara said.

Keith leaned closer. "Big question is—would you eat it again?"

I smiled, swallowing. "If I was out here, yeah."

They both laughed.

It settled on me how light everything felt here, like the rest of the world was on mute. Which, in a way, is the real luxury of America. The country works well enough—supply lines reliable, fuel at the pumps, no mobs threatening to overrun your rural settlement—that people can choose to live out on the edge and not worry. The order of the outside world allows the frontier to survive. Out here in the bayou, you could chart your own course and still sleep easy, knowing the nation kept the ground (or the waters) steady beneath you.

After dinner, Keith boated me back to shore. I had a ninety-minute drive ahead of me, and so I shut my car door on the rising hum of crickets and turned on my headlights, the dark swamp fading into the rearview. Out there was a life with its own rules and rewards, a life that asked for respect but gave back an untethered feeling of freedom.

I found it comforting to know that wild places like this one still existed—and I sure hope I'll be living as audaciously as Carlis if I reach eighty-two—and yet already I felt a familiar excitement growing in my chest, a pull toward the next destination.

Even before I was old enough to drive, I'd felt a yearning to explore, to learn, to experience the unexpected, to live a life that was rarely safe or predictable. Driving back across the eighteen-mile bridge over the Atchafalaya Basin, toward the neon swagger of New Orleans, I found my thoughts drifting back to the first time I'd ever chased the idea of adventure, and the thousands of different roads that chase had sent me down since.

CHAPTER 10

The Road Trip That Started It All

I still remember the bright September sun cutting through the sugar maples, their leaves just starting to turn red and purple and yellow, as my best friend Steve drove down my parents' gravel driveway, honking the horn of a stripped-down cargo van.

It looked more like a plumbing-company vehicle than something built for travel: blue sliding side door, bare metal interior, a single overhead light, its wire taped to the ceiling. The cassette deck had a glitch we could never figure out, playing the frequency of the engine along with the music. The van belonged to Steve's dad. But for the next few months, until our money ran out, this old GMC Vandura was ours.

I'd spent the summer mowing lawns and holing up weekends at Steve's to prep. We bought a small fridge that plugged into Vandura's cigarette lighter and stashed clothes and cooking gear in plastic bins bungeed to the van's walls. We practiced lying down in our mummy bags on top of thin Therm-a-Rest blow-up mattresses—my head between the front seats, Steve's at the rear doors—our legs nearly touching from the hip down.

There wasn't much room to sleep between the bins and our two mountain bikes, but there was enough.

In a few weeks, I'd be eighteen, and what came after high school was a question I didn't want to think about yet. Nobody in my family had a college degree, and as the last of three boys, my parents, probably exhausted, had given up on trying to push me in any sort of immediate direction, not even mentioning college once. But that didn't mean I didn't have plans. Steve and I were about to see the United States for ourselves, mile by mile, and I figured that maybe whatever questions I had about the rest of my life might be answered out there on the open road.

* * *

Childhood was simple in Vermont in the '80s and '90s. No helicopter parenting. No cell phones, no tracking or tracing. No social media. You came home when the dinner bell rang.

We were so free-range, so unsupervised, that I could tell my mom I was spending the night at Steve's house when really, as soon as he got his license at sixteen, we'd drive two and a half hours north to Montreal. Steve and I would slip over the Canadian border without passports—back then you didn't need one—and find ourselves in the front row at Club Super Sexe. The legal age to visit a strip club was eighteen, but somehow, we got around that. (When I'd come home the next day, I'd tell my mother Steve and I had a great time riding around BMX bikes. Steve ran the same play with his mom, saying he was at my place.) Even at sixteen, that urge to cross borders was already pushing me beyond Vermont.

I wanted a car of my own badly. A car meant freedom, independence. And our schools fed that pioneering spirit, teaching fifteen-year-olds—some of whom could barely see over the steering wheel—driver's ed as part of a basic public school curriculum. I'd been mowing lawns for $25 a pop, landscaping, stockpiling cash in a shoebox for my first ride: a 1984 VW Rabbit GTI that I bought for $1,550 half a year before my sixteenth birthday. It sat idle in the driveway, waiting for September 27 to arrive. Or at least that's what my parents thought. Some weekends, when they met up with friends in the evenings and left me home alone, I'd drive as far and as fast as I could—crossing the Champlain Bridge into New York State, heading deep into the Adirondacks. The smell of hot oil and smoking brake pads filled the car as I tore down back roads—windows down and blasting Rush, or Pearl Jam or The Police, competing for decibels with the overworked engine. I kept one eye on my black digital Casio watch—the one that everyone had in those days—turning back just in time to make it home before my parents. Some nights I'd cut it so close, I'd worry they'd hear my engine pinging and clattering under the hot hood of my clapped-out Rabbit. The risk of getting busted was pure adrenaline.

Before that, my experiences on the road were mostly closer to home. Growing up, every spring my parents had a dump truck unload a new pile of sand near the woods. (I think sometimes about how that small detail—it being a loose pile and not sand in a contained box—became a metaphor for the direction my life would take.) Our driveway was long and surrounded by forest, deep in the countryside. With each new pile, I'd spend hours pushing sand into roads for my toy trucks, carving them into the forest, winding down rocky ledges and out toward the field below. From there, you could see the waters of Lake

Champlain and the high peaks of the Adirondack Mountains. The air smelled of thawed earth and blossoms in spring, pine sap and sweetgrass in summer, damp decaying leaves in fall, and then the metallic cold of winter. With no boundaries marking property lines, my roads went as far as my imagination allowed.

When it rained, my little roads washed out, and fixing them felt like a matter of life or death. Before winter snow piled too deep, I'd plow them clear. I could spend six hours straight playing in the sand—looking out over the lake and mountains, dreaming about what the world was like, lost in it all, with only an occasional drink from the garden hose back at the house taking me away from it. Sand was the cheapest babysitter.

By the end of each year, the sandpile evolved into a nine-inch-wide road network stretching across our land and crossing over to a neighbor's property far away. Then the dump truck would return in the spring, unload another pile of sand, and I'd get to work again.

I spent years lost in those imaginary worlds, long enough that the transition from making truck noises in the sand to sitting front-row at the strip club was a pretty quick one. There might have even been a few weeks where those two activities overlapped.

From early on, I'd wanted to travel—not just west over the Adirondacks, but to the Mississippi River, the Rockies, following the highway all the way until it ended at the Pacific Coast. And then fly off to see Europe and the world. Neither of my parents—or any of my aunts and uncles that I knew of—had even been out West. Our family only went to three places for getaways: the New York/New Jersey metro area, where my parents had grown up and my cousins still lived; Rhode Island, where my grandmom lived; and Montreal. And by seventeen, Steve and I had both decided Montreal's strip clubs were lame. We had more audacious plans.

* * *

We left my parents' house high on each other, bouncing in our seats as Vandura rattled on, carrying us south on I-87, then west on I-90. We giggled like kids—because in many ways we still were.

We had about $3,500 each in savings and an unfettered confidence that everything would work out. Maybe it came from growing up in a place where we never worried about having enough food at home or gas running out or crime. My parents didn't even have the keys for our lock on the front door. You could trust the roads would be plowed in winter, that water would come from the faucet clean, that the community would come together each summer for parades. Maybe most people felt that way in the mid-'90s, when the weather in America was gale-force optimism. Or maybe our confidence was just due to youth itself—that weightless moment before rent and responsibilities kicked in.

Our only plan was to return when the money ran out. We knew our savings could vanish quickly if we weren't careful. Gas was around $1.15 a gallon back then, but Vandura only got about twenty miles per gallon at best. So, we agreed: no hotels, no restaurants, nothing to drink but free water. Nothing but what we needed to keep us on the road.

In the classes Steve and I weren't interested in, we'd been terrible students. On graduation day, we were among the only ones not to receive any kind of award. Regurgitating algebraic formulas wasn't our strength; counting dots on the ceiling while fantasizing about our upcoming adventure was. But we'd learned enough history to know we were embarking on an American tradition.

Since the very first people came here from Asia some twenty thousand years ago, the American frontier has tugged at mankind in a way that's hard to explain unless you've felt it. Good land. A fresh start. A chance to plant your feet somewhere and say, *All right, this is mine.* Or maybe *This is where I finally get to decide who I am.*

Long before the American Revolution turned into the familiar story about taxes and tea, it was already a story about geography. When the last battles of the French and Indian War ended in 1763, the British drew a hard line along the Appalachian Mountains, essentially saying to the colonists, *That's far enough. Stay where you are.* From the Crown's point of view, it made sense: fewer frontier skirmishes to manage, fewer negotiations with Native nations to bankroll. Some historians argue that this one restriction—this understanding that the British Empire meant to halt westward expansion—did more to provoke the American Revolution than any tax parliament could have dreamed up.

Then, less than thirty years after independence, the Louisiana Purchase doubled the country on paper. Newspapers fretted that the United States had become so large it would be impossible to govern and wondered if citizens could ever feel allegiance to a nation so vast. Yet by the 1850s, Americans were spilling eagerly into territories whose names they couldn't yet pronounce, following rumors of fertile river valleys, grazing land, and gold. All this happened within a single lifetime. A child born in Philadelphia the year the Declaration of Independence was signed would have been alive to see the flag raised on the Pacific.

We often think of this kind of progress as inevitable, but it wasn't. It was an improbable swell of wanderer's fire. An enormous gamble pulled forward by thousands upon thousands of ordinary people convinced that life had more to offer than what they'd been handed.

And somehow, each new generation seemed to find a way to keep that pioneering spirit alive, to promote the courage—the thrill of possibility—needed to leave what you knew, travel into the unknown, stake your claim, and build a new life from scratch. In 1862, Congress passed the Homestead Act, granting 160 acres of public land to any adult citizen (or intended citizen) who had never borne arms against the government, provided they lived on and "improved" that land for five years. One and a half million families (out of a total American population of thirty million at the time) would benefit—renters becoming owners, the wealthy prevented from fully monopolizing the rich land of the frontier. By 1869, the transcontinental railroad had shortened the trip from New York to San Francisco from six months to one week, opening up the possibility of westward migration at scale.

Pioneering spirit. It meant early mornings, broken plows, frigid winters, dusty summers, loved ones left thousands of miles behind. And yet it trained something deep inside the soul of Americans: independence, endurance, the belief in a better day tomorrow. It created a people who believed that a profound sense of self-agency was necessary to get the most out of life.

* * *

New York surprised us with its size. It took most of the day to get across, my first introduction to the massive scale of this country. I looked at the atlas and saw the much bigger Western states and thought, *How long will it take to get across those?* We watched the sun set into the waters of Lake Erie, which looked like an ocean with no visible land on the other side. That night, we pulled into a roadside hotel parking lot outside Cleveland, a dull orange light flickering through Vandura's front window as the night settled around us, the steady hum of passing big rigs on the highway putting us to sleep. We'd practiced getting into our sleeping bags, but this was the real thing. I think that was when the raw reality of our adventure set in.

The country moved like a treadmill in those early days—rolling toward us, then dropping off in the rearview mirror. Somewhere outside Davenport, Iowa, I looked down at the large Rand McNally Road Atlas in my lap and directed Steve to change interstates to I-80. We'd been talking about it for years: Now it was time to cross the Mississippi.

I remember pulling off to the side of the interstate on the far side of the river, jumping and yelling. I don't know if it was Mark Twain or Jack Kerouac or what, but there was something deeply ingrained about that line of water as a demarcation between East and West, the known and the unknown.

Soon, the cornfields of Nebraska stretched under big, puffy clouds into a dream state of freedom. We pulled off the highway and drove down random country roads etched between the crops. For the first time, we saw one of those huge agricultural sprinkler systems, its wheels towering over the fields. We parked the van and checked it out like something foreign that had landed on Earth. We climbed its metal frame high above the field like the jungle gym at our elementary school, taking pictures—one hand gripping tight, the other raised high to the sky. Simple things felt so alive.

Back on the interstate, fellow travelers became our family. For hours at a time, we'd ride alongside the same cars and trucks, passing each other back and forth, sometimes shooting a smile to each other; it felt as if we were on the same mission together. All of us driving into the night under the starry Midwestern sky.

It had just turned fall, 1995. Alanis Morissette's "You Oughta Know" and "Mr. Jones" by the Counting Crows were in constant rotation on the radio. Cal Ripken Jr. had broken Lou Gehrig's record for the most consecutive games played, and O. J. Simpson was found not guilty. And I know I might be guilty of some nostalgia here, but the country felt like the open road—free and full of possibility. America was in this sweet spot where it had pushed through not *all* but a *lot* of its social issues. This was before the hypersensitivity of social media, before "going viral" could mean fame or ruin, before information silos divided groups of people. Before media went fully partisan. I don't recall people being so worried about saying the "wrong thing" that'd get them ostracized. In my high school, we had a few standout teachers who pushed us to keep our minds open to different perspectives and taught us critical-thinking skills by making us take turns debating for and against third-rail issues with respect. There was a lot of rebel energy in many of us, and we loved to challenge authority, but we still lived by the nursery rhymes our elementary teachers drilled into our heads: *"Sticks and stones may break my bones, but words will never hurt me."* We shrugged off insults and strove to be resilient against things outside our control, realizing someone else's insecurities didn't need to make us insecure.

We were barreling down an interstate highway system built by our parents' and grandparents' hard-earned tax dollars, tracing the same paths our great-great-grandparents had once cut with horses and wagons—together across the centuries, all going west, chasing the same dream.

Eventually, each of our companions peeled away at an exit, leaving a flicker of melancholy as their headlights disappeared in the rearview mirror. Then we were back on our own, swallowed by the electric pulse of the interstate, carried through the night.

* * *

Once I turned eighteen, I was on my own financially. Since then, every plane ticket, every tank of gas has come through my own labor. Every mile. Maybe that's why I paid such close attention to the world when I finally got out into it—because I knew exactly what it cost me to get there and how quickly the lifestyle would end once the money dried up.

After a couple of nights in hotel parking lots, we were learning the ways of cheap travel. These places were perfect: safe, well-lit, free, and conveniently right off the highway, with many out-of-state license plates and, in those days, no cameras or security tracking who belonged there and who didn't. Each night before sundown, Steve and I would pull over, fire up the camping stove, and boil water for pasta. We'd strain it, dump it back into the pot, and pour in cold jarred sauce and a dusting of parmesan from one of those green canisters—the baby-powder kind that causes coughing fits if you inhale at the wrong time. Breakfasts were Raisin Bran with lukewarm milk from the fridge we unplugged at night so it wouldn't drain Vandura's battery.

Waking up one morning in a parking lot outside of a Days Inn, I remember slipping in to use the bathroom and passing a large Continental breakfast—one of those spreads people go all-in on to make beautiful. A woman looked up and smiled at me.

"Good morning! Enjoy your breakfast."

I looked over my shoulder to see who she was talking to, but nobody was there.

After using the restroom, I passed through the lobby again.

"We've got eggs and crispy bacon coming out soon. Make sure you get them while they're hot," she called, as if she were cooking them just for me.

I smiled back. *Bacon.* It was a nice thought.

Back in the van, Steve was sitting cross-legged on the rubber mat, pouring warm milk over another bowl of Raisin Bran. As I told him about the eggs and bacon I'd just smelled, I could feel the adrenaline we'd shared so many times before—sneaking out late on a warm summer night to jump the fence and swim in the town pool, or climbing the roof of our high school—starting to surge. We walked into the hotel confidently, smiling; moments later, our plates were piled high.

We thought we were getting away with something, thought we were proving ourselves the sort of risk-takers who knew the worst reaction we could get was a no. But I think we weren't fooling anyone, and that the woman probably knew what she was doing—giving scrappy road trippers like us some breakfast and helping us along our journey.

* * *

The Rockies didn't appear all at once—they crept closer, slowly, like we'd been driving toward them our whole lives. At least three plays of "You Oughta Know" passed on the radio before we could see the texture of the mountains. Their grays and greens.

A hundred miles later, Steve and I found ourselves above ten thousand feet up in the middle of an early fall snowstorm. We pulled off and decided there'd be nothing better than to ride our bikes in the snow. A herd of deer moved in the distance. We threw snowballs at each other, perched on top of the world.

For a curious mind, travel has an addicting feel. You're driven by wanting to explore around every next corner, thriving in the unknown. Late at night, we'd lie on Vandura's floor, the atlas open between us with our headlamps on, scanning the names of new places and wondering what they might be like. Our big atlas was already getting scruffy, notes scribbled in the margins about people we met, phone numbers written in the corners of worn pages for strangers who told us to call them if we ever returned to their towns. From time to time, I'd pump a few coins into a gas station pay phone to let my parents know I was alive: "*Yep. All good. Yes, we're having fun. It's beautiful. Yep, okay, bye.*" That was the extent of it. Even thinking of home detracted from the adventure.

Colorado was beautiful, but October brought more snow. Someone told us at a rest stop about a place called Moab, Utah—out in the desert. We'd never been to a desert.

We climbed for what felt like forever, Vandura choking on the thin air, topping eleven thousand feet through the Eisenhower Tunnel on I-70—which awed us with its long passage through the mountain—then dropping us back into warm sunshine. The light turned gold, and the smell of pine gave way to desert sandstone. For the first time, I experienced how two places forty-five minutes apart could look and feel like different worlds, everything hinging on big Western elevation changes.

It was strange, almost extraordinary, to know that we were following, in a loose way, the tracks left by earlier travelers, like the Mormon pioneers who had traveled through the Great Basin by horse and carriage just 140 years before. And of course, the Mormon Trail was only one thread in the vast network of westward routes that once pulled Americans into the interior. The California Trail, running hot to the gold fields. The Santa Fe Trail, a long mercantile artery flowing to New Mexico. The 2,170-mile-long Oregon Trail, tramped by fur traders and trappers. What amazed me, tracing even the faintest outline of those journeys, was how varied the destinations were and yet how similar the impulse. People moving toward some imagined better life, often with no idea of what was waiting on the other end. These days, our trails were I-70, I-20, I-90, but the longing that drove all of us voyagers was the same.

In Moab, we had the famous Slickrock Trail to ourselves, our bike tires gripping red rock under a deep blue desert sky, the snowcapped La Sal Mountains peeking in the distance. We'd hang out at Poison Spider Bicycles and shoot the breeze with the mechanics and anyone else who came through the door, absorbing information like desert plants during a monsoon rain. We just wanted to experience life, and we did through those random conversations—stories about places we hadn't seen, lives we didn't know.

At the time, striking up conversations with older adults felt natural, but I realize now, as I watch some of my friends raise their kids, how much our upbringings gave us the skills to be able to talk to much-older strangers, the ability to navigate the unknown.

In junior high, I went from the star player in Little League to riding the bench full-time. It wasn't about talent; it was about politics. My best guess is the coach didn't like my father, who was from out of state, and was taking it out on me for not being "local" enough. For a little while, it was devastating, but in hindsight it turned out to be the greatest gift. After a few long bus rides to away games and zero playing time, I quit. All that spring, I'd come home from school itching to do something. I begged my mother to drive me to my friends' houses in town. "If you want to see your friends, ride your bike there," she'd say. Fourteen miles round trip to Vergennes, down a country road with pickup trucks and tractors, and then a busy road with no shoulder and tractor-trailer trucks.

One thing led to another, and I found myself at a bike shop in Burlington, forty-five minutes away. The owner took me under his wing and introduced me to bike racing. Before long I was traveling to Massachusetts, New Hampshire, Pennsylvania. I got talking with older racers, people with different backgrounds from mine. It was the first glimpse of how travel—how different people—could influence my world. Looking back, cycling was also where I learned that to get results, you have to put in a lot of work. So much of it was often a grind, like training long miles in the cold Vermont rain, but that was what great things came from. The sport taught me discipline and delayed gratification and what it was like to know that my accomplishments came from the work I'd put in, not from group dynamics I had no control over. And, of course, getting sidelined from baseball taught me to strike out on my own, to find my own unorthodox path. It fostered the independence that had led me two thousand miles from home.

* * *

We kept moving, camping along the sandy shores of the Colorado River, where the water cut swift and cold between red cliffs. At night, the temperature dropped the instant the sun set, frost caressing Vandura by midnight. It was my first experience of a true diurnal climate in a desert stripped bare. With no clouds to hold down the warmth at night or block the sun's powerful rays during the day, the temperature could change by as much as fifty degrees between 2:00 a.m. and 2:00 p.m.

We woke to crisp mornings, the sky cloudless day after day. It felt like we'd cheated the season, getting this late into October without the rain and gray we'd known our whole lives. We found a Best Western—or maybe it was a Holiday Inn—and met Connie at the Continental breakfast, where she was serving up omelets. Her uniform was always clean, but her shoes were blackened and caked with tar. Being curious, we asked about them. Connie laughed and said she and her husband ran a driveway-sealing business on the side.

I started noticing a pattern: When we showed strangers honest interest, they showed it back in volumes. Connie became a kind of mother figure to us—asking about our plans, checking in each morning like we were her own. "Enjoy your breakfast, boys. Will I see you tomorrow?" she'd say with a smile, knowing that we weren't staying at the hotel. (One morning she'd caught us parking Vandura before breakfast. I'm happy we grew out of our occasional Continental breakfast stage and I'm not suggesting it to anyone.)

"Of course, Connie. We'll be back."

And then, one day, we weren't.

Our plan was to get up to Bozeman, Montana, where Steve's sister had a friend willing to let us crash on the floor for a few nights. Vandura's spartan comforts were wearing thin—our pillows flat, the cold nights biting—and the thought of a warm shower sounded better by the day.

We wound our way north through Utah's mountains, coasting in neutral down the passes to save on gas. Late one Friday night, Vandura coughed its last breath outside Afton, Wyoming. A burly, long-bearded tow truck driver hauled us into town, headlights bouncing off shuttered storefronts, the World's Largest Elkhorn Arch stretching skeletally across Main Street. This was a different West: raw, cold, unforgiving. The scent of burning logs and hard labor in the air.

He dropped us behind a mechanic's shop that reeked of grease and wet iron. "You'll have to wait it out here 'til Monday," he said. "Ronny's gone for the weekend—either fishin' or huntin'." He handed over a $125 bill for the tow.

So far, our money had trickled out of us predictably, we were probably down to around $5,000 now, but this unexpected bill landed like a punch. Money wasn't just money anymore—it was time on the road. I fooled myself into thinking we might be on a permanent adventure, never thinking too far ahead, even though we were roughly one-third into our journey. This was a crack in the illusion. The first reminder life on the road wouldn't last forever.

After weeks of twenty-four hours a day together, Steve and I had learned to grow quiet with each other, relaxed in the comfort of silence without anxiety—a skill that would help me years later during hours of silence with people I couldn't speak a common language with. Our long, still stretches broke only with a laugh, a stray observation, a heavier thought about life. While our classmates sat clocked into jobs—as mechanics, on farms, in the military—or college, we were in the classroom of the country, learning its scale, its moods, the edges where one region bled into another, the accents that shifted between long stretches of road. Where I grew up no longer felt like the center of the world; it was a place I was starting to outgrow. I hadn't showered in many days. After eating a bowl of Raisin Bran with flaked ice milk for breakfast—by this point, an unplugged refrigerator was colder than a plugged-in one—I carried two one-gallon jugs of water and a bar of soap behind the forklift by Ronny's shop. The sky hung low and gray, the temperature in the high teens. I stripped down and poured water over my head, steam hissing up from the clash of a warm body and frigid water. A stabbing ice-cream headache shot behind my eyes. I dried fast and ran for the van, diving feet first into my sleeping bag to thaw. I spent the afternoon in that position, flipping through the atlas.

Monday finally came, and after a day of repairs—a new fuel pump and another $220 bill—we rolled out of town, pressing days-cold fingertips against the lukewarm air blowing through Vandura's vents. The road carried us between extremes: trapped when Vandura was sick, untouchably free the moment it ran. We hiked Jackson Hole, saw bison, watched geysers blast in Yellowstone, trekked through Bridger Bowl and Big Sky ski resorts in the snow. We were fascinated by the sheer expansiveness of everything—the freedom of a lone driver in a pickup truck turning off the open road toward his ranch.

In Bozeman, we took long, hot showers at Steve's sister's friend's place and slept toasty warm for the first time in weeks, then hit the open road again before we overstayed our welcome.

* * *

The freezing temperatures of Wyoming and Montana aimed our thoughts and steering wheel toward Seattle, somewhere the milder Pacific Northwest winter would make sleeping in the van somewhat easy again—or so we thought.

By this point, our bodies felt a nutritional imbalance. The great majority of our calorie intake was simple carbs. It honestly didn't register that we could spend a little money at a restaurant, even for one meal, and eat some protein. We were obsessed with sticking to our thinning budget.

Our first evening in the city, I remember cruising around looking for a parking lot. The lights and street life felt so alive after so many small towns. We rolled past a luxury car dealership on a hilltop, trays of hors d'oeuvres and shimmering dresses glinting amid chrome and glass.

"What do you think, Steve? Check it out?" I asked half kidding as we circled the block again, windows down, the coastal air warm and damp on our skin.

Steve giggled through his nose, as he often did. But the look between us held a charge—it was *that* look.

Steve parked the van, and we crossed the street and stood on the sidewalk in front of ground-to-ceiling windows. On the other side was a long table loaded with shrimp and steak and every side dish imaginable. Fizzing champagne flutes in front of shiny Ferraris, Lamborghinis, and Porsches.

"Yeah," he said. "Let's take a look."

This is probably where I should tell you that Steve grew up around cars. His father came from an era when it was still possible—rare, but possible—to stumble on a valuable car decaying in a barn. Steve's father grew up on a dairy farm in rural Vermont, which is the last place you'd expect to find a red 1950 Ferrari 340 Barchetta. But a military veteran had imported one from Italy after his service and squirreled it away with other broken and worthless (at the time) old cars from overseas. He couldn't get them going. But Steve's father, at age fifteen, paid something like $500 for the Barchetta—a partial payment, the rest of which he paid for in work to get the other cars up and running. This experience eventually led to Steve's dad starting a business fixing old exotic cars. Vermont wasn't the center of the car world, or even an especially thriving economy, but it became one of those "If you build it, they will come" ventures.

By the time Steve was eight, he already knew how to wrench on some of the most luxurious European rides.

He grew up in that shop, smelling like a combination of solvent, rubber, and leather conditioner, his fingernails permanently packed with grease. There was always a burnt hole in his shirt from a welding flare or a tear in his jeans from fabricating some metal part. His thick curly hair stood almost as a line of defense against the materials thrown at his body over the course of long workdays. Steve's parents left town sometimes for the weekend to go to car shows, and we'd go into the shop to stare at Ferraris, Porsches, and rare models like the BMW M1, sitting in the driver's seats pretending to turn the steering wheels back and forth while making car noises, dreaming about taking them out one day. By thirteen, we were.

The first car we snuck from the shop was an Audi (I forget the model), which we quickly pushed to its limits, the velocity making everything stress and flex. I remember a draft whistling through the doors, the engine screaming. I glanced at the speedometer: 157, 158, 159, 160. We'd done it! Our challenge had been to hit 160. (And remember, this was hilly Vermont, not straight-road Nebraska.)

Whoosh—a car blurred past in the other direction, blue and red lights flipping on. For a second I thought we were done for. But at 160, the cop was out of view in the blink of an eye. I looked at Steve, his eyes bulging out of his head just barely above the steering wheel. Everything moved in fast-forward as we yelled with excitement. The world around us became a smear. It was like that *Back to the Future* scene right before Marty's DeLorean vanished.

There was no way that cop was turning around and catching us, not without backup. We made it from Shelburne to Vergennes—a twenty-five-minute drive—in eight minutes. Steve killed the lights as we came down to 110 mph, slipping under the moonlight in stealth mode. If we got busted, it would be game over for us in so many ways.

Back at Steve's parents' place, I bolted from the car and threw open the shop doors. As we snuck the car in, I set my hand on the hood—it was burning hot. The smell of scorched oil and rubber smoked up the air. We crept out to the side of the road and hid under some brush, poking our heads out to see if any cars were coming. Ten minutes later, the cop car rolled by. We watched its red taillights fade into the distance and laughed. We were lucky—this could've gone so wrong, but our brains, all rogue hormones, couldn't calibrate the danger.

So anyway, all this is to say that when we sauntered into the dealership in Seattle, we'd done way more risky things around cars.

We walked into the gala, our Rocky Mountain–worn shoes, shaggy hair, shredded jeans, and sun-faded shirts clashing with the glossy white floors of polished marble. The women wore stylish dresses and glittering jewelry, the men fine suits and heavy watches. A few people near the door looked our way, eyes narrowing at the two grubby kids off the street.

Steve and I made our way to the buffet table, loaded our plates like we hadn't eaten in weeks. I bit into a massive prawn so fast I forgot to peel it. A second later I ducked behind a planter and spit the shell by a tree, then looked up just in time to see a couple of people staring at me in disgust.

Two men marched over, faces stern.

Steve and I froze, our bodies still except for the chewing motion of our mouths. I knew we were about to be removed.

One man raised his hand, ready to grab my plate. And then I heard Steve's voice beside me.

"This Ferrari Dino 246 GTS looks fast but accelerates like a slouch, doesn't it?"

The man stopped, annoyed.

Steve went on, unbothered. "Yeah, the carburetor idle jets were typically too small to pass US emissions back in the day. If you replace the number fifty-five jet with a number sixty, all the problems disappear."

The man's eyes narrowed as Steve doubled down, pointing to his right.

"That Ferrari 365 GTB/4 Daytona over there isn't running so good, is it?"

The other man looked at Steve and shrugged. "The mechanics in the back room have tried everything."

"What they should be doing is setting camshaft timing using a .050 mm valve clearance instead of the specs in the workshop manual. That gives a more precise contact area on the camshaft lobe and finds crankshaft degrees halfway between when the intake valve opens and exhaust valve closes. You'll get way more top-end speed that way."

A few men and their wives gathered in closely, eyes bright with interest, Steve's esoteric knowledge cutting through class lines. Our ragged looks and young age seemed suddenly unimportant; it was all substance now. They wanted more, and Steve delivered. He pointed to a Ferrari 308 GTS with evidence of a slight leak under the engine. "This is the ubiquitous *Magnum, P.I.* Ferrari. Oh, what an interesting one this is."

"Yeah, this one's been a problem," said the man who appeared to be the manager of the dealership. "We haven't been able to stop the leak, and locating a new water pump from Italy has been a challenge. We almost sold it last week, but then the potential customer noticed the leak and backed out."

"Look, these cars are exotic and all, but sometimes it's a simple fix," said Steve. "Go to the local hardware store and order a generic basement sump-pump rebuild kit. Use the ceramic seals and springs to restore the pump. You don't have to pay a fortune or wait forever for a new one from Ferrari that might be faulty anyway."

By now, I'd loosened my shoulders and sunk my teeth into a strip of rare steak, my body jolting at the sudden hit of protein. I hadn't eaten red meat since leaving home two months before.

An hour later, with full stomachs and a circle of fans, we left the event to extended hands. I remember looking at Steve with a grin, in awe of his knowledge and suave execution. One couple even invited us to another car gathering in a few weeks and for us to stay at their place. We smiled, politely declined, and said we had business on the road.

* * *

A few years after I asked my mom for a book about the Soviet Union for Christmas (at around thirteen years old), I subscribed to a magazine called *Russian Life*, which covered all the vast territory of the fifteen Soviet states. (In retrospect, I was quite possibly the youngest subscriber.) The Cold War was in its final throes. But the Soviet Union was still our adversary, and the more I was told by media and my teachers to fear it, the more curious I became. I'm so thankful to my parents for the way they encouraged my curiosity as a child, rather than shutting it down. It made all the difference. There are few lessons as important as replacing fear with curiosity.

I remember flipping through the pages of the magazine,

mesmerized by the exotic names: Kyiv, Yekaterinburg, Dushanbe, Ukraine, Russia, Tajikistan. . . . I was captivated by the images of colorful, dome-shaped Orthodox churches beside heavy Soviet apartment blocks. The strange juxtapositions that made the USSR look mysterious, forbidden, adventurous.

One day, my seventh-grade substitute algebra teacher was on the receiving end of my countercultural fixation when she asked my name and I replied, "Joseph."

"Joseph who?" she asked.

I paused, scrambling for a last name that could go well with Joseph. I didn't know why, but I knew it would shock her, so I went with it.

"Joseph Stalin," I announced with gusto.

Watching adults tense up over anything Soviet was somehow amusing for our rebellious teenage brains.

But my curiosity wasn't limited to the former USSR. I remember watching the 1991 bombing of Iraq on the news. It dominated the media for a couple of days and then went away, but I wondered for months afterward what it was like there. How were the people living now?

And though Steve and I weren't (yet) overseas, sneaking into a luxury car dealership in Seattle gave me an early hint at not just the thrill of getting a little uncomfortable but the confidence that could come with connecting with others with whom I had little in common.

* * *

It rained nonstop in Seattle. The cool Pacific air felt good on the skin, but the dampness sank deeper by the hour. From behind the wet windshield, the city looked intriguing, but there wasn't much we could do outside. So we pointed Vandura north and crossed into Canada.

We got lucky—the weather eased, breaking into off-and-on showers with dry spells in between. We wandered through Vancouver, drifting into a seedier part of town and striking up conversations with locals in shops and on the streets.

At one corner, a barely dressed woman said to Steve, "It's so cold out." She looked him up and down. "I need to get warm somehow. Can you help me?"

You'd think Steve wouldn't have been that dumb, but his mechanical, fix-it mentality kicked in. "Well, duh," he said. "It's cold out. Put on pants and a jacket."

The next day we walked the streets some more. Vancouver felt unmistakably Canadian, but in small ways: the Queen staring back at you from your coins, the king-size Reese's Peanut Butter Cups packaged with three cups instead of four. The buildings stood next to the bay, with mountains shooting up to the clouds behind. The place felt far north—the sun didn't climb as high in the sky.

We turned a corner onto a pedestrian square, where a man stood commanding a small crowd.

"Who wants to get rich?" he called out.

A few heads turned, people shuffled closer. Steve and I drifted in, curious.

"Who wants to get rich?" he repeated, louder.

The man's cadence had a hypnotic pull. He was good-looking—blond wavy hair combed back, a sharp suit, a wide salesman's smile. He let the silence hang just long enough to pass from intriguing to awkward, right at the point where people might drift away. Then . . .

"Who wants to get rich?!" he thundered, his voice dropping into a bass register.

Even my spine straightened.

"I want to get rich!" a man blurted out, unable to hold back. His clothes hung loose, shredded, like he'd peeled himself off the sidewalk after a drunken night.

Jake—that was the showman's name—stretched out his hand to the crowd, coaxing a response.

We responded in unison: "*I want to get rich!*"

A wave of euphoria filled the air. Jake held the silence, keeping the crowd expectant, on our toes. Then another guy—out of sync and a couple of years older—jumped forward, stumbling, in a lime-green polo with a popped collar. "I want to get rich!" he yelled.

It wasn't the most professional bunch.

It went on like that for a while, call-and-response. The crowd buzzed, as if we'd already made thousands. Steve and I glanced at each other, laughing. Whatever this was, we were in.

Finally, Jake raised his hand for silence.

He dropped his voice into a quiet, confidential tone. "If you want to get rich, meet me here tomorrow morning at ten o'clock."

* * *

I started cutting grass at eight years old and kept at it right up until Steve and I headed West. At around twelve years old I was up to seven lawns at twenty-five dollars each every week from April to October. Between that and other landscaping jobs, I could pull in around $350 a week—good money for those times, and definitely for that age.

Vermont back then carried a strong puritanical ethos, at

least when it came to work. Work was pride, work was identity, and that was instilled early on. Sitting around watching TV wasn't an option in my family. My parents were big believers in that classic line, "Go find something to do or I'll find something for you to do."

To put into perspective just how renegade the late 1980s and early 1990s were: There was a lawn I mowed in front of my mother's office that had a brutally steep section. If I pushed the mower across the slope, the mower would lift up on two wheels and tip over as my ankles twisted to keep the machine steady. When I complained about not being able to finish that part of the lawn, my mother and her coworkers came up with a solution. They handed me a rope and told me to tie it to the mower handle and creep it down the hill from the top. The pep talk ended with a pat on the back and a "You've got this."

Sometimes I'd slip attempting to pull the mower up the hill, trying not to crash into it as I slid down. I did this in front of their office windows as they sat at work. Cars drove by and observed this as if it was normal, and it *was* normal in the late '80s.

Another yard had old stumps with beehives underneath. When I mowed around them, I stirred up a hive—and the bees chased me down, stinging me as I sprinted for the house, the mower still roaring in the background with a swarm circling it like something out of a cartoon. My neighbors, a husband and wife, sat me down in their kitchen, dabbed toothpaste on the stings, and handed me a cold lemonade with big ice cubes that cracked around in the glass. We chatted for a few minutes, and then the husband patted me on the back. "All right, Peter," he'd said. "Time to get back out there and finish the job."

Forced independence, resilience by necessity: traits of a common Gen X upbringing. Nothing was going to happen on its own or by some outside force, at least not in the environment I was in. And no, I'm not going to start talking about walking to school both ways uphill and backward in a blizzard, but I do want to make this point: If you wanted it, you had to earn it. So, get-rich-quick schemes? Steve and I didn't believe in them. But out here on the road, we never said no to an adventure.

* * *

We couldn't find a parking spot in Vancouver that evening, so we drove south to one of the colleges and parked there. The Pacific Northwest in winter was gnarly. The rain poured in sheets for hours, and inside the muffled world of the Vandura, things went damp and sour. The skin on my feet kept a permanent wrinkle from living in shoes that never fully dried. We tied a clothesline across the van and hung our clothes during the day, but they never dried either. At night we slid into clammy sleeping bags, my skin sticking to the nylon with a loud, tacky peel.

Most nights, exhaustion won. We fell asleep fast, our brains overloaded. But this night was different. I woke to a splash on my forehead. Seconds later, another. I flicked on my headlamp and hinged up from the waist—had Vandura sprung a leak?

Droplets clung everywhere on the ceiling like the inside of a wet cave, our breath turning Vandura into a cloudburst. It was raining inside. When I rolled to the side to dodge the dripping, a drop shot straight into my ear canal like a sniper hit. Another nailed me on the crown. Eventually, I threw my damp, stained towel over my skull and surrendered.

While I lay there getting waterboarded, Steve snored through all of it.

If it wasn't for our upbringings—my lawn mowing bee

stings and the hot metal flares that burned through Steve's clothes—we probably would have turned Vandura back to Vermont the next morning, seeking the comforts of home: a warm shower and a soft bed. But giving in wasn't an option. Despite the discomfort, we were having the time of our lives.

When Steve and I showed up in downtown Vancouver the next day, Jake stood in the middle of a group of about thirty people. He lowered his head, eyes up, and in a hushed voice said, "I'm happy to see you all here this morning." He sounded almost priestly. His girlfriend, Sandra, who looked like a cheerleader, unfolded a stepladder and Jake climbed up, standing high above us.

A long pause. Attention tightened.

"What we're selling are pub cards," he announced, like they were valuable collectibles. "Thirty-two dollars each. When someone buys one, they get half off their tab at these select pubs and restaurants." He held one up, flipping it to show the list on the back. "There are forty-seven pubs and restaurants in Vancouver where the pub card works."

Jake ran through the sales pitch, then started dividing us into pairs. To our surprise, he handed stacks of cards to us complete strangers and set us loose.

"Be back here by five o'clock," he shouted. "Now get out there, sell some pub cards, and get rich!" He couldn't help himself with one last "*Who wants to get rich?*"

We erupted into our trained response, fists pumping: "I want to get rich!"

Steve and I were sent to (if I remember correctly) the Gastown neighborhood, an established part of the city with older brick-and-masonry buildings and a fair amount of people walking around.

"We're going to sell so many cards here," Steve said with his signature nasal laugh.

We stood on the corner watching pedestrians stream past, played a best-of-three round of roshambo to decide who'd go first. After I lost, I took a deep breath, clutching the stack of cards.

Scanning the crowd, I spotted an older lady headed our way. I stepped in front of her, trying to sound confident.

"Hello, ma'am, how would you like half off your next meal?"

She breezed right by without slowing.

I pivoted to the next man.

"How would you like to drink for half price?"

He raised an eyebrow. "How do I do that?"

"Let me introduce you to the power of the pub card." I held it up like Jake did—like I was unveiling something important.

"How much?"

"Thirty-two dollars."

He laughed. "You expect me to give thirty-two bucks to some kid on the street?"

"I know it's a big ask, but the savings are huge," I said, trying to keep a straight face, telling myself that each card sold would keep us on the road longer.

He smirked. There was no way he was handing over thirty-two dollars.

It went on like that all afternoon. We felt like Mormon missionaries without the nice clothes, organization, or training . . . and a worse conversion rate.

At five o'clock we circled back to Jake. He clapped his hands. "So, who's getting rich today?"

Heads hung low. Out of thirty of us, only one person had made a single sale. He held up the thirty-two bucks like it was gold. Jake peeled off five dollars, gave it to him, and pocketed the rest. Strangely, the man didn't seem upset. Since he was the only one who made anything, he lightened his step and puffed out his chest.

"Okay, team," Jake boomed. "First days are first days. Tomorrow we're going to get rich. Who wants to get rich?"

"I want to get rich," we mumbled in unison.

Everyone dispersed. Only Steve and I lagged behind, trying to wrap our heads around how this pyramid scheme was supposed to work.

"Hey, you two," Jake called us over. "Want to grab a bite with me and Sandra?"

Soon we were bouncing in the back of Jake's old Trans Am—burnouts at stoplights, '80s hair bands blasting, Jake's hot girlfriend flirting with us, cruising Vancouver's streets from pub to pub. Life was good. That night, when Vandura's interior rain came pouring down, I didn't fight it.

We stuck with the pub card hustle for about a week. Steve sold one. I sold one. That was it. The real payoff was sliding into pubs like locals, eating and drinking for free. Meeting people, dancing to live bands. Experiencing the city.

The business model? I still don't understand it. Hardly anyone made a sale, yet Jake never seemed rattled. He kept smiling, kept the food and drinks flowing. Steve and I didn't ask too many questions. On the road, we were learning—and maybe in life too—you just went with the flow.

* * *

And then, one morning, I turned to Steve and said what we'd both been waiting to hear from the other: the best for last. "It's time we go to California."

Weeks of rain broke right at the California border, as if the weather itself respected state lines. The sun felt warm on our faces in the middle of winter. Everything seemed freer, lighter. We pedaled our bikes through the rugged Northern California coast and cooked our pasta off the shoulder of Highway 1, looking out over the golden sun falling into the Pacific. The ocean felt nothing like the Atlantic—it was wild, untamed, powerful. We swam in the frigid waves that crashed near the elk that roamed the long empty beaches, and played in the sand like little kids. Though it was maybe sixty degrees, we sat shirtless as if it were a summer heat wave.

While riding my bike, my mind wandered. I thought about how timelines in life only matter if you know the day you're going to die. If I was only going to live to fifty and wanted a successful career, then sure, better to start early. But if I lived to a hundred, what difference would a year or two or five make? Especially if years on the road gave me experiences and knowledge that I could carry through the rest of life and set me up for what I was truly meant to do. I was realizing that what I wanted, really wanted, out of life was to follow my heart, to follow my curiosity about other places and people, to live an adventurous life—not to be locked down and have it "all figured out" by age twenty-five. Not to wait until retirement to do what truly interested me.

The next day, I smelled eucalyptus for the first time, sharp and sweet in the air. We parked among redwoods that put us—small and insignificant humans—in our place. The forest absorbed sound, shards of light beaming through gaps in the canopy, hitting the ground like spotlights. Massive ferns rose from the fertile soil. Here was a place where things thrived.

The road kept pulling us south, each turn opening to something new. Hawks glided alongside Vandura as we wound along the cliffs of the Pacific Coast Highway, and before long the road carried us over the Golden Gate Bridge and into San Francisco. The way urban and natural worlds fused in the city felt unreal. One moment we were walking crowded streets, past colorful Victorians, the next we'd turned a corner into a eucalyptus forest alive with ferns and robins and coyotes. At the edge of the city, waves hammered the rocks, foghorns bellowing in the distance while gulls wheeled overhead, their cries echoing through the mist. A light winter salty haze drifted over the city at night and burned off by day. The light stayed in a constant dream state.

It was also a place with a gritty side we'd never experienced before. On 5th and Market, we caught wind that someone was selling fake IDs for twenty-five dollars. We walked through the Tenderloin neighborhood in search of the guy, drugs changing hands and a few people's screams echoing around us. One guy was having an argument with a lamppost. We stepped into a Carl's Jr. and saw a homeless man carving his skin with a razor blade. Everyone ignored it. Steve and I froze. If this were happening at home, everyone would have rushed in to help.

Eventually, we climbed a narrow flight of stairs behind an unmarked door to a dingy room, where a Chinese man who spoke little English took our pictures and laminated them into Illinois IDs with birthdates over twenty-one. That was when we started to slip up on our budgeting. Inspired by the fun we'd had in Vancouver, we started to go out, visiting bars around the city. Soon, we were down to our last $1,600.

Our trip continued into 1996: Lake Tahoe, the water clear as glass under snowcapped peaks. Big Sur, where the highway wound along cliffs that dropped straight into the Pacific. Los

Angeles, sprawling, the air buzzing with traffic, neon, and the smoke from taco trucks. San Diego, sun-washed and laid-back, palm trees towering over convertibles. Tijuana, chaotic and colorful, Mexican music and every type of vendor crowding the streets. Joshua Tree, dry desert wind and alien rock formations scattered beneath an endless sky. And Death Valley, the trip's biggest surprise and to this day one of my favorite places in the world.

It felt otherworldly. There was no wind, no birds chirping, no leaves to rustle, no trace of urban hum—just wide-open valleys with rugged mountains on both sides, sometimes with green rocks, sometimes reds or purples.

The name Death Valley came from a party of pioneers known as the Death Valley '49ers who were making their way to the gold mines of California. Three years earlier, the Donner Party—stranded just a few hundred miles north in the Sierra Nevada—resorted to cannibalism to survive until spring. This southern route was warmer but challenging nonetheless. After getting stuck for over a month in the dry and inhospitable land, one of the pioneers, upon their escape, turned around and said, "Goodbye, Death Valley." The name has stuck ever since.

The desert widened as Steve and I drove north, descending mile by mile. By the time we reached the valley floor, we were below sea level. I don't know if it was just placebo or something real in the brain, but it felt like being under an ocean with no water above. We slept under bright stars near Furnace Creek at two hundred feet below sea level and woke up looking up at 11,000-foot Telescope Peak. I'd never seen such sheer elevation gain in one frame. We ran barefoot across the empty sand dunes, hiked the mountains, enjoyed the comfort of temperatures in the seventies in late January. I remember thinking back East was a sandbox compared to this. This was an endless, freeing sandpile.

I still remember how Death Valley seemed to stare right through me, its deafening silence forcing me to go deeper into my thoughts, to ponder where I came from and how far I had come. That the dream I'd dreamed all my youth—out in the sandpile and on bike rides—had at last become reality.

As we headed back West again to see Mount Whitney, the Lower 48's tallest peak, Vandura acted up once more. I stared down the road in both directions: not a single soul in sight. We knew the next town was a long way off. In the atlas, it looked like two more passes and roughly eighty-five miles to Lone Pine.

I kicked a rock off the pavement into the desert. The crack was deafening—concert volume in the silence. It carried on forever, because there was nothing to dampen it: no trees, no humidity.

Steve lifted the hood, fixed the rod in place. About thirty minutes later, a shimmer appeared on the horizon—first a dot, then a square, then the slow emergence of a faded orange pickup truck that rolled to a stop beside us. The driver stepped out, cowboy hat brim low, his skin cracked and faded like an old leather chair.

"You know," he said, "I can call you a tow truck when I get to Stovepipe Wells. But you boys better have some money. Out here it's five bucks a mile."

We couldn't do it. That kind of tow would wipe us out—weeks of the trip gone, maybe the end of the adventure altogether.

I stared up at the long gradual pass stretching into the horizon. Out here, distance was impossible to gauge without trees or buildings.

"How far away is the top of the pass?" I asked.

"Oh . . .'bout twenty-five miles from here."

I felt a flicker of hope. "And on the other side, how long's the downhill?"

"I'd say . . . 'bout another fifteen."

I did the math fast. Forty miles. Two hundred dollars saved. I looked at Steve—by this point in the trip, we didn't need words.

"We've got a rope in the van," I said. "Any chance you could tow us up to the top?"

The man looked like he might say no. But he paused, squinting toward the gradual pass as he thought it over. Then a slow smile formed, as if he remembered a younger, more adventurous version of himself, and he nodded.

"All right," he said. "Let's give it a shot, kid."

After a long tow behind the pickup, we reached the top of Towne Pass, nearly five thousand feet of climbing. "Be careful on the descent, boys," the man warned. "There are truck runaway ramps if you get too much speed and lose your brakes."

We didn't think it through at all. We just flew down the mountain, screaming with excitement, flashing back to that day we hit 160 in the Audi, to the rush that being on the edge of out of control brings. Vandura rattled and moaned on the wide, sweeping curves, barely holding together.

Another valley opened before us, a straight road stretching to the horizon. Steve let off the brakes completely, and Vandura accelerated forward, the speedometer pinned all the way to the right as we kept gaining speed. The van shook like it had the DTs as we coasted for miles, finally rolling to a crawl in the empty valley, euphoric.

* * *

I think there's no better way to explore America than by setting off on an adventure—and you don't need a lot of money or a set itinerary. You don't even need a whole lot of time. Epic road trips are great, but so is a weekend somewhere unfamiliar, a road you've never taken, or a town you've driven past but never pulled over to explore. An adventure might even be waiting for you on the other side of your own city: on streets you've never walked, inside random places you've never ducked into, with a person you would have never come across in your normal routine.

Exploration doesn't have to be dramatic. All it requires is curiosity, a bit of creativity, and a willingness to tune in to what's around you. When you do—when you slow down just enough to give a place your full attention—things start to happen. Conversations open up and strangers share their world. That's the real magic of this country: our ability to so easily connect despite the differences we might have. And then you walk away knowing something you didn't before, carrying a thought or a feeling that you bring with you on your way home, something that maybe lets you see your own life from a different perspective.

It's a great way to get fired up about this country again. And I find it often gets me excited about the possibilities for my own life too, seeing the brilliant, daring, fascinating things my fellow Americans are doing.

I've always tried to keep an open mind, to think that what I'm looking for might be somewhere else. I've traveled across continents, through eighty-five countries, all of which rewarded me greatly, but also reminded me why *this* is the place I love the most. I feel so fortunate to call America home.

It can be easy sometimes to dwell on whatever's wrong. I

think that's probably just human nature. Which is why it often takes an outside perspective to help to shake us out of our rut, to see what we've already got and why it's so important to appreciate it. Not because we should be complacent, but so that we don't lose hope. So that we remain grateful for this unique experiment that for 250 years has marched to the unmistakable beat of its own drum.

* * *

And then, suddenly, the dream was over. A tow truck hauled us into Lone Pine. We found the cheapest motel we could, and in the morning stepped outside to see the snowcapped peak of Mount Whitney rising 14,505 feet straight up from town. Later we stood at the edge of the shop, watching as a mechanic shuffled between his toolbox and Vandura. He moved slow, glassy-eyed, like he was working through a hangover. Each trip back to the toolbox felt like a countdown clock on our adventure—our money evaporating by the minute. The bill came in at $587. It hit like a hammer. We were done.

For the first time on the trip, Steve and I clashed. He was excited to get home. He had his father's shop, his brothers, the steady stream of characters who came through their lives each day. I was coming up with wild ideas to extend the trip. What if we found work somewhere out here for a time? I couldn't get psyched about heading back to frigid Vermont in midwinter—to cold gray skies that got dark at 5:00 p.m., and my childhood room that I'd left four and a half months earlier. To a house out in the woods that was empty most of the time, with my parents working long hours and my older brothers no longer living at home. To the odd job I ended up taking that winter organizing a wealthy man's massive basement, where, beneath the dust and the fluorescent lights, I'd dream about the trip Steve and I had just taken and all the rest of the world I'd yet to see, stuffing my sock drawer again and counting down the days before I'd hit the road once more.

Because I knew the adventure wasn't over, not really. It couldn't be. There was so much of this world left to explore.

Acknowledgments

This book exists because people across America welcomed a stranger with a camera and trusted me enough to share their stories. Many of the people who opened their homes and lives to me appear in these pages, and many more show up in the videos that led to this book. I'm grateful to all of you.

Thank you to my fantastic YouTube audience who sends me fascinating story ideas that allow us all to learn about our fellow Americans.

The book itself would not exist without the team behind it. Megan Hogan and Gin Smith guided me editorially with professionalism and great wisdom. A special thanks to Megan, who allowed me the freedom to roam in my writing while bringing order to my ideas. Sean Manning at Simon & Schuster gave a first-time writer the opportunity—and the trust—to bring this project to life. And thanks to the rest of the Simon & Schuster team, from book design to marketing and everything in between, for helping carry this book into the world.

Long before this book, there were teachers who molded the way I think about documenting stories. Dr. Gary Cage at Truckee Meadows Community College pushed me to treat every perspective fairly and to understand the many sides of a story. Dr. Michael Branch at the University of Nevada, Reno, introduced me to great filmmakers and the storytelling process that later influenced how I approach my videos.

Several friends helped push this project forward when it was still uncertain. Cody Shirk encouraged me to move ahead with this book concept when I wasn't sure if the time was right. Richie McGinniss helped guide me through the writing process. Steven Haste connected me with many of the stories that eventually made their way into these pages.

My best friend Steve Markowski has been my wingman since day one, joining me on that transformational road trip we took together across the country.

My brother, Spencer Santenello, has supported my creative work from the beginning.

The foundation for all of this starts with my parents, who provided me with a sandpile instead of a sandbox and created an environment where my curiosity could wander and my dreams could take shape unrestricted. To my mother, with her can-do attitude, and to my father, who has since passed, whose ability to talk to anyone—and make people feel comfortable in any setting—left a lasting impression on me.

And to the audience who has followed these journeys on YouTube: Your curiosity about this country made this all possible. Without you, the travels, the conversations, and ultimately this book would not exist.

To all my fellow Americans for being such a cool, interesting, mixed-up, dynamic bunch. I'm glad to be in this together with you.

Finally, to my wife, Natalia. She's fully supported me since the very beginning of my YouTube journey when it was just a crazy idea, and throughout the process of writing this book. Her support, encouragement, and work behind the scenes have made this possible. My partner, my best friend, and my co-creator.

About the Author

PETER SANTENELLO is an independent journalist and filmmaker with more than four million subscribers on YouTube. He's traveled to eighty-five countries and lived in five, building a global audience by letting people tell their stories in their own words. For the past six years, Peter's lens has been focused squarely on the United States, where he explores the diverse, complex, and often misrepresented communities that make up the fabric of America. To watch these stories in full (and hundreds more), check out @PeterSantenello on YouTube.